Bronze and Iron Age Tombs at Tel Gezer, Israel

Finds from Raymond-Charles Weill's excavations in 1914 and 1921

Aren M. Maeir

with contributions by
Nava Panitz-Cohen, Dan Barag, Othmar Keel,
Nachum Applbaum and Yaakov H. Applbaum

BAR International Series 1206
2004

Published in 2016 by
BAR Publishing, Oxford

BAR International Series 1206

Bronze and Iron Age Tombs at Tel Gezer, Israel

ISBN 978 1 8417 1569 8

© A M Maeir and the Publisher 2004

The author's moral rights under the 1988 UK Copyright,
Designs and Patents Act are hereby expressly asserted.

All rights reserved. No part of this work may be copied, reproduced, stored,
sold, distributed, scanned, saved in any form of digital format or transmitted
in any form digitally, without the written permission of the Publisher.

BAR Publishing is the trading name of British Archaeological Reports (Oxford) Ltd.
British Archaeological Reports was first incorporated in 1974 to publish the BAR
Series, International and British. In 1992 Hadrian Books Ltd became part of the BAR
group. This volume was originally published by Archaeopress in conjunction with
British Archaeological Reports (Oxford) Ltd / Hadrian Books Ltd, the Series principal
publisher, in 2004. This present volume is published by BAR Publishing, 2016.

Printed in England

PUBLISHING

BAR titles are available from:

	BAR Publishing
	122 Banbury Rd, Oxford, OX2 7BP, UK
EMAIL	info@barpublishing.com
PHONE	+44 (0)1865 310431
FAX	+44 (0)1865 316916
	www.barpublishing.com

TABLE OF CONTENTS

Table of Contents I

List of Tables II

List of Figures III

List of Plates IV

List of Contributors V

Abbreviations VI

Preface - *Aren M. Maeir* .... VII-VIII

Chapter 1: Introduction - *Aren M. Maeir* 1-8

Chapter 2: The Pottery Assemblage - *Nava Panitz-Cohen and Aren M. Maeir* 9-41

Chapter 3: The Stone, Faience, Bone, and Metal Objects -

      Nava Panitz-Cohen and Aren M. Maeir 41-46

Chapter 4: An Egyptian 18th Dynasty Glass Vessel - *Dan Barag* 47-49

Chapter 5: The Glyptic Finds: Stamp Seal Amulets - *Othmar Keel* 51-54

Chapter 6: Medical Computed Tomography (CT) Analysis of Selected Pottery: Preliminary Results -

      Nachum Applbaum and Yaakov H. Applbaum 55-60

Chapter 7: Summary - *Aren M. Maeir* 61-65

Figures 1-3

Plates 1-30

LIST OF TABLES

Table 1: Chronological Range of Pottery Types .... p. 34

Table 2: Distribution of Vessel Classes .... p. 35

Table 3: Distribution of Imported Pottery .... p. 35

Table 4: Distribution of Finds in Tomb I (Late Bronze Age/Iron Age I) .... p. 35

Table 5: Distribution of Finds in Tomb III (Late Bronze Age) .... p. 35

Table 6: Distribution of Finds in Tomb IX (Iron Age I) .... p. 35

Table 7: Stratigraphy of the Excavations at Gezer (e.g., *Gezer V*: 6-7: Dever 1998) .... p. 63

LIST OF FIGURES

Fig. 1 - Map of the Southern Levant with the Location of Gezer and Selected Ancient and Modern Sites.

Fig. 2 - Map of Central Israel with the Primary Sites Mentioned in Text.

Fig. 3 - Plan of Tel Gezer with the Location of the Excavations by the Various Expeditions. The Location of the Tombs Excavated by R. Weill is not known.

LIST OF PLATES

Plate 1 - Line Drawings of Pottery: Bowls

Plate 2 - Line Drawings of Pottery: Bowls

Plate 3 - Line Drawings of Pottery: Bowls, Chalices and Krater

Plate 4 - Line Drawings of Pottery: Lamps

Plate 5 - Line Drawings of Pottery: Jugs and Bottle

Plate 6 - Line Drawings of Pottery: Juglets

Plate 7 - Line Drawings of Pottery: Flasks and Pyxides

Plate 8 - Line Drawings of Pottery: Imported Vessels

Plate 9 - Line Drawings of Pottery: Imitations of Cypriot Jugs

Plate 10 – Schematic Line Drawings of Pottery: Miscellaneous Missing Vessels

Plate 11 - Line Drawings of the Non-Ceramic Objects

Plate 12 - Line Drawings of Local Pottery Attributed to Tomb I

Plate 13 - Line Drawings of the Imported Vessels, Imitations of Imported Vessels, and Other Objects Attributed to Tomb I

Plate 14 - 1) Group Photograph of Objects Known to Have Originated from Tomb I; 2) Line Drawing and Photograph of the Egyptian Late Bronze Age Glass Vessel (HU 214)

Plate 15 - Line Drawings and Photographs of the Glyptic Finds

Plate 16 - Line Drawings and Photographs of the Glyptic Finds

Plate 17 - Photographs of Selected Bowls from Plate 1 (HU Collection)

Plate 18 - Photographs of Selected Bowls from Plate 2 (HU Collection)

Plate 19 - Photographs of Selected Bowls, Chalices and a Krater from Plate 3 (HU Collection)

Plate 20 - Photographs of Selected Lamps, Flasks and a Pyxis from Plates 4 and 7 (HU Collection)

Plate 21 - Photographs of Selected Jugs from Plate 5 (HU Collection)

Plate 22 - Photographs of Selected Ceramics from Plate 6 (HU Collection)

Plate 23 - Photographs of Selected Imported Wares from Plate 8 (HU Collection)

Plate 24 - Photographs of Selected Imitation Base Ring Vessels from Plate 9 (HU Collection)

Plate 25 - Photographs of Selected Vessels (SG Collection)

Plate 26 - Photographs of Selected Vessels (SG Collection)

Plate 27 - Photographs of Selected Vessels (AO Collection)

Plate 28 - Photographs of Selected Non-Ceramic Objects from Plate 11 (HU Collection)

Plate 29 - Digital Radiographic Images of Selected Vessels

Plate 30 - Digital Radiographic Images of Selected Vessels

LIST OF CONTRIBUTORS

- **Dr. Aren M. Maeir** - The Institute of Archaeology, The Martin (Szusz) Department of Land of Israel Studies and Archaeology, Bar-Ilan University, Ramat Gan, 52900, ISRAEL (maeira@mail.biu.ac.il). Principal investigator and editor of volume; author of Preface, and Chapters 1 and 7; co-author of Chapters 2 and 3.

- **Ms. Nava Panitz-Cohen** - The Institute of Archaeology, The Hebrew University of Jerusalem, Jerusalem 91904, ISRAEL (panitz@h2.hum.huji.ac.il). Co-author of Chapters 2 and 3.

- **Prof. Dan Barag** - The Institute of Archaeology, The Hebrew University of Jerusalem, Jerusalem 91904, ISRAEL. Author of Chapter 4.

- **Prof. Othmar Keel** - Biblische Institut, University, Miséricorde, CH-1700 Fribourg, SWITZERLAND (Othmar.Keel@unifr.ch). Author of Chapter 5.

- **Mr. Nachum Applbaum** - The Institute of Archaeology, The Hebrew University of Jerusalem, Jerusalem 91904, ISRAEL (applebau@h2.hum.huji.ac.il). Co-author of Chapter 6.

- **Dr. Yaakov H. Applbaum** - The Institute of Radiology, Haddasah University Medical Center, Jerusalem 91120, ISRAEL (applbaum@hadassah.org.il). Co-author of Chapter 6.

ABBREVIATIONS

AO - Archéologie Orientale (Musée de Louvre, Paris)
cm - centimeter
CRM – Collection Room Number (Hebrew University)
CT – Medical Computed Tomography
EA - el Amarna Letter Number
EB - Early Bronze Age
Fig. - Figure
FS - Furumark Shape
HU – Hebrew University
HUC - Hebrew Union College
LB - Late Bronze Age
LH - Late Helladic
LM - Late Minoan
MB - Middle Bronze Age
MYC - Mycenaean
n. - note
No. - Number
Pl. – Plate
RM – Rockefeller Museum
SG - Saint Germain en-Laye

PREFACE

This volume, in which the tombs that excavated by Raymond Weill at Gezer and the objects found within them are described and discussed, can be defined as being the final product of a long and drawn out story. Starting from the special circumstances behind the excavation of the tombs, followed by the wide dispersal and numerous transferals of the finds, and finally, the manner in which the tombs and finds were brought to light, all contribute to "the spinning of quite a yarn".

To begin with, the story behind the excavations illuminates interesting aspects of the history of the archaeological exploration of the Land of Israel, as well as provide an additional perspective on the early Zionist settlement activities in the land during the early part of the 20th century CE. In addition, the finds themselves, some of them of intrinsic archaeological interest, are yet another example of the many "excavated, yet buried" archaeological discoveries, which, due primarily to chance circumstances, have finally been brought to light (for a description of the circumstances related to the excavations and the various post-excavation stages, see Introduction, Chapter 1, below).

Unfortunately, due to the long time that has elapsed since the excavation, much of even the most basic information has been lost. None of the original excavators are still alive, and little, if any documentation has survived. Thus, only a small amount of information could be culled, despite the fact that a wide range of sources were searched. In effect, a major portion of the archaeological data on these tombs have been permanently lost, and thus, one must unfortunately suffice, for the most part, with the description and discussion of the various finds.

The process of bringing the finds from these tombs to publication was a long, drawn out procedure. Throughout this long process I was assisted by many people from numerous institutions, and to all of them I would like to express my deepest gratitude.

I was first informed of the existence of these tombs and finds by my former teacher, and now colleague, Prof. D. Barag. Without this initial information, these finds would still be unknown to the public. Following his initial lead (and some important data on the background of the excavation), a long journey began, in which an attempt was made to track down information on the excavations and the excavators, the location of the finds and documentation, and other relevant aspects.

I would like to gratefully acknowledge the financial assistance that I received for this project, assistance that was provided, in part, by a minor research grant from the *Robert H. and Claris Smith Center for Art History*, of the Hebrew University of Jerusalem, and a larger grant from *Yad Avi Ha-Yishuv* (The Rothschild Foundation), Jerusalem. In addition, the opportunity to examine the finds in Paris, France, was funded by a travel grant from Bar-Ilan University, Ramat Gan. The manuscript was completed while I was a post-doctoral fellow at the Dibner Institute for the History of Science and Technology at MIT.

The lion's share of the finds that are discussed in the present volume are currently located in the Collections Room of the Institute of Archaeology, at the Hebrew University of Jerusalem (Mt. Scopus Campus). I would like to thank: G. Horowitz (Curator) and D. Tsoran (Assistant Curator), for their generous help in locating the finds and the surviving documentation; Y. Strauss, who served as a research assistant in the initial stages of the work; N. Panitz-Cohen, who continued the analyses of the finds, and did most of the research and writing on the pottery and small finds (Chapters 2 and 3 below). In addition, she style-edited most of the chapters of the volume; E. Sachar, who style-edited Chapter 5; H. Bitan and D. Weinblatt, who drew the pottery located in Jerusalem; M. Caplan, who arranged the pottery plates; and M. Cohen, who photographed most of the objects from the Hebrew University.

In addition, I would like to thank the following:

A. Caubet, E. Fontain and M. Pic, from the Musée de Louvre, Paris, who assisted me both in receiving permission to access, and in examining the relevant finds located in the collections of the Department d'Archéologie Orientale, as well as for supplying line drawings and photographs of these objects (the photographs were taken by C. Larrieu - ©).

Ch. Lorre of the Musée des Antiquités Nationales, St.-Germain-en-Laye, France, for assistance in obtaining permission, and with the actual examination, of the relevant finds in the Museum, and for supplying photographs and line drawings of the vessels.

A. Drori (former Director, Israel Antiquities Authority), R. Peled, A. Sabriano-Shukrun and A. Rochman of the Israel Antiquities Authority and J. Zias (formely of the Israel Antiquities Authority), for assistance in locating the finds and administrative records kept in the Rockefeller Museum in Jerusalem; for supplying relevant information; and for permission to publish the two vessels from the Museum.

Numerous people assisted in obtaining (or attempting to obtain) information on the excavation, the finds, and the related circumstances, and I would like to thank them all. This includes: P. Amiet, G. Barkay, W.G. Dever, P. de

Miroschedji, G. Godron, J. Leclant, G. Sheinfeld, R. Tenen, R. Veil, and B. Zohar. My apologies to anyone that I may have accidentally omitted.

During the course of the research I utilized the bibliographic resources of numerous institutional libraries. I wish to acknowledge and thank these institutions and their staff for the use of their facilities and their gracious assistance. This includes the libraries at the following institutions: The Institute of Archaeology, The Hebrew University of Jerusalem; The Jewish National Library, Jerusalem; The Israel Antiquities Authority, Rockefeller Museum, Jerusalem; The Albright Institute for Archaeological Research, Jerusalem; The École Biblique et Archéologique Française, Jerusalem; The Institute of Archaeology, Tel Aviv University, Tel Aviv; Bar Ilan University, Ramat Gan; The Zionist Archives, Jerusalem; The Library of Congress, Washington; The Bibliotèque Nationale, Paris; and finally, the Tozzer, Widener, and Andover libraries at Harvard University, Cambridge, Massachusetts.

Special thanks go to the respective contributors to this volume, N. Panitz-Cohen (pottery and small finds, Chapters 2 and 3), D. Barag (an Egyptian glass vessel, Chapter 4), O. Keel (glyptic finds, Chapter 5), and N. Applbaum and Y. Applbaum (Medical Computed Tomography analyses of selected pottery, Chapter 6) for their willingness to study and publish selected portions of the finds, and for their patience in waiting for the appearance of this volume.

Last but not least, I would like to thank my wife and loving partner Adina, the love of my life, who has been at my side through thick and thin, and our sons, Noam, Uri and Netanel, for their ever-present love and support. And also to our dog Nona, who lay on the floor snoring as the volume was being completed ...

Aren M. Maeir
Cambridge/Brookline, MA
July, 2003

CHAPTER 1: INTRODUCTION

Aren M. Maeir

1.1. INTRODUCTION

The ancient site of Tel Gezer (*Abū-Shûsheh/Tell Jezer/Tell el-Jazari*) is located in Central Israel (Levant Grid 1425/1407), approximately halfway between Jerusalem and Tel Aviv (Fig. 1). It is situated in the northern section of the Judean foothills (Shephelah), not far from the southernmost hills of south-western Samaria (Fig. 2). The site is part of a ridge that commands the Ayalon valley to the north and the Soreq valley to the south (e.g. Orni and Efrat 1980:62-66), offering a magnificent view of the entire countryside for miles in every direction.[1] The long-term cultural prominence of the site can be explained in light of several circumstances: it is located in the vicinity of several roads of primary or secondary importance (e.g. Aharoni 1979:25-26; Dorsey 1991: 181-189, map 13); it commands an imposing view; it is surrounded by extremely fertile agricultural tracts; and, it has a sufficient water supply (adjacent springs and adequate precipitation). Thus, the site was settled, almost continuously, from the Proto-Historic periods until Modern times (for an overview of the cultural history of the site, see, e.g., Dever 1991; 1992; 1993; 1998).

The site, whose peak is 225 m above sea level, is some 13 hectares (33 acres) large (Figs. 3-4), and as such be classified as one of the medium-to-large Bronze and Iron Age sites in the Land of Israel. It is also one of the rare examples of an ancient site that can be identified beyond doubt. This identification is based primarily on the Hellenistic period "Gezer boundary inscriptions" (the first having been found by Clermont-Ganneau [1896:257-267]; for those discovered since then, see Reich 1985), which provide a water-tight identification of the site. The site is mentioned in many ancient sources, including several appearances in the Akkadian letters from the archive that was found in El-Amarna, Egypt, dating to the mid-14th century BCE, in which the kings/mayors of Gezer, *Milkilu* and *Yapahu*, are mentioned (EA 249; 250; 253:22; 254; 287; 290; 292; 298; 297; 298; 299; 300; 369; 378; see, e.g., Ross 1967; Moran 1992), numerous Biblical passages (e.g. Josh 10:33; 16:10; Judg 1:29; 2 Sam 5:25; 1 Kgs 9:16; I Chron 6:52; 20:4), and other texts (for a survey of these references, see, e.g., Lance 1967).

Following the identification of the site in the late 19th century CE, Gezer attracted the interest of various biblical, historical and archaeological scholars. The first intensive explorations of the site were conducted by R.A.S. Macalister between 1902 and 1909, under the auspices of the Palestine Exploration Fund. This excavation, for which preliminary reports on the ongoing excavation appeared regularly in the *Palestine Exploration Fund Quarterly Statement*, was published in three large volumes in 1912 (*Macalister I-III*). Macalister in fact excavated major portions of the tel, uncovering remains from virtually all periods represented on the site. Unfortunately, the methods of excavation, analysis and subsequent publication were quite primitive. Due to this, the inherent scientific value of these reports was quite limited. Thus, although major portions of the site had been excavated and permanently damaged, not enough was known about this important site. Due to this problem, subsequent excavations at the site were first and foremost interested in trying to restudy the site and understand its history. Both by defining and excavating portions of the site that had not been explored by Macalister, and based on the finds, to reinterpret the finds that had been reported by Macalister (on this issue, see, e.g., Dever 1998:29-31).

This in fact was the initial aim and strategy of the re-excavation of the site by the Palestine Exploration Fund in 1934 (Rowe 1935a; 1935b). Although originally expected to continue for several seasons, it was terminated after a short, and quite unsuccessful, season. Likewise, this same reasoning stood behind much of the initial planning of the American excavation. As opposed to earlier British excavations, the American endeavor continued for quite a few seasons (1964-1972, 1984, 1990), and was quite successful (for summaries of the finds from all the various expeditions [save for Weill's], with emphasis on the finds from the American excavations, see Dever 1991; 1993; 1998; see below, p. 63, Table 7).

The results of the American excavations enabled a substantial improvement of the understanding of the history of the site, providing a firm stratigraphic sequence from the Chalcolithic period through to Modern times. In particular, the finds of the Middle and Late Bronze Ages and those of the Iron Ages are of importance. These remains have played (and still play) a major role in the ongoing interpretation, and occasional controversies, on these respective periods.

In addition to the stratigraphic data that was attained from the American excavations, several virtually undisturbed cave-tombs were excavated, containing finds from the Early Bronze and Late Bronze Ages (*Gezer V*). Besides the fact that some quite unique finds were recovered from these graves, in particular from the one dating to the Late Bronze

---

[1] For a report on a regional archaeological study of the environs of Tel Gezer and the Ayalon valley (based primarily on an intensive archaeological surface survey of the region), with emphasis on the remains from the Bronze and Iron Ages, see Shavit 2000. For an archaeological study of the Ayalon valley and its vicinity during the late Iron I/early Iron II periods, see Ortiz 2000.

Age (Cave I.10A), they served as an excellent comparison to the many tombs that had been inadequately excavated and published by Macalister (for the location of the various excavation areas, see Fig. 3).

1.2. THE EXCAVATION BACKGROUND

Following the general introduction on the site of Gezer, one can now proceed to present a background on Raymond Weill's excavations at Gezer, which lead to the discovery of the tombs published in the present volume.

From the mid-19th century CE, there was an intensive interest in various aspects relating to the Near East by many of the European countries (for surveys of this topic, see, e.g. Ben-Arieh 1979; Silberman 1982; 1995; 1997 and there further literature). It is from this time onwards that there is much European (and to a lesser extent, American) activity in the region. These activities included the first modern explorations of the region, including numerous geographical, historical and archaeological studies. Needless to say, much of this work was dictated by political, economic and strategic interests, and not only due to scientific curiosity and/or religious convictions. Probably the best example for this is the British *Survey of Western Palestine* (Conder and Kitchener 1882). Although to this day this work is an unparalleled study of major portions of the southern Levant, of striking utility for modern historical and archaeological research, the information collected by this investigation was of paramount strategic importance for the British Army. And in fact, it served as one of the primary intelligence sources during the British campaign in Palestine in 1918 CE (see e.g., Tibawi 1961; Tuchman 1982; Moscrop 2000). To varying degrees, the same can be said of most of the other western "scientific activities" in the Near East (to a certain extent continuing even to this very day) -- ulterior motives were, and are, often omnipresent (e.g., Silberman 1982; 1990a; 1990b; Broshi 1987; Ben-Yehuda 1995; Abu el-Haj 1999; 2001; Benvenisti 2000).[2]

During the second half of the 19th century, when the Jewish immigration and settlement of Palestine started to increase (e.g. Lacquer 1977), little attention was paid to connecting the archaeological remains from the region to the nascent Zionist national agenda (Shavit 1987). The new Jewish settlers (and those that were already in the land), focused on other aspects to serve as the ideological foundations for their claims to the land. In fact, it was only during the beginning of the 20th century CE that the close relationship between the modern Zionist national agenda and the historical and archaeological study of the Land of Israel began to appear (e.g., Shavit 1987; 1997). By the second decade of the 20th century CE, the Jewish settlers started to take an active role in the study of the history and archaeology of the land. Among the events that mark this change, one can note the founding of the Jewish Palestine Exploration Society in December 1912 (and its subsequent revival, after the First World War, in 1919), and the first excavation conducted under its auspices, the discovery and excavation of an ancient Synagogue in Hamath Tiberias directed by N. Slouschz (e.g. Brawer 1965; Shavit 1987; Ben-Arieh 2001).

During the late 19th and early 20th centuries CE, one of the important engines behind the Jewish settlement in Palestine was the support and activities of the late Baron Edmond James de Rothschild (1845-1934). Commencing in the early 1880s, the Baron Rothschild (who was popularly known as "the Baron", "*Avi Ha-Yishuv*" [= father of the settlement] or "*Ha-Nadiv Ha-Yaduah*" [= the well-known benefactor]), provided extensive financial and organizational support for existing Jewish settlements, and purchased lands for the erection of new settlements. Furthermore, the various activities conducted in the settlements that were supported by the Baron Rothschild were closely monitored by quite a large bureaucratic system working for the Baron, at times to the chagrin of the settlers (see, e.g., Margalith 1957; Aaronsohn 2000). During the initial years of his activities he paid little attention to the archaeological study of the land. But in the early 20th century CE, in line with the change in the intellectual interests in the *Yishuv* (the Jewish settlement), the Baron Rothschild commenced to initiate and support archaeological research in the land.[3]

In the late 19th century CE, the Baron Rothschild had purchased lands in Jerusalem, including tracts on the hill to the south of the Temple Mount, in the village of Silwan (in the area known today as the "City of David", or "the southeastern hill"). Once the purchase was made, the Baron decided to conduct archaeological explorations on the site. It is safe to assume that among the reasons that the Baron had decided to conduct the excavations was the fact that several European teams had been working in Jerusalem in the last decades of the 19th century and the beginning of the 20th century CE, and this very work had led to the discovery of some very interesting, and in some cases, extraordinary remains (for overviews of the earlier archaeological research in Jerusalem, see, e.g., Kenyon 1974:1-35; Bahat 1990:16-19). In addition, Silberman (1982: 185) reports that Rothschild had been upset by the scandalous results of M. Parker's work in Jerusalem, and decided to hire an archaeologist who would excavate under his patronage in the

---

[2] A close reading of some of the studies noted here will reveal (and one might add, quite unsurprisingly), strong preconceptions and personal ideologies guiding these observers as well. This is seen, quite categorically, in Abu el-Haj's work (1999; 2001). For a critique of this, see, e.g., Maeir, In Press.

[3] It should be noted that this can be seen as the commencement of the long term commitment by the late Baron Rothschild, and subsequently by the Yad Hanadiv foundation (who has continued his legacy), to support archaeological research in the Land of Israel. Among the numerous projects that have been supported over the years (subsequent to the work by R. Weill discussed below), one can note, e.g.: the et-Tell/Ai Excavations, directed by Marquet-Krause (1935); the Hazor Expedition (both the earlier stages directed by Yadin [e.g. Yadin 1972] and the current project directed by Ben-Tor [e.g. Ben-Tor 1996]); and the Ramat Hanadiv Excavations, directed by Hirschfeld (2000).

Chapter 1 - Introduction

plots that he had purchased in the "City of David" (for a general survey of the so-called "Parker scandal", see ibid: 180-188).

1.3. R. WEILL'S EXCAVATIONS IN GEZER

Raymond-Charles Weill, commenced his career in archaeology and Egyptology at a relatively late age. After having received his training in Egyptology and archaeology in France, he subsequently had some brief archaeological experiences in Egypt and Sinai (see Vandier 1951; Clère 1951; Dawson and Uphill 1972:300). Apparently, due to his being of Jewish descent, the Baron Rothschild invited him to excavate (needless to say, with the Baron's financial support) in Jerusalem, on lands belonging to the Baron. These excavations were conducted both before (in 1913-1914) and after (in 1923-1924) the First World War, and were duly reported by Weill (1920; 1947). Noteworthy, although this is often overlooked (e.g., Albright 1970:57-58; King 1983:104-106; Shavit 1987), Raymond Weill was in fact the first Jewish archaeologist to excavate in modern day Palestine. To a certain extent, he may seen as the harbinger of the local Jewish, and later, Israeli profession of field archaeology,[4] a vocation which has now been vibrant and active for close to a century (see, e.g. Bar-Yosef and Mazar 1982; Broshi 1987:26-30; Mazar 1988).

It was during the course of his excavations in Jerusalem that Weill excavated at Gezer. The Baron Rothschild had acquired lands on and around the site of Gezer, lands which were settled and farmed by Jewish settlers. Apparently, ancient tombs had been revealed on the site by the settlers, and Weill, who by chance was excavating at the time for the Baron in Jerusalem, was called in to excavate at Gezer. Both seasons of Weill's excavations at Gezer (in 1914 and 1924) coincided with his work in Jerusalem.[5]

Unfortunately, very little is known about R. Weill's excavations at Gezer. Asides from a very brief description of the tombs that appeared in the second volume on his excavations in the City of David (Weill 1947:19, 128-129), a detailed report was never published. Even the location of the tombs on the site itself is not known (Fig. 3). To add to this, in the general archaeological and popular literature, these excavations were hardly ever mentioned (briefly mentioned in: Albright 1924:11; ΝΕΑ ΣΙΩΝ 1924:164; Syria 1924:78; Vandier 1951:III-IV; Ussishkin and Wright 1970:115), such as in the various general surveys, bibliographies and lists of the archaeological work during this period (e.g. Meyer 1931; Abel 1938; Barrois 1939; 1953; Vogel 1971:30-32; Vogel and Holtzclaw 1981:30-31). Macalister (1925), who undoubtedly was aware of this work, does not mention Weill's excavations at Gezer in his survey of the archaeological work in Palestine that had been carried out until 1925. Likewise, Vincent, in his, at the time, seminal study comparing the "Royal Tombs" at Gezer and Byblos (Vincent 1923; 1924) does not mention Weill's excavations, despite the fact that they had been conducted by his compatriot so very recently. Even the American excavators of Gezer were not aware of Weill's excavations (e.g. Dever 1992; 1993; 1998; pers. comm.; see as well Finkelstein 2002), despite the many similarities between the finds from both excavations.

Based on the little that is known (primarily from Weill 1947:19, 128-129), the following information about the excavations can be gleaned. In 1914, three tombs were excavated (Tombs I-III), of which Tombs I and III were dated by Weill to the Late Bronze Age, and Tomb II to the Middle Bronze Age. In 1924, an additional six tombs were excavated (Tombs IV-IX). Of these latter tombs, Weill mentions the dating of only three of them. Accordingly, Tombs IV and V primarily contained finds dating to the Late Bronze Age, while Tomb IX contained finds dating to the Middle Bronze Age and Iron Age I periods (it should be stressed that these are the datings suggested by Weill).

1.4. THE POST-EXCAVATION PROCESSING

In his brief description of the excavations, Weill (1947:128-129) also mentions that the finds were given to various museums. The majority of the finds from the 1914 season were given to the now defunct Museum of the *Alliance Israélite* in Jerusalem. Immediately after the first season, three vessels were apparently given to the Jerusalem Municipal Museum (which was located in the Citadel [near Jaffa Gate in Jerusalem]) and thirteen vessels were presented to the Musée de Louvre in Paris. In the early 1930's the finds that had been located in the *Alliance Israélite* were transferred to the newly opened Archaeological Museum of the Hebrew University, while the finds from the by-then defunct Jerusalem Municipal Museum, were transferred to the newly opened Rockefeller Museum.

From the 1924 season, most of the finds were also given to the Archaeological Museum of the Hebrew University, though quite a few vessels were also given to Musée de Louvre in Paris and to the Musée des Antiquités Nationales, in Châteaux de Saint-Germain-en-Laye, outside of Paris.

---

[4] This must be qualified. Although Weill was in fact the first archaeologist of Jewish descent to direct an excavation in Palestine, he should not be seen as a figure who initiated and/or set the directions and agendas for the development of the local Jewish/Israeli archaeology. From an historical point of view, this last role should probably be conferred to the late E.L. Sukenik, the father of well-known archaeologist Yigael Yadin (see, e.g., Shavit 1987; Silberman 1993).

[5] The first season of excavation, in 1914, was conducted under the Ottoman rule. Details about the official permits that were granted for this work could not be located. For the second season of excavation, in 1924, which was carried out under the British Mandate in Palestine, an excavation permit was granted by the Department of Antiquities of Palestine (Excavation Permit 12, granted on January 4, 1924, by the acting director of the Department, P.L.O. Guy [document 3200/ATQ/627, located in the British Mandate Period Archive, The Israel Antiquities Authority Archive, Rockefeller Museum, Jerusalem]).

The original plan of publication for the tombs and their contents, as explained by Weill (1947:128-129) was that they would be studied and published by Mme Paula Zilberberg (née Zelwer), who had been Weill's assistant in the 1923-1924 excavations at the City of David and Gezer (along with A.B. Duff).[6] The publication was to be titled: *Neuf tombes de Gezer*. As one may assume, this volume was never completed. Although Mme Zilberberg commenced working on this project in the 1930's, she did not manage to conclude it. During the Second World War, in 1940, after the German conquest of France, she was forcibly deported to the concentration and death camps by the Nazis, along with thousands of other French Jews. During this period, under uncertain, although undoubtedly horrific circumstances, she was murdered. In addition to her dreadful personal tragedy, her scientific legacy was lost as well. Sadly, none of the materials that had been prepared by Mme Zilberberg could be located. Undoubtedly, this lost work (if even only partially completed) would have been able to provide important information on the tombs, the context of the finds, and other details.

Subsequently, this excavation was virtually forgotten. Save for a cursory note by Ussishkin and Wright (1970:115),[7] these tombs and finds do not appear in any of the archaeological publications relating to Gezer (see above), various studies relating to the Late Bronze Age (e.g. Bunimovitz 1989; Gonen 1992), or any related aspect (e.g. Bloch-Smith 1992; Hallote 1994).

1.5. THE CURRENT RESEARCH

In 1989, the present author was contemplating writing his doctoral dissertation on burial customs in Palestine during the Middle Bronze Age, and was informed of these tombs by Prof. D.B. Barag. Although subsequently, this topic was not chosen for the actual doctoral dissertation (Maeir 1997), it was nevertheless decided that the finds from these tombs (those that were located in the Collections Room of the Hebrew University), warranted an in-depth study of this excavation. In the early 1990's after receiving grants to process and publish the finds from the *Yad Hanadiv* (Rothschild) Foundation and from the Smith Center for the History of Art at the Hebrew University, a long process of research commenced. For more than a decade, an effort was made to track down the finds from the excavation (in five museums and two continents); to retrieve as much information as possible about the excavation; about the people who had been involved in it; about the background of the excavation; and finally, to process the finds and prepare them for publication.

---

[6] Abraham Baer Duff subsequently became Professor of French Civilization at the Hebrew University of Jerusalem, and eventually founded the Department of French Civilization and Language at the same institution.

[7] Surprisingly, the excacavations were not mentioned by Ussishkin in his unpublished M.A. thesis on the Gezer excavations (Ussishkin n.d.).

Unfortunately, despite the fact that quite a substantial amount of information was collected about the excavations, the finds and other related aspects, most of the crucial data is missing. It was not possible to locate any detailed information about the tombs themselves (such as shape, type, number of burials, exact location, etc.), the exact division of the finds to the respective tombs (only some could be related to specific tombs, especially to Tomb 1, see below, p. 32, Pls. 12-14:1), and such details as stratigraphy, location of the finds within the tombs, etc. In addition, some of the original finds from the tombs may be missing, and there does not appear to be any way to ascertain this. Although, without a doubt, this seriously impinges on the ability to interpret the tombs and the finds within them, the unique collection of finds, their comparison to other finds and tombs from Gezer and other sites, as well as the general background of this excavation, insures that the publication of the finds from the tombs is a worthwhile endeavor.

Following the introductory chapter, the respective contributors discuss and analyze finds from the tombs. In Chapter 2, N. Panitz Cohen and the present author discuss the pottery from the tomb. In the following chapter, Chapter 3, the same authors discuss the stone, faience, bone, and metal objects. In Chapter 4, D. Barag discusses the Egyptian 18th Dynasty glass vessel from the tombs, a unique vessel and one of the more important finds from the tombs. In Chapter 5, O. Keel discusses the glyptic finds from the tombs, which included three scaraboids and one stamp seal. In Chapter 6, N. Applebaum, who conducted radiographic analyses of a sample group of vessels from the tombs, discusses the technological conclusions reached from this analysis. And finally, in Chapter 6, I present a summary discussion of the all the various finds.

1.6. TECHNICAL NOTES

Several technical comments on the finds and their registration are warranted. Following the transfer of the find from the *Alliance Israélite* to the Collections Room of the Institute of Archaeology, the Hebrew University, they were registered by the late Prof. Nahman Avigad. This registration consisted of a short entry in the Collection's catalogue, in which basic information (site, ceramic type, dating, and if possible, in this case, from which tomb) was noted. In addition, miniature, although, on the whole, quite accurate line drawings of the objects were added. In the end, these drawings were of some importance. Due to the fact that the contents of the Collections Room were transferred several times over the last several decades (from the Mt. Scopus campus after 1948, and eventually back to the Mt. Scopus, after 1967), ten objects from among finds from the tombs that had been registered in the catalogue could not be located. Thus, N. Avigad's miniature drawings and short descriptions supplied the only available information on these objects (see Pl. 10).

The registration numbers of the respective finds from the various museums and collections are referred to by the use of the following system:

* Hebrew University, Jerusalem: a two or three digit number.
* The Rockefeller Museum, Jerusalem: "V" (= vase), followed by a four digit number. The objects are listed in the British Mandate period inventory books (so-called "Army Books") that are located in the British Mandate Period Archive in the Rockefeller Museum.
* Musée de Louvre, Paris: "AO" (= Archéologie Orientale), followed by a four digit number.
* Musée de Antiquités Nationales, Saint-Germain-en-Laye: "SG" (=Saint-Germain), followed by a five to seven digit number.

These registration numbers are the original registration numbers used in the respective institutions, save for the registration numbers at the Musée de Antiquités Nationales, Saint-Germain-en-Laye. In the latter case, an "SG" (not appearing in the original museum registration numbers) has been added in the text before the actual registration number, so as to insure that these vessels are not mistaken with the registration numbers from the other museums.

All the finds that could be located from the respective collections in Jerusalem were both drawn and photographed. Most, but not all of the finds located in the Museums in France, were drawn and photographed. Nevertheless, due to the different methods used in the drawing of the vessels, and the different photographic guidelines, these illustrations were not always compatible with the graphic information available for the majority of the finds, e.g., those located in Jerusalem. Thus, the illustrations appearing in this volume are, for the most part, items from the Jerusalem collections, although when necessary (if there was a type not represented in the vessels from Jerusalem and a photograph was available), photographs of the vessels from France were included as well.

REFERENCES

Aaronsohn, R.
2000 *Rothschild and Early Jewish Colonization*. Israel Studies in Historical Geography. Jerusalem: Magnes.

Abu el-Haj, N.
1999 Translating Truths: Nationalism, the Practice of Archaeology, and the Remaking of the Past and Present in Contemporary Jerusalem. *American Ethnologist* 25:166-188.

Abu el-Haj, N.
2001 *Facts on the Ground: Archaeological Practice and Territorial Self-Fashioning in Israeli Society*. Chicago: The University of Chicago Press.

Aharoni, Y.
1979 *The Land of the Bible: A Historical Geography*. Revised and Enlarged Edition (A.F. Rainey [trans. and ed.]). Philadelphia: Westminster Press.

Albright, W.F.
1924 Report of the Director of the School in Jerusalem. *Bulletin of the American Schools of Oriental Research* 16:9-15.

Albright, W.F.
1970 The Phenomemon of Israeli Archaeology. Pp. 57-63 in *Essays in Honor of Nelson Glueck: Near Eastern Archaeology in the Twentieth Century*, ed. J.A. Sanders. Garden City, NY: Doubleday.

Bahat, D.
1990 *The Illustrated Atlas of Jerusalem*. Jerusalem: Carta.

Barrois, A.-G.
1939 *Manuel d'archéologie biblique, Tome I*. Paris: Auguste Picard.

Barrois, A.-G.
1953 *Manuel d'archéologie biblique, Tome II*. Paris: Auguste Picard.

Bar-Yosef, O. and Mazar, A.
1982 Israeli Archaeology. *World Archaeology* 13:310-325.

Ben-Arieh, Y.
1979 *The Rediscovery of the Holy Land in the Nineteenth Century*. Jerusalem: Magnes.

Ben-Arieh, Y.
2001 Developments in the Study of Yediat Ha'aretz in Modern Times, up to the Establishment of the State of Israel. *Cathedra* 100:305-338, 400-401 (Hebrew with English Abstract).

Benevenisti, M.
2000 *Sacred Landscapes: The Buried History of the Holy Land since 1948*. Berkeley: University of California Press.

Ben-Tor, A.
1996 The Yigael Yadin Memorial Excavations at Hazor: Aims and Preliminary Results of the 1990-1992 Seasons. *Eretz Israel* 25:67-81 (Hebrew with English Abstract).

Ben-Yehuda, N.
1995 *The Masada Myth: Collective Memory and Mythmaking in Israel*. Madison: University of Wisconsin Press.

Bloch-Smith, E.
1992 *Judahite Burial Practices and Beliefs about the Dead*. Journal for the Study of the Old Testament Supplement Series 123; JSOT/ASOR Monograph Series 7. Sheffield: JSOT Press.

Brawer, A.J.
1965 From the Early Days of the Israel Exploration Society. Pp. 228-236 in *Western Galilee and the Coast of Galilee*, ed. J. Aviram. Jerusalem: Israel Exploration Society.

Broshi, M.
1987 Religion, Ideology, and Politics and their Impact on Palestinian Archaeology. *Israel Museum Journal* 6: 17-32.

Bunimovitz, S.
1989 *The Land of Israel in the Late Bronze Age: A Case Study of Socio-Cultural Change in a Complex Society*. Unpublished Dissertation. Tel Aviv: Tel Aviv University (in Hebrew with English Summary).

Clère, J.J.
1951 Bibliographie de Raymond Weill. *Revue d'Égyptologie* 8:VII-XVI.

Clermont-Ganneau, C.S.
1896 *Archaeological Researches in Palestine during the Years 1873-1874, Vol. II*. London: Palestine Exploration Fund.

Conder, C.R., and Kitchener, H.H.
1882 *The Survey of Western Palestine*. London: Palestine Exploration Fund.

Dawson, W.R., and Uphill, E.P.
1972 *Who was Who in Egyptology*. London: Egypt Exploration Society.

Dever, W.G.
1976 Gezer. Pp. 428-443 in *The Encyclopedia of Archaeological Excavations in the Holy Land, Volume 2*, eds. M. Avi-Yonah and E. Stern. Jerusalem: Israel Exploration Society.

Dever, W.G.
1992 Gezer. Pp. 998-1003 in *The Anchor Bible Dictionary, Vol. II*, ed. D.N. Freedman. New York: Doubleday.

Dever, W.G.
1993 Gezer. Pp. 496-506 in *The New Encyclopedia of Archaeological Excavations in the Holy Land, Vol. 2*, eds. E. Stern and A. Gilboa. Jerusalem: Exploration Society (Hebrew).

Dever, W.G.
1998 *Gezer: A Crossroads in Ancient Israel*. Jerusalem: Ha-Kibbutz Ha-Meuchad (Hebrew).

Dorsey, D.A.
1991 *The Roads and Highways of Ancient Israel*. The ASOR Library of Biblical and Ancient Near Eastern Archaeology. Baltimore: The Johns Hopkins University Press.

Finkelstein, I.
2002 Gezer revisited and revised. *Tel Aviv* 29/2:262-296.

Gezer I = Dever, W.G., Lance, H.D., and Wright G.E.
1970 *Preliminary Report of the 1964-1966 Seasons*. Jerusalem: Hebrew Union College Biblical and Archaeological School in Jerusalem.

Gezer II = Dever, W.G. (ed.)
1974 *Report of the 1967-70 Seasons in Fields I and II*. Jerusalem: Nelson Glueck School of Biblical Archaeology.

Gezer IV = Dever, W.G., et al.
1986 *Gezer IV: The 1969-71 Seasons in Field VI, the "Acropolis"*. Jerusalem: Nelson Glueck School of Biblical Archaeology.

Gezer V = Seger, J.D., and Lance, H.D. (eds.)
1988 *Gezer V: The Field I Caves*. Jerusalem: Nelson Glueck School of Biblical Archaeology.

Gonen, R.
1992 *Burial Patterns and Cultural Diversity in Late Bronze Age Canaan*. American Schools of Oriental Research Dissertation Series Volume 7. Winona Lake, IN: Eisenbrauns.

Hallote, R.S.
1994 *Mortuary Practices and their Implications for Social Organization in the Middle Bronze Southern Levant*. Unpublished Dissertation. Chicago: University of Chicago.

Hirschfeld, Y.
2000 *Ramat Hanadiv Excavations: Final Report of the 1984-1998 Excavations*. Jerusalem: Israel Exploration Society.

Kenyon, K.M.
1974 *Digging up Jerusalem*. London: Ernest Benn.

King, P.J.
1983 *American Archaeology in the Mideast: A History of the American Schools of Oriental Research*. Philadelphia: American Schools of Oriental Research.

Lance, H.D.
1967 Gezer in the Land and in History. *Biblical Archaeologist* 30:34-47.

Lacquer, W.Z.
1977 *A History of Zionism*. London: Weidenfeld and Nicolson

Chapter 1 - Introduction

Macalister I = Macalister, R.A.S.
1912 *The Excavation of Gezer, Volume I*. London: John Murray.

Macalister II = Macalister, R.A.S.
1912 *The Excavation of Gezer, Volume II*. London: John Murray.

Macalister III = Macalister, R.A.S.
1912 *The Excavation of Gezer, Volume III*. London: John Murray.

Macalister, R.A.S.
1925 *A Century of Excavation in Palestine*. London: Religious Tract Society.

Maeir, A.M.
1997 *The Material Culture of the Central Jordan Valley during the Middle Bronze II Period: Pottery and Settlement Pattern*. Unpublished Dissertation. Jerusalem: Hebrew University.

Maeir, A.M.
In Press Review of Abu el-Haj 2001. *Isis*.

Margalith, I.
1957 *Le Baron Edmond de Rothschild et la colonisation juive en Palestine, 1882-1899*. Paris: M. Riviere.

Marquet-Krause, J.
1949 *Les fouilles de 'Ay (et-Tell)*. Paris: Paul Geuthner.

Mazar, A.
1988 Israeli Archaeologists. Pp. 109-128 in *Benchmarks in Time and Culture: Essays in Honor of Joseph A. Callaway*, eds. J.F. Drinkard, G.L. Mattingly and J.M. Miller. Atlanta: Scholars Press.

Meyer, L.A.
1931 Concise Bibliography of Excavations in Palestine. *Quarterly of the Department of Antiquities of Palestine* 1/2:86-94.

Moran, W.L.
1992 *The Amarna Letters*. Baltimore: The Johns Hopkins University Press.

Moscrop, J.J.
2000 *Measuring Jerusalem: The Palestine Exploration Fund and British Interests in the Holy Land*. Leicester: Leicester University Press.

ΝΕΑ ΣΙΩΝ
1924 Ἐχχλησιαστιχά Χρουιχά. *ΝΕΑ ΣΙΩΝ* 1924:160-164.

Orni, E., and Efrat, E.
1980 *Geography of Israel*. 4th Revised Edition. Jerusalem: Israel Universities Press.

Ortiz, S.M.
2000 *The 11/10th Century B.C.E. Transition in the Aijalon Valley Region: New Evidence from Tel Miqne-Ekron Stratum IV*. Unpublished Ph.D. Dissertation. Tucson: University of Arizona.

Reich, R.
1985 The 'Boundary of Gezer" - On the Jewish Settlement at Gezer in Hasmonaean Times. *Eretz Israel* 18:167-179, 71* (Hebrew with English abstract).

Ross, J.F.
1967 Gezer in the Tell el-Amarna Letters. *Biblical Archaeologist* 30: 62-70.

Rowe, A.
1935a The 1934 Excavations at Gezer. *Palestine Exploration Fund, Quarterly Statement* 1935: 19-33.

Rowe, A.
1935b Gezer. *Quarterly of the Department of Antiquities of Palestine* IV: 198-201.

Shavit, A.
2000 Settlement Patterns in the Ayalon Valley in the Bronze and Iron Ages. *Tel Aviv* 27:189-230.

Shavit, Y.
1987 'Truth Shall Spring out of the Earth': The Development of Jewish Popular Interest in Archaeology in Eretz-Israel. *Cathedra* 44: 27-54 (Hebrew with English summary).

Shavit, Y.
1997 Archaeology, Political Structure, and Culture in Israel. Pp. 48-61 in *The Archaeology of Israel: Constructing the Past, Interpreting the Present*, eds. N.A. Silberman and D. Small. Supplement of the Journal for the Study of the Old Testament 237. Sheffield: Sheffield Academic Press.

Silberman, N.A.
1982 *Digging for God and Country: Exploration, Archeology, and the Secret Struggle for the Holy Land, 1799-1917*. New York: Alfred A. Knopf.

Silberman, N.A.
1990a The Politics of the Past: Archaeology and Nationalism in the Eastern Mediterranean. *Mediterranean Quarterly* 1:99-110.

Silberman, N.A.
1990b *Between Past and Present: Archaeology, Ideology, and Nationalism in the Modern Middle East*. New York: Doubleday.

Silberman, N.A.
1993 *A Prophet from Amongst You: The Life of Yigael Yadin*. Reading, MA: Addison-Wesley.

Silberman, N.A.
1995 Power, Politics and the Past: The Social Construction of Antiquity in the Holy Land. Pp. 9-23 in *The Archaeology of Society in the Holy Land*, ed. T.E. Levy. London: Leicester University Press.

Silberman, N.A.
1997 Structuring the Past: Israelis, Palestinians, and the Symbolic Authority of Archaeological Monuments. Pp. 62-81 in *The Archaeology of Israel: Constructing the Past, Interpreting the Present*, eds. N.A. Silberman and D. Small. Supplement of the Journal for the Study of the Old Testament 237. Sheffield: Sheffield Academic Press.

Syria
1924 Nouvelles Archéologiques. *Syria* 5: 78-81.

Tibawi, A.L.
1961 *British Interests in Palestine, 1800-1901*. Oxford: Oxford University Press.

Tuchman, B.
1982 *Bible and Sword: How the British Came to Palestine*. London: Macmillan.

Ussishkin, D
n.d. *R.A.S. Macalister's Excavations at Gezer*. Unpublished Master's Thesis. Jerusalem: Hebrew University (in Hebrew).

Ussishkin, D., and Wright, G.E.
1970 Gezer. Pp. 111-117 in *The Encyclopedia of Archaeological Excavations in the Holy Land, Volume I*, eds. B. Mazar et al.. Jerusalem: Israel Exploration Society (in Hebrew)

Vandier, J.
1951 Raymond Weill (1874-1950). *Revue d'Égyptologie* 8:I-VI.

Vincent, H.
1923 Le Nouvel Hypogée de Byblos et l'Hypogée Royal de Gézer, I. *Revue Biblique* 32:552-574.

Vincent, H.
1924 Le Nouvel Hypogée de Byblos et l'Hypogée Royal de Gézer, II. *Revue Biblique* 33:161-185.

Vogel, E.K.
1971 Bibliography of Holy Land Sites Compiled in Honor of Dr. Nelson Glueck. *Hebrew Union College Annual* 42:1-96.

Vogel, E.K., and Holtzclaw, B.
1981 Bibliography of Holy Land Sites, Part II. *Hebrew Union College Annual* 52:1-92.

Weill, R.
1920 *La Cité de David. Compte-rendu des fouilles exécutées à Jérusalem, sur le site de la ville primitive. Campagne de 1913-1914*. Paris: Paul Geuthner.

Weill, R.
1947 *La Cité de David. Compte-rendu des fouilles exécutées à Jérusalem, sur le site de la ville primitive. Campagne de 1923-1924*. Paris: Paul Geuthner.

Yadin, Y.
1972 *Hazor: The Head of All Those Kingdoms*. The Schweich Lectures, 1970. London: The British Academy.

CHAPTER 2: THE POTTERY ASSEMBLAGE

Nava Panitz-Cohen and Aren M. Maeir

2.1. INTRODUCTION

In this chapter, the pottery assemblage, which constitutes the primary material evidence from the tombs, will be presented. The 186 vessels from the tombs that have been located, represent some of the finest published examples of the respective types. However, as stated in the introduction, the exact location of these tombs is unknown, as are their particular contents. This makes it impossible to study the respective tomb assemblages as separate tomb groups, save for a small number of vessels that can be assigned to specific tombs. Thus, the vessels are presented in catalogue form, attempting to group them together typologically with the primary purpose of facilitating the presentation and general dating. The few vessels that can be assigned to a specific tomb (below, p. 32; e.g., Tomb I, Pls. 12-14:1) are grouped together, even if the information about these tombs is limited as well.

The wide chronological range of the vessels spans the Early Bronze IV/Middle Bronze Age I to the Iron Age II, with the main bulk of finds from the Middle Bronze Age IIB/C to the Late Bronze Age II (see Table 4). In addition, one jug dating to the Hellenistic period was also found.[1] The assemblage includes mainly local ceramic vessels, with an assortment of Late Bronze Age Cypriote and Mycenaean imports as well. Other finds include stone, metal, bone, ivory and glass vessels and implements, as well as glyptics (see Chapters 3-5, below).

Due to the nature of the assemblage, parallels were sought only from a selection of proximate sites that afford accessible published comparisons. These sites are: Lachish, Beth Shemesh, Tell Beit Mirsim, Tel Batash-Timnah, Tel Miqne-Ekron and Gezer itself; several relevant tomb groups from Jerusalem were checked as well. Whenever possible, care was taken to mention similar vessels found in the other excavations at Gezer (see the Introduction, above, Chapter 1, and the references provided in the bibliography); the finds from the tombs of these latter excavations were of particular interest, despite the obvious problems in dating (vis-à-vis some of the tombs that had been excavated by Macalister as well as the tombs discussed here). In a few relevant cases, comparisons from other regions are suggested as well. General parallels for each typological group are cited at the end of its description; however, when a comparison was especially suited to one particular vessel within the general group, it is referred to immediately after the description of that vessel.

As explained in the introductory chapter, the largest selection of finds from these tombs is currently situated in the Hebrew University. Over the years, due to various contingencies, the finds have been moved several times, and it appears that some of the original vessels from these tombs have been lost. The only existing documentation for these lost vessels is a series of miniature drawings (along with a brief description, recorded by the late Prof. Nahman Avigad) in the registration logbook of the Collections Room at the Hebrew University's Institute of Archaeology. These drawings are collected below on Pl. 10, and are discussed respectively with their assumed typological groups, if this attribution could in fact be discerned from the schematic drawings and the accompanying description.

Most of the vessels from the Gezer tombs that are presently in the Musée de Louvre and the Musée des Antiquités de Saint-Germain-en-Laye were not drawn, and are not presented graphically in the plates; most of these are identical to the types that appear in the plates. For those vessels from these two sources that are not already represented typologically in the corpus of the Hebrew University Collections Room, photos are provided.

Most of the vessels were found intact and those that underwent restoration did so, for the most part, due to breakage that occurred over the years during storage and display. Such mending is specified in the plate descriptions wherever possible.

2.2. THE POTTERY

2.2.1. BOWLS

2.2.1.1. BOWL TYPE A - LARGE SHALLOW BOWLS WITH MOLDED RIM
Pls. 1:1-5; Nos. 58, 68, 81, 80, 79; Pl. 10: No. 82?; Pl. 17:1.

---

[1] All dates are BCE unless otherwise specified. Note the possibility that the earliest vessel (EB IV/MB I) and the latest vessel (Hellenistic period) may have been mistakenly included with the tomb groups from Gezer (for the discussion of these vessels, see in this chapter, below). It should be noted that 10 vessels are marked in the Hebrew University Collection Room inventory as belonging to the tombs from Gezer that were excavated by R. Weill, but they are missing from the collection and no drawings or other documentation are available. These are: Bowls: Inventory Nos. 71, 106, 130, 133, 134, 138, 140, 201; Lamps: 193, 194. They were not included in the total count of the assemblage.

Gezer - Tombs

NOT DRAWN: SG 77.211B.[2]

These are large shallow bowls (averaging c. 23 cm diameter) with thick rounded walls and a thick disc base (flat or convex, straight or everted exterior). The rim top is slightly molded: flat-topped, thickened or incurving.

-**Pl. 1:1 (No. 58)**: traces of red band on rim; slightly convex disc base with sharp everted exterior.

-**Pls. 1:2; 17:1 (No. 68)**: rim circumference distorted; flat disc base with sharp everted exterior.

-**Pl. 1:3 (No. 81)**: rim circumference distorted; flat disc base.

-**Pl. 1:4 (No. 80)**: slightly incurving rim; very convex disc base; red band on rim. *Gezer I*: Pl. 31:20-21, Stratum XIX.

-**Pl. 1:5 (No. 79)**: very slightly everted rim exterior; wide disc base.

-**SG 77.211B (Pl. 25:1**; *Saint Germain-en-Laye*: 149): a large bowl (25 cm rim diameter), reddish yellow fabric; pockmarked and encrusted; mended.

General Parallels:
Gezer: *Gezer I*: Pl. 31:1,19, Stratum XIX; *Gezer IV*: Pl. 3:24, red painted radial band inside, red on rim, Stratum XXII; Pls. 7:1; 8:23, red on rim, Stratum XVIII; *Gezer V*: Pl. 12:1, base missing, Cave I.10A entrance, Stratum XVI (LB IIA); Pl. 33: 35, rim only, Cave I.10A, construction phase of lower burial cave, (MB IIC[3]-LB IA); *Macalister III*: Pl. LXII:44, Tomb 1.

Lachish: *Lachish II*: Pl. XXXVIIB:8, ring base, Fosse Temple I; Pl. XXXVIIB:15, Fosse Temple II; *Lachish IV*: Pl. 70:596, tapering rim, Tomb 129 (MB IIB/C).

Beth Shemesh: *Ain Shems I:* Pl. XXIX: 222, Tomb 17.

Tell Beit Mirsim: *TBM 1a*: Pl. 10:5, Stratum E.

Discussion
Similarly shaped bowls, generically called 'platter bowls', have a long chronological range. They begin as early as MB IIA and are common in MB IIB/C contexts with both plain and molded rims; many have a red band painted on the rim. The bases at this time are ring bases, or more rarely, convex disc bases (e.g. Amiran 1969: 91; Pl. 26: 2-3, 7-8, all from Megiddo, Strata XII-XI).

Such bowls continue to be found in Late Bronze Age I and II contexts as well, though the later bowls are generally deeper, heavier and with straighter sides (see our Bowl E below). Early Late Bronze Age examples often have painted decoration or burnish inside, or a red band painted on the rim. The rim tops tend to be tapering or rounded. Tufnell's 'Bowls Without Flare, Class 1' (*Lachish II*:78, Pl. XXXVII) include examples similar to those from the Gezer tombs and are present in all three phases of the Fosse Temple; the notable changes are in the proportions and the base, with the bowls in Temple I having ring bases, those in Temple II having both ring and disc bases and those in Temple III - only disc bases. These bowls are Classes G (plain) and H (curved) from the Lachish tomb deposits, dating to MB IIB/C (*Lachish IV*: 181-182).

Thus, the parallels to the shallow platter bowls with slightly molded rims from the Gezer tombs suggest that they span the MB IIB/C to early LB horizon; the disc base common to all of the bowls of this type found at Gezer indicates that they should be placed on the later end of this spectrum.

2.2.1.2. BOWL TYPE B - SMALL- MEDIUM SHALLOW BOWLS WITH THICKENED INNER RIMS
Pl.1: 6-14; Nos. 135,200,132,131,137,136, 202,139,211; Pl. 17:2-4.

NOT DRAWN: SG 77.211B (see, above, n. 2)

These are small to medium sized bowls (averaging ca. 20 cm diameter) with a thickened inner rim, either rounded or truncated; the contact line of the folded inner rim to the body is sometimes emphasized with a groove. The sides are rounded, rising to a straight or everted rim exterior. Bases are generally variations of a thick disc base, flat or slightly convex.

-**Pls. 1:6; 17:2 (No. 135)**: rounded inner rim; everted rim exterior; very distorted rim circumference; low disc base.

-**Pl. 1:7 (No. 200)**: rounded inner rim; slightly everted rim exterior; thick, slightly convex disc base with everted exterior.

-**Pls. 1:8; 17:3 (No. 132)**: rounded inner rim; everted rim exterior; rim circumference slightly distorted; disc base with a slightly prominent, untrimmed bottom.

-**Pl. 1:9 (No. 131)**: Same as No. 135 (Pl. 1:6).

-**Pl. 1:10 (No. 137)**: truncated inner rim; everted rim exterior; wheel\coil marks prominent on body; flat disc base with everted exterior.

-**Pl. 1:11 (No. 136)**: rounded inner rim; straight rim exterior; rim circumference distorted; disc base. For a discussion of the pottery technology of this bowl, as seen through Computed Tomography Analysis, see below, Chapter 6.

---

[2] The catalogue of the Saint Germain-en-Laye Museum (*Saint Germain-en-Laye*: 149) records five bowls registered with this number (77.211B). Only three were available and photographed. They appear in our catalogue with the same registration number, though they represent three separate bowls.

[3] It should be noted that the use of the nomenclature MB IIC is not without problems. See, e.g., Kempinski 1983; Maeir 1997:148-149.

-**Pls. 1:12; 17:4 (No. 202)**: rounded inner rim; everted rim exterior; thick disc base. *Gezer I*: Pl.29: 5, Stratum XV.

-**Pl. 1:13 (No. 139)**: truncated inner rim; everted rim exterior; rim circumference slightly distorted; thick disc base.

-**Pl. 1:14 (No. 211)**: rounded inner rim; everted rim exterior; rim circumference slightly distorted; unique, very wide flat base.

-**SG 77.211B (Pl. 25:1**; *Saint Germain-en-Laye*: 149): a medium sized bowl with a slightly thickened inner rim and everted exterior rim; disc base.

General Parallels:
Gezer: *Gezer II*: Pl. 24:24, thick, base missing, Stratum XV; *Gezer IV*: Pl. 13:16, rim only, Strata XV; *Gezer V*: Pl.8: 1, no base, Cave I.10A, post-burial phase (LB IIB); Pl. 14:4, 14, Cave I.10A, Upper Burial phase (LB IIA).

Lachish: *Lachish II*: Pl. XLB: 93,94, Fosse Temple III.

Tel Beit Mirsim: *TBM 1a*: Pl. 12:13, low ring base, Stratum D.

Beth Shemesh: *Ain Shems II*: Pl. XXX: 30, Stratum IV.

Tel Batash-Timnah: Kelm and Mazar 1995: Fig. 4.13:1, Stratum VIII (LB IB).

Tel Miqne-Ekron: Killebrew 1996: Pl. 1:3, Stratum X (LB I-LB IIA).

Discussion
These bowls are related to the generic group of 'platter bowls' (see Group A above). However, they are smaller and deeper, representing a somewhat later stage in the development of this type. Their distinguishing characteristic is their thickened inner rim, as opposed to the plain or slightly molded rim top of Group A.

It is notable that small to medium sized bowls with this inner rim shape were not common in the Lachish Fosse Temples. The two comparisons cited above from Fosse Temple III appear to have a thickened inner rim, though Tufnell included them in her category of 'Flared Bowls, Class 1', which were defined as having plain rims (*Lachish II*: 78, Pl. XLI). In her category of 'Flared Bowls - Class 3', which were defined as having internally flanged rims, only large bowls are presented; these correlate with our Group C and will be discussed below. Thus, small sized bowls with internally thickened rims appear to be relatively uncommon at Bronze Age Lachish, both in the Fosse Temple and in the tombs. At Gezer as well, based on the published pottery, this bowl type does not appear to have been very common.

The parallels reflect that the main appearance of this shape was in LB II, though they do begin earlier. Most of the examples from the Gezer tombs have a rim distortion, which is a common characteristic of bowls in LB II, suggesting rather careless stacking in the kiln resulting from the mass production of these utilitarian vessels. Alternatively, this might have been the result of the proposed handmade (coil) or slow wheel technology that several scholars suggest was used in pottery production in LB II, especially in the 13th century, resulting in "careless formation" (Killebrew 1998: 399; and see the additional discussion on the technology of one of these bowls, as seen through Computed Tomography Analysis, below, Chapter 6).

2.2.1.3. BOWL TYPE C - LARGE SHALLOW BOWLS WITH THICKENED INNER RIM
Pl. 1:15-21; Nos. 207,206,209,205, 72, 208,57; Pl. 17:5-8.

These are similar to Type B, but larger (averaging ca. 30 cm diameter). The sides are thick and rounded, rising to a straight or everted rim exterior. Bases are generally variations of a thick disc base, flat or convex.

-**Pls. 1:15; 17:5 (No. 207)**: slightly everted rim exterior; truncated inner rim; prominent wheel\coil marks on body; rim circumference slightly distorted; convex disc base.

-**Pl. 1:16 (No. 206)**: rounded inner rim; very everted rim exterior; flat disc base. Heavy bowl.

-**Pls. 1:17; 17:6 (No. 209)**: slightly thickened inner rim with varying asymmetrical width, slightly everted rim exterior; convex disc base with slight ompholos inside.

-**Pl. 1:18 (No. 205)**: truncated inner rim, straight rim exterior with slight bulge; concave disc base with dip in center.

-**Pls. 1:19; 17:7 (No. 72)**: rounded inner rim; straight rim exterior; thick flat disc base.

-**Pl. 1:20 (No. 208)**: truncated inner rim; straight rim exterior; rim circumference slightly distorted; concave disc base with dip in center.

-**Pls. 1:21; 17:8 (No. 57)**: truncated inner rim, almost horizontal; straight rim exterior; rim circumference slightly distorted during manufacture; slightly convex disc base.

General Parallels
Gezer: *Macalister III*: Pl. LXXXVIII: 18, Tomb 84 (LB-early Iron Age I); *Gezer II*: Pl. 22:6, rim only, Stratum XVI; Pls. 23:8, 24:23, base missing Stratum XV; *Gezer IV*: Pl. 7:13, Stratum XVIII.

Lachish: *Lachish II*: Pl. XXXVIIIB: 43 (see our Nos. 205, 208), Fosse Temple II and III; Pl. XLB: 71, Fosse Temple I and II (see our Nos. 206, 207); *Lachish IV*: Pl. 70: 584 (MB IIC); Pl. 70:593 (MB IIB/C).

Tell Beit Mirsim: *TBM Ia*: Pl. 10:10, everted rim exterior, Stratum E.

Beth Shemesh: *Ain Shems IV*: Pl. LVIII: 1, Stratum IV.

Tel Batash-Timnah: Kelm and Mazar 1995: Fig. 4.28:1, Stratum VII (LB IIA).

Tel Miqne-Ekron: Killebrew 1996: Pl. 2:1-3, Stratum X (LB I-IIA); Pls. 4:9-11, 6:4, Stratum IX (LB IIA-B).

Derivative Variation:
-**Pls. 1:22; 17:9 (No. 70)**: round-topped 'hammer head' rim with very flaring exterior, forming a horizontal "shelf"; rim circumference distorted; wheel\coil marks visible on body; slightly convex disc base.

Parallels:
Lachish: *Lachish IV*: Pl. 71:611, similar rim, high ring base, MB IIB/C.

Tel Beit Mirsim: *TBM I*: Pl. 44:7-8, smaller, Stratum D.

Discussion
The separation of these from their smaller counterparts (Group B above), though arbitrary, shows that while both were contemporary during the Late Bronze Age, the larger bowls had already begun to appear in MB IIC. At this time, the folded inner rim is usually shorter and rounder than the later successors (e.g. *Gezer IV*: Pl. 8:14, Stratum XIX), although longer examples may be found. Several MB IIB/C parallels to this bowl have two handles, e.g. Gezer, *Macalister III*: Pl. CLIV:6, wide and shallow; *Lachish IV*: Pl. 69:579,580; *TBM Ia*: Pl. 12:18, Stratum D. Dever contends that a slightly everted exterior on bowls of this type places them late in the Late Bronze Age (*Gezer IV*: 79, note 132). Some of the bowls classified as Bowl B from the Gezer tombs are slightly everted and the heavy flat or concave disc base that is characteristic of all of them also points to a later date in the sequence, i.e. LB IIB.

2.2.1.4. BOWL TYPE C1 - LARGE ROUNDED BOWL WITH LEDGE RIM

-**Pls. 1:23; 17:10 (No. 210)**: short truncated inner rim and everted rim exterior; ring base; red slip and irregular hand burnish inside and outside.

Parallels:
Gezer: *Macalister III*: Pl. LXXXIII: 12, Tomb 28 (Iron Age II).

Tell Beit Mirsim: *TBM III*: Pl. 21:15, horizontal ledge rim, Stratum A.

Beth Shemesh: *Ain Shems IV*: Pl. LXVI: 4, smaller, red slipped and burnished, Stratum IIb.

Lachish: *Lachish V*: Pl. 41: 11, rim and upper body, red slipped and burnished, Stratum V.

Discussion
This bowl is presented at the end of the thickened inner rim bowls, though its ledge rim sets it apart from the Bronze Age bowls, as does its surface treatment. As the parallels indicate, similar bowls may be found in early Iron Age II contexts, when they are usually covered with the red slip and hand burnish typical of this period. It is generally accepted that this combination of surface treatment began to appear in the late 11th and early 10th centuries (Mazar 1985: 83-86).[4] Although its basic shape - large, open, with rounded sides - may be reminiscent of similarly shaped bowls in the Bronze Age, it may be considered that such bowls were a utilitarian product more than a continuation of a singular long running pottery tradition. The rim shape and red slip on the bowl from Gezer point to an Iron Age IIA date.

2.2.1.5. BOWL TYPE D - DEEP BOWL WITH MOLDED RIM
Pl. 2:1-3; Nos. 87,96,76; Pl. 18:1.

These are three deep bowls (averaging 22.5 cm diameter) with rounded sides and a short, truncated inner rim creating a small angled "shelf". The rim top is tapered, with a straight or flaring exterior. The base is a slightly convex disc base with everted exterior.

-**Pl. 2:1 (No. 87)**: sharply-angled inner rim; straight rim exterior; rim circumference slightly distorted.

-**Pl. 2:2 (No. 96)**: sharply-angled inner rim, flaring rim exterior; rim circumference slightly distorted.

-**Pl. 2:3 (No. 76)**: thinner walls; flaring rim exterior.

General Parallels:
Lachish: *Lachish II*: Pl. XLB:83 (smaller, but similar rim and base), Fosse Temples II and III; *Lachish IV*: Pl. 70: 609, different rim, red band on inner rim, Tomb 539 (LB IIB).

Tell Beit Mirsim: *TBM Ia*, Pl. 16:15, Stratum C.

Discussion
Although these three bowls share several features, they are not a homogeneous group and do not constitute a common type. Their relative large size and deep proportions might indicate a krater-like function (such as food preparation). Comparisons to the general features of this type, especially the base, suggest a date in LB II.

2.2.1.6. BOWL TYPE E - DEEP ROUNDED BOWLS WITH PLAIN RIM
Pl. 2:4-7; Nos. 83,203,126,127; also Pl. 10: Nos. 77,78,142,143,204[5]; Pls. 18:2-3.

NOT DRAWN: SG 77.211C

These are small to medium bowls (averaging 15 cm diameter) with rounded walls and average proportion of 1:2.8

---

[4] Holladay (1990; 1995) has proposed lowering the date of the beginning of red slip and irregular burnish to the second half of the 10th century. See though Mazar 1998 for a rebuttal of his suggestion.

[5] Since a cross section of the bowls was not provided in the miniature drawings, it is impossible to know whether the inner rim was thickened (see especially No. 78, whose everted outer profile suggests this); thus, these bowls might be included with Type BL B as well.

(though No. 83, Pl. 2:4, is deeper at 1:2). The rim is plain, with a round or tapering top. The base is a thick flat disc base, with a straight or rounded exterior.

2.2.1.6.1. BOWL TYPE E1 - MEDIUM SIZED WITH WIDE DISC BASE

-**Pls. 2:4; 18:2 (No. 83)**: tapering rim; rim circumference slightly distorted during manufacture; roughly finished base. Note the deeper stance, relating it to the proportions of the bowls in Group A (see above).

-**Pl. 2:5 (No. 203)**: tapering rim; rounded exterior disc base.

-**SG 77.211C (Pl. 25:2**; *Saint Germain-en-Laye*: 149): small bowl (13.8 cm diameter; red band painted on rim interior and exterior.

Parallels (83 and 203):
Gezer: *Gezer I*: Pl. 28:20, Stratum XV-XIV; *Gezer IV*: Pl. 23:21, Stratum XIII (Iron Age I, though from a locus mixed with MB II and LB II - ibid: 193); *Gezer V*: Pls. 20:2; 26:3-7, variations in proportions, Cave I.10A, Lower Burial Phase (LB IB/LB IIA).

Lachish: *Lachish II*: Pl. XXXVIIIB: 36-39, 51-52, some ring and mostly disc bases, Fosse Temple II and III; *Lachish IV*: Pl. 70:606, Tomb 1003 (LB IIA); *Lachish V*: Pl. 39: 9-10, convex ring bases, Stratum VI.

Tell Beit Mirsim: *TBM Ia*: Pl. 16:1,4, Stratum C.

Beth Shemesh: *Ain Shems II*: Pl. XXXII:51, Stratum Sub-III; *Ain Shems IV*: Pl. LVIII:2,5-6,14, thick, Stratum IV.

2.2.1.6.2. BOWL TYPE E2 - SMALL SIZED WITH NARROW BASE - CONCAVE DISC OR FLAT

-**Pls. 2:6; 18:3 (No. 126)**: the proportions of this bowl are similar to 127, though the walls are thinner and the rim is slightly flaring, with a tapering top; rim circumference slightly distorted during manufacture; highly convex disc base with a straight exterior; red line painted on rim interior and exterior.

-**Pl. 2:7 (No. 127)**: slightly incurving, rounded rim top; rim circumference slightly distorted during manufacture; thick flat base with a bulge in the interior.

Parallels (Nos. 126 and 127):
Gezer: *Gezer I*: Pl. 28:13; Stratum XV-XIV; *Gezer IV*: Pl. 42:1, 20, red line on rim, Stratum XI.

Lachish: *Lachish IV*: Pl. 70: 599 (see 127), Tomb 501 (LB II).

Tell Beit Mirsim: *TBM Ia*: Pl. 16:12, Stratum C.

Beth Shemesh: *Ain Shems IV*: Pl. LXII: 18-19,23-25, Stratum III.

Discussion
Despite the variation in proportions, these bowls may be grouped together as one of the simplest and most basic shapes of the Late Bronze Age bowls. This shape may be traced from LB IIA (see also Amiran 1969: Pl. 38:1, from Megiddo Stratum IX, for a similar shape in LB I) while a deeper, slightly more hemispherical version may be found continuing into early Iron Age I as well, as the parallels indicate. The heavy flat disc base that is found on most of the bowls of this group is a common feature in LB II.

This bowl is included in Tufnell's 'Bowls Without Flare, Class 2' (*Lachish II*: 78, Pl. XXXVIII) and 'Class H, Curved Bowls' (*Lachish IV*: 181-182), dated by Tufnell to LB II. Thus, our bowls probably belong to a general LB II horizon.

2.2.1.7. BOWL TYPE F - HEMISPHERIC BOWLS
Pl. 2:8-10; Nos. 184,186,185; 18:4.

These are small bowls (15 cm diameter) with round incurving sides; the rim is plain and rounded on top. The base is a heavy ring base.

-**Pl. 2:8 (No. 184)**: red band painted on outer rim, with "drizzles" of paint inside.

-**Pl. 2:9 (No. 186)**: center of base is slightly convex. The bowl is red-slipped inside and outside, with no visible traces of burnish.

General Parallels:
Gezer: *Gezer I*: Pl. 28:21, larger, red slipped and burnished, base missing, Stratum XIV; Pl. 29:6, red slip, no burnish, base missing; Stratum XV; Pl. 35:8, Stratum IX; *Gezer II*: Pl. 28:34, red slip, base missing, Strata XIII-XII; Pl. 29:7, deeper proportion, with red band painted on rim, convex ring base, Strata XII-XI.

Lachish: Zimhoni 1997: 75, Fig. 3.5:3, red slip inside and halfway outside, Level V.

Variation:
-**Pls. 2:10; 18:4 (No. 185)**: A small deep bowl with rounded sides incurving below an everted, slightly thickened rim top. The inner lower walls and inner base of the bowl are thickened, apparently as a result of their not having been properly trimmed during manufacture; the base is flat. The bowl is red-slipped inside and outside, with traces of burnish.

No exact parallels were found for this bowl, but its shape and surface treatment indicate that it probably should be attributed to Iron Age IIA.

Discussion
Small hemispherical bowls with plain rounded rims and heavy ring bases are characteristic of Iron Age I and continue into early Iron Age II. They may be considered a development of the round-sided, plain-rimmed bowls that were so common in Late Bronze Age II, as discussed above (Group F). See, for example, a similarly shaped bowl with a disc base found in Lachish Fosse Temple III (*Lachish II*: Pl. XLIIB:145) belonging to Tufnell's 'In-curving Bowls'; see also the red slipped bowl from Gezer Stratum XV, above). However, the surface treatment on our bowls indicates that they should probably be ascribed to Iron Age I or IIA. Based

2.2.1.8. BOWL TYPE G - ROUND BOWL WITH HIGH SOFT CARINATION
Pls. 2:11; 18:5-6. No. 109[6]

This is a large bowl (28.5 cm diameter) with thick, rounded walls rising to a soft carination below a long flaring rim which creates a short "neck", forming a 'cyma' profile. The rim circumference was distorted during manufacture; the thick ring base has a convex center. The bowl's interior is decorated in red with a schematic palm motif between two triglyphs.[7] The wide, shelf-like rim top has traces of red paint, which covers the outer "neck" as well. This bowl was found in Tomb 1.

Parallels to 109:
Gezer: *Gezer I*: Pl. 26:19, Stratum XI; *Gezer IV*: Pls. 22:1-2,7; 30:4-6, Stratum XIII; Pl. 36:1-2, Stratum XI; Pl. 38:9, Stratum XII; *Macalister III*: Pl. CLXXIII: 4,6.

Lachish: *Lachish II*: Pl. XLIB: 117, 125, Fosse Temple II and III; *Lachish IV*: Pls. 69: 555, more sharply carinated, Tomb 527 (LB II).

Tell Beit Mirsim: *TBM I*: Pl. 29:13; *TBM III*: Pl. 12:1, Stratum B.

2.2.1.8.1. BOWL TYPE G1 - ROUND BOWL WITH TRUNCATED INNER RIM
Pl. 2:12; No. 86

This is a medium sized bowl (21 cm diameter) with very slightly rounded sides rising to a soft carination, above which the straight rim stance creates a short vertical "neck;" the inner rim is truncated and angles down, while the rim top is tapered. The rim circumference was distorted during manufacture. The flat disc base has an everted exterior and an ompholos interior.

Parallels to 86:
Gezer: *Macalister III*: Pl. CLXXIII:4.

Lachish: *Lachish IV*: Pl. 72: 630, two small bar handles near rim, with palm and zigzag motif painted inside, Tomb 571 (late LB IIB- Iron Age I).

Discussion

---

[6] Photographs of this bowl have already been published by Amiran (1969: 162, Photo 162) and Ussishkin and Wright (1970:114).

[7] As one can be seen from the parallels quoted in this discussion, such bowls were not only found at Gezer. Nevertheless, these bowls have been popularly nicknamed as "Gezer-Type Bowls" (e.g. Dothan 2000:153). The origin of this appellation is not clear.

The shape of Bowl 109 is included in Tufnell's 'Flared Bowls, Class 6' (*Lachish II*: 78, Pl. XLI) or 'Carinated Bowls - Classes B and C (*Lachish IV*: 179). It first appears in LB IIA and makes its final appearance in the late Iron Age I; the longevity of this bowl's existence and its design is notable. The shape of Bowl No. 86 was typologically defined by Tufnell as 'Miscellaneous' (ibid: 183). These bowls are presented here together despite the difference in rim shape, since the parallels show that both these bowl shapes may be found decorated with the distinctive motif, termed by Macalister a "palm and paneled zigzag". This was a common motif on the bowls at Gezer, with a number of variations (*Macalister II*: 190-191, Figs. 346-347). These variations include a straight line instead of a tree (ibid: Fig. 347); a double ended tree intersecting a panelled zigzag at a right angle (ibid: Fig. 346); and the same as the latter, but with the double ended tree enclosed by zigzags (*Macalister III*: Pl. CLXVII: 10).

Note that several round-sided 'platter' bowls (see our Groups A-C above) were also decorated with a radial triangular division made of red painted zigzag lines in the interior (see our Group A above), e.g. *Lachish II*: Pl. XXXVIIB: 27,31, Fosse Temple II and III, and *Lachish IV*: Pl. 71:615, Tomb 216, LB IIA-B. Remains of a similar motif may also be found on a straight sided flaring bowl from Stratum B at Tell Beit Mirsim (*TBM III*: Pl. 12:4). At Gezer, Dever noted that the carinated bowl shape appeared as early as Stratum XV (*Gezer II*: 49), but the initial appearance of the "palm tree-and-panel" motif (as well as simple painted red bands on the rim) on such bowls occurred in Stratum XIV (ibid: 51). The subsequent appearance of this motif on bowl shapes other than the cyma profile took place at a slightly later phase at Gezer, during Stratum XIII, in the course of the 12th century (*Gezer IV*: 80, n. 137). Based on the parallels from Gezer, our Bowl No. 109 may be dated as early as the late 13th century, but also as late as the mid-11th century. However, the rather careless and simplistic depiction of the traditional motif on our Bowl No. 109 alludes to a date towards the end of the range, reflecting the gradual decline of the common Late Bronze Age Canaanite motifs (Amiran 1969: 162; for a recent discussion of the appearance and significance of the "palm-tree" motif in the LB, see, e.g., Keel 1998:30-36). Since our Bowl No. 86 lacks decoration, it is difficult to place it in the developmental sequence that Dever maintained; its shape points to a similar initial date, continuing until the 12th century.

It appears that the datable examples from the Fosse Temple II at Lachish are the earliest and possibly this is where these bowls and their specific decorative motif originated. Its appearance at Gezer is a development and continuation of this bowl type at the end of the Late Bronze Age and in the early Iron Age. Though this shape spread to the north during Iron Age I, the painted motif on such bowls remained an exclusively southern trait.

2.2.1.9. BOWL TYPE H - CARINATED BOWLS
Pl. 3:1-9, Nos. 85,103,92,56,141,102,101,105, 93; Pl. 10: Nos. 88, 104; 19:1-7

NOT DRAWN: SG 77.211B (see, above, n. 2)

The carinated bowls found in the Gezer tombs are varied both in their proportion and their standards of manufacture. They are a representation of the numerous variations of carinated bowls found in the Bronze Age.

-Pls. 3:1; 19:1 (No. 85): a finely made, medium-sized bowl with an almost horizontal stance below a sharp, pinched carination at the lower third of the body. The sides, eggshell thin, flare out above the carination to a tapering rim top; the base is a high trumpet base with an everted bottom. For a discussion of the pottery technology of this bowl, as seen through Computed Tomography Analysis, see below, Chapter 6.

Parallels and Discussion
Bowls with low, sharp carinations can be found initially in MB IIB/C contexts (e.g. Amiran 1969: Pl. 27:18, from Megiddo, Stratum XII). This shape bowl may be found on chalices of this period as well (ibid: Pl. 28:10, also from Megiddo, Stratum XI). A body sherd of such a bowl was found in the pre-burial phase of Cave I.10A at Gezer, dated to MB IIC (*Gezer V*: Pl. 32:26). These bowls are more common in the north during the MB IIB/C, and they appear in the center and south of the country only sporadically (Maeir 1997:94).

This shape continues into LB I: *Lachish II*: Pl. XLIIB: 129, carination slightly higher, low ring base, Fosse Temple I (and one in Temple II); *Lachish IV*: Pl. 68:502, shallower, similar base, creme slip, Locus 129, MB IIA/B. These are Tufnell's 'Carinated Bowls, Class A'. These are most likely heirlooms. Bowls like No. 85, wheel made and usually burnished to a polish, are technologically among the finest wares to be produced during the Bronze Age. It is, in fact, the finest made bowl in the material from the Gezer tombs discussed here.

-Pl. 3:2 (No. 103): a medium sized bowl, wider in proportion than its depth, with a sharp carination slightly above mid-body and inverted walls above it. The long everted rim creates a kind of short flaring neck. The carination is on the same line as the rim edge, dictating the proportion of this bowl. The base is a convex disc. A red line is painted on the rim exterior.

-Pls. 3:3; 19:2 (No. 92): a medium sized bowl, wider in proportion than its depth; the carination is just about at mid-body, with inverted walls above it. Like in Bowl No. 103, the carination is on line with the flaring rim edge. The base is a narrow, very high ring base.

-Pl. 10: Nos. 88 and 104 apparently belong to this shape as well.

-SG 77.211B: (not illustrated in plates; *Saint Germain-en-Laye*: 149): medium sized bowl (18 cm diameter); low sharp carination; string cut disc base; reddish brown fabric, peeling, many small white and black inclusions. Possibly from Tomb X.

Parallels:
Gezer: *Gezer I*: Pl. 31:8, Stratum XIX; *Gezer II*: Pl. 20:29, Strata XIX-XVIII.

Lachish: *Lachish IV*: 69:544, Tomb 216 (LB IIA-B).

Beth Shemesh: *Ain Shems IV*: Pl. LV: 5, Stratum V.

Jerusalem: Sallers 1964: Fig. 10:7, Dominus Flevit Tomb.

-Pl. 3:4 (No. 56): This is a medium sized, thin-walled bowl, wider in proportion than its depth; it has a soft curve at mid-body, above which the slightly rounded stance flares at the rim. It has a convex disc base.

Parallels:
Lachish: *Lachish II*: Pl. XXXIXB:61, slightly thicker, Fosse Temples II and III; *Lachish IV*: Pl. 68: 508, slightly more angular carination, Locus 4008 (MB IIC). This is Tufnell's "Carinated Bowls Class A"; however, despite its similarity and early date, the parallel quoted here is understood by Tufnell to be relatively late in the Bronze Age sequence and represents a "degradation" of the form (ibid: 178).

-Pl. 3:5 (No. 141): a medium sized bowl, whose proportion is deeper than its width, with a blunt carination just above mid-body. The walls above the carination are almost vertical, and the long rim is everted. The base is a thick, slightly convex disc.

-Pls. 3:6; 19:4 (No. 102): a medium sized bowl, whose proportion is deeper than its width, with a carination just above mid-body. The walls above the carination are inverted and the short everted rim top is slightly angled in.

Parallels:
Gezer: *Gezer I*: Pl. 30:23, Stratum XVIII; *Gezer II*: Pl. 14:29, Stratum XX; *Gezer IV*: Pl. 3:21,23, Stratum XXII; *Gezer V*: Pl. 32:3, slightly shallower, Cave I.10A, pre-burial phase (MB IIC/LB IA).

Lachish: *Lachish IV*: Pl. 69: 544, Locus 129 (MB IIB/C).

Tell Beit Mirsim: *TBM I*: Pl. 42:4-6, Stratum D; *TBM Ia*: Pl. 8:9, Stratum E.

Beth Shemesh: *Ain Shems I*: Pl. XXIX: 221-224, Tomb 17.

Jerusalem: Saller 1964: Figs. 11:4, 12:5, Dominus Flevit Tomb.

-Pls. 3:7; 19:5 (No. 101): a medium sized bowl, deeper in proportion than its width, with a carination above mid-body; the walls turn sharply in above the carination, forming a sloping "shoulder". The carination protrudes beyond the line of the long flaring rim, which creates a kind of short neck. This differentiates this bowl from Nos. 103 and 92, despite the general affinity, and sets this shape apart from the ordinary carinated bowls. The base is a wide very high ring base. A red line is painted on the rim interior and exterior.

Gezer - Tombs

Parallels:
Lachish: *Lachish II*: Pl. XLIB: 104-105, Pl. XLIIB: 127, Fosse Temple I; *Lachish IV*: Pl. 69:546, shorter rim, Tomb 129 (MB IIB/C); this is related to Tufnell's "Carinated Bowls Class C", that Tufnell claims are among the earliest forms among the angular carinated bowls (ibid: 179-180).

-Pls. 3:8; 19:6 (No. 105): a large, heavy bowl with a round carination above mid-body, topped by long flaring walls; rounded rim top with red band painted inside and outside; ring base with concave center.

-Pls. 3:9; 19:7 (No. 93): a large, thick-walled bowl with a blunt carination at mid-body topped by long flaring walls; rounded rim top; ring base with concave center.

Parallels:
Gezer: *Macalister III*: Pl. CLIV:12, "Second Semitic Pottery", lower carination.

Lachish: *Lachish IV*: Pl. 68:512, 513, Tomb 119 (MB IIC); Pl. 68:517 (vertical upper walls), Locus 129 (MB IIB/C).

Discussion
These carinated bowls represent fine examples of the high stage of development of this type, with most of them in the chronological range of MB IIC-LB IB; some of the shapes may be found continuing into LB II as well, though usually more degenerate. The technological decline in the production of the carinated bowls that is noticed at many sites at the end of the Late Bronze Age (Amiran 1969: 125, 129; *Lachish IV*: 178) is not particularly marked among the bowls from the Gezer tombs, suggesting that they span the earlier part of the sequence.[8] The bowls in Pl.3: 5-6 are more common in the south (Kempinski 1983: 187).

2.2.1.10. BOWL TYPE I - SHALLOW CARINATED BOWLS
Pl. 10: Nos. 144, 145, 146

These three bowls represent a shape that is difficult to reconstruct based solely on the miniature drawings. The drawings appear to indicate a wide flat base, though this would be unique in the corpus. No indication was given in the records of the presence of red slip or burnish. These possibly may be what are termed "degenerated" carinated bowls, found at the end of the Late Bronze Age sequence (e.g. Amiran 1969: Pl. 39:8-11; Edelstein and Avrant 1992: Fig. 11:14 [though with different bases]).

---

[8] Although note Dever's contention that a red band painted on the rim is a relatively late characteristic, typical of many late 13th-early 12th century bowls at Gezer (*Gezer IV*: 58). It seems that the red band on our carinated bowls is a separate phenomenon, in light of the earlier morphological comparisons.

2.2.2. CHALICES
Pls. 3:10-11; 19:8-9. Nos. 172, 128.
Pl. 25:3-4. SG 77.211F1, SG 77.211F2

Four chalices were found in the tombs: two from the Hebrew University Collection and two in the Saint Germain en-Laye Museum. They all differ from each other:

-Pls. 3:10; 19:8 (No. 172): This chalice is thick-walled, and its bowl has rounded sides and a hammerhead rim top protruding in and out. The high pedestal base has a ridge above its bottom and an everted edge. This chalice was found in Tomb 1.

Parallels:
Gezer: *Macalister III*: Pls. XC:1; XCI: 12-13, Tomb 96, 10th c.; *Gezer IV*: Pl. 37:8, narrower and higher, but similar stance, bowl mostly missing, Stratum XI.

Beth Shemesh: *Ain Shems III*: Fig. 6: 3-77, chalice base, Room 317 (Iron Age I); *Ain Shems IV*: Pl. LIX:22, no ridge on base but similar rim, angled out, Stratum III.

Discussion
No exact parallels could be found to match this chalice, whose proportions are relatively stout and whose rim is quite unique. The characteristics of a ridged lower foot and out-turning rim would place this chalice in Iron Age I (Amiran 1969: 213, Pl. 68; though note a ridged pedestal on several LB II chalices at Lachish (e.g. *Lachish IV*: Pl. 72:634, 637).

-Pls. 3:11; 19:9 (No. 128): This chalice is stout, with a very thick join between bowl and base. The wide shallow bowl has slightly rounded outer walls, with a flat rim top. The short pedestal base is flaring.

Parallels:
Gezer: *Macalister III*: Pl. LXXIV:1, wider bowl and higher base, Tomb 30 (LB IB-LB IIB); *Gezer V*: Pls. 21:1, 23:6, 27:19, wider bowl, Cave I.10A, construction phase (LB IB).

Lachish: *Lachish IV*: Pl. 72:636, slight ridge at mid-foot, Locus 1006 (LB IIA).

Tell Beit Mirsim: *TBM Ia*: Pl. 8:16, Stratum E.

Discussion
Most of the few parallels found for this chalice point to an early to mid-LB range; the general characteristics of this chalice, despite its rather unusual stout proportions, points to this date as well (see also Amiran 1969: 95, Pl. 28:14 from Megiddo, Stratum X; Pl. 40:3 from Megiddo, Stratum VIII, and Pl. 40:13-14 from Hazor, Strata IA-B). The close similarity with the chalice from Tell Beit Mirsim Stratum E may suggest the appearance of this shape as early as MB IIB, although this is not certain.

-SG 77.211F1 (Pl. 25:3; *Saint Germain-en-Laye*: 149): this chalice is relatively small (13 cm extant height, with base broken). It has a round bowl with a pronounced horizontal shelf rim. The rim is painted red and splotches of red paint stain the outer and inner body. The fabric is reddish yellow with small white and black inclusions; prominent wheel marks inside and outside. This chalice comes from Tomb IX.

Parallels:
Beth Shemesh: *Ain Shems III*: Figs. 5:4-100, 6:3-54 (Stratum IIa); *Ain Shems IV*: Pl. LXII: 48,50,53; LXIV: 35.

-SG 77.211F2 (Pl. **25**:4; *Saint Germain-en-Laye*: 149): a small chalice with a rounded bowl and long everted rim. The pedestal base is short and is topped by a ridge.

Parallels:
Beth Shemesh: *Ain Shems IV*: Pl. LIX:26 (Stratum III); *Ain Shems III*: Fig. 6:3-54 (Stratum IIa).

Lachish: *Lachish V:* Pl. 41: 14-21 (Level V).

Tell Qasile: Mazar 1985: Figs. 32:4-5; 43:22; 52:15 (Strata XII-X, Type Chalice 2; discussion on p. 49).

Discussion:
Chalices with everted rims are a common shape in the Iron Age I and many examples of this shape may be found in 10th century contexts. The ridge on the foot of these chalices points to an Iron Age I to early Iron Age II date as well. Grant and Wright claimed that the cyma-shaped flaring rim chalices are typical of Strata III at Beth Shemesh, while in Stratum IIa, the horizontal ledge rim develops (*Ain Shems* V: 135).

2.2.3. KRATER
Pls. 3:12; 19:10. No. 119

This is the only krater found in the Gezer tombs excavated by Weill.[9] It was found in Tomb I.

Generally, kraters are not a common vessel in Iron Age I tomb deposits (although see Edelstein and Aurant 1992: Fig. 11:18). Its presence might be due to its special design, which prompted placing it in a funerary setting.

-Pls. 3:12; 19:10 (No. 119): A deep, bell-shaped krater with a short slightly flaring neck and everted, shelf-like rim; two horizontal handles slant up diagonally. The base is a convex ring base. The exterior is decorated with overlapping groups of zigzag lines. It has faint traces of the white slip characteristic of many Philistine bichrome vessels.

This krater was published with Dothan's Krater Type 2 (Dothan 1982: Fig. 11:7, although note the somewhat different rim stance in the drawing there). It is fully discussed by her (ibid: 106-115; Fig. 7; see also Mazar 1985: 90-93, 103-104).

Our krater differs somewhat from the norm in its short neck and emphasized convex ring base, which appear to be less common on kraters of this type. These kraters are usually decorated on the upper half of the body with intricate geometric bichrome designs from the Philistine repertoire. The decoration on the Gezer krater bears a pattern of "composite zigzags" (as Dothan defines this motif), which is very rare. A similar decoration appears on a krater from Tell el-Far'ah (S) (Dothan 1982: Fig. 11:8) and on a cup (rhyton?) from Tell Qasile (Mazar 1985: Fig. 20:1). A somewhat similar motif also appears on the upper and middle part of a cyma-shaped bowl from Gezer (*Gezer IV*: Pl. 14:6, Stratum XIV) considered imitation 'White Slip II', though Macalister interpreted this motif as an imitation of basket work (*Macalister II*: 190). Compared to the intricate and well-drawn Philistine motifs on other kraters of this type, the decoration of our krater is somewhat schematic, crude and inferior. There are very faint traces of the whitish slip that is typical of Philistine bichrome pottery, particularly in its early stages.

This krater type is fully developed in the 12th century, and eventually disappears sometimes in the 11th century, when the "degenerate" version of this krater appears at a limited amount of sites (Dothan's Krater Type 18, see Dothan 1982: 197-198; Fig. 60; Mazar 1985: 45-47).[10] Although the execution of its design is somewhat unorthodox, the shape of our krater places it in a relatively early phase in the developmental sequence of the Philistine bell-shaped krater. The initial appearance of Philistine pottery at Gezer is in Stratum XIII (*Gezer IV*: 79-80) and it continues to be found until Stratum XI (mid-11th century). The placement of a Philistine krater in the tombs is of chronological significance vis-a-vis the periods of use of the tombs, and may also indicate the cultural connections of the tomb users at this time.

2.2.4. LAMPS
Pls. 4:1-13; 20:1-4. Nos. 95, 190, 94, 125, 196, 198, 117, 194, 189, 197, 191, 195, 118.

Pl. 25:5. SG 72.356b.

NOT ILLUSTRATED IN PLATES: SG 77.211D, SG 72.356a.

The lamps found in the Gezer tombs are of three main types (A, B and C), with sub-variations:

2.2.4.1. LAMP TYPE A - A SMALL TO MEDIUM SIZED LAMP WITH A STRAIGHT RIM EXTERIOR.

In some examples (e.g. Nos. 94 and 125) the inner rim is thickened, similar to that of bowls of Groups B and C. The wide base is round.

---

[9] Note that the krater published in Dothan 1982: Fig. 5:4=Pl. 18 is marked HU 243, from Gezer. However, this is not part of the assemblage under discussion and the designation is apparently erroneous.

[10] The traditional chronological framework for the dating of the Philistine material culture is used here, following, e.g., Mazar (1997). One should note the alternative (and lower) chronological system that has been espoused recently (e.g. Finkelstein 1995).

Gezer - Tombs

-Pls. 4:1; 20:1 (No. 95): very slightly pinched mouth.

Parallels:
Lachish: *Lachish II*: Pl. XLV: 188, Fosse Temple I; *Lachish IV*: Pl. 73:649-654, MB IIB/C. This is Tufnell's Lamp Class A (ibid: 185)

Tell Beit Mirsim: *TBM Ia*: Pl. 15:18,20, Stratum D (MB II).

Beth Shemesh: *Ain Shems IV*: Pl. LV: 18, Stratum V (MB II).

Jerusalem: Saller 1964: Fig. 54:3, Dominus Flevit Tomb.

-Pls. 4:2; 20:2 (No. 190): slight rounded thickening at base.

-Pl. 4:3 (No. 94)

-Pl. 4:4 (No. 125)

General Parallels:
Gezer: *Gezer IV*: Pl. 22:12,18, Stratum XV; *Gezer V*: Pls. 18:5-6,8; 20:12, Cave I.10A, Lower Burial Phase (LB IB-LB IIA); Pls. 13:11, 14:6, Cave I.10A, Upper Burial phase (LB IIA). No differences in lamps were discerned between the two burial phases in this cave: ibid: 82).

Lachish: *Lachish II*: Pl. XLB: 189, Fosse Temple I; XLB:197, Fosse Temple II; XLB: 200, Fosse Temple III; *Lachish IV*: Pl. 73:663, LB I-LB IIB.

Tell Beit Mirsim: *TBM I*: Pl. 48 (Stratum C).

Tel Batash-Timnah: Kelm and Mazar 1995: Fig. 4.28: lamp, Stratum VII (LB IIA).

Jerusalem: Amiran 1960: Fig. 3:50-51, Nahlat Ahim tomb (LB IIA).

2.2.4.2. LAMP TYPE B - A SMALL TO MEDIUM-SIZED LAMP WITH AN EVERTED, SHELF-LIKE RIM

The wide bases of this type are rounded or somewhat flattened.
-Pl. 4:5 (No. 196)

-Pl. 4:6 (No. 198)

-Pl. 4:7 (No. 117)

-Pl. 4:8 (No. 194): slight carination above base.

-Pls. 4:9; 20:3 (No. 189)

-Pl. 4:10 (No. 197)

-Pl. 4:11 (No. 191)

-Pl. 4:12 (No. 195)

-SG 77.211D (not illustrated in plates; *Saint Germain-en-Laye*: 149): a medium sized lamp with red slip on rim with splotches of red paint outside; slip extends 2 cm beyond rim inside and outside; yellowish fabric with small white inclusions; wheel marks. It was found in Tomb IX.

-SG 72.356a (not illustrated in plates; *Saint Germain en-Laye*: 149): reddish yellow fabric, some small and a few large white inclusions; mended.

Variation:
-Pls. 4:13; 20:4 (No. 118): thick-walled, wide flat base, non-everted flat rim.

Gezer: *Gezer I*: Pl. 28:12, narrower base, Stratum XV.

General Parallels:
Gezer: *Gezer IV*: Pl. 33:1, Stratum XIII; Pl. 35:11, Pl. 38:12-13, Stratum XII.

Lachish: *Lachish II*: Pl. XLB: 203-204, Fosse Temple III.

Tell Beit Mirsim: *TBM I*: Pl. 51:1,6, Stratum B.

2.2.4.3. LAMP TYPE C - HIGH DISC BASE LAMP

-SG 72.356b (Pl. 25:5; *Saint Germain-en-Laye*: 149): a small lamp with a thick high disc-base (3 cm high); a high, pinched, rounded mouth and a flaring rim-top; coarse reddish fabric with many white and black inclusions; rim chipped away.

Discussion
This is the only example of this well-known late Iron Age II type (Amiran 1969: 291). The lamp with high disc-base is one of clearest criteria for differentiation between 8th and 7th centuries assemblages in Judah. During the 7th century, the bases became progressively higher and thicker and the ware coarser (Aharoni and Aharoni 1976: 84). Tufnell concluded that the disc-based lamps were introduced sometime in the late 8th and early 7th centuries (*Lachish III*: 282-283; Pl. 83:153; Tufnell's L.9-10). Among the many examples, one can note, e.g., *Ain Shems IV*: Pl. XLVIII: Pl. 8,12 (Stratum IIc; and Tombs 2 and 4-8).

General Discussion
The saucer lamps in the Gezer tombs span the development of Middle Bronze IIB-Late Bronze IIB lamps (a sequence that essentially continues into Iron Age I, as the parallels indicate). From small, plain-rimmed bowls with slightly pinched mouths, to well-developed everted rims and more tightly pinched mouths (Amiran 1969: Pl. 59, 190). Tufnell concluded that lamps with non-flaring rims existed in all three phases of the Fosse Temple, but the everted-rim lamps were found only in Temples II and III, and possibly did not continue until the very end of Temple III (*Lachish II*: Pl. XLB, note that only Temple III examples are presented in this plate; *Lachish IV*: 186, Tufnell's Class E, dated to the 14th century).

Aside from one lamp that can be dated to the MB IIB/C, the straight rim lamps of sub-group A have parallels dating to the span of LB IB to LB IIB. The everted-rim lamps of sub-group B may be compared to similar lamps beginning in LB IIB and continuing into Iron Age I. It is notable that no everted-rim lamps are found among the published LB material from Gezer excavations, and only Iron Age I parallels exist, suggesting the latter as the possible date for this sub-group.

The single example of a high disc or stump-based lamp points to the use (though possibly of a limited nature) of the tombs at the very end of the Iron Age II. This is also supported by the appearance of other ceramic types in our assemblage, such as the small 'black juglets', and the Judean decanter (see below).

Almost all the lamps in the Gezer tombs show signs of use.

2.2.5. JUGS
Pl. 5: 1-12; Nos. 28,55,213,21,65,182,179, 183,216,177, 188, 215.

NOT ILLUSTRATED IN PLATES: SG 77.211H4.

2.2.5.1. JUGS - GENERAL

The wide variety of jugs found in the tombs does not permit grouping of types, so that each will be presented individually, save for the last two types which are distinctive and of particular chronological and regional significance.

-**Pls. 5:1; 21:1 (No. 28)**: a medium-sized jug with a wide flat base, slightly thickened inside. The squat body is round, topped by a long very flaring neck. The rim is missing; a rather crude handle extends from below the rim to the shoulder. The vessel is covered with a light red wash which is streaky and patchy, so that it is difficult to determine whether an intentional pattern was applied, especially on the shoulders and on the handle.

A close comparison to this jug is found in the Northern Cemetery of Beth Shean (e.g. Oren 1973: Fig. 1:13, similar decoration, Tomb 74). Numerous additional examples of this type jug, mostly undecorated, were found in the tombs from Beth Shean dating to EB IV/MB I. This jug, called a "one handled pitcher" by Oren, is quite common in tomb deposits in northern Palestine and in the northern Jordan Valley (e.g. Palumbo and Peterman 1993; MicNicoll 1992: 31, Pls. 23: 17-18; 24:23,26-28; 25: 30,32), but very rare in the south. Oren cites an unpainted example from Jerusalem and their appearance in the Jericho tombs (Oren 1973: 28).

Thus, the appearance of this EB IV/MB I jug in the Gezer tombs would represent a very rare phenomenon in the south and alludes to northern connections. Its presence is especially questionable in light of the occupation gap at Gezer spanning most of the EB III through MB IIA (Dever 1993: 498). This is the earliest vessel in the entire tomb groups. It is so entirely out of the general chronological range of the assemblage that the possibility exists that this jug was not found at Gezer and it was mistakenly included in the group during some earlier stage of the handling of the finds in the Hebrew University collections.[11]

-**Pls. 5:2; 21:2 (No. 55)**: a nicely formed medium-sized jug with an ovoid body with high rounded shoulders and a narrow slightly concave neck. The everted rim has a concave interior. A double strand handle beginning at mid-neck, rises to the rim and extends down to the shoulder. The disc base is slightly convex, with everted edges.

This jug is Tufnell's Jug Class A, found in MB IIA/B contexts, with a double handle attached to the rim, and a ring base (*Lachish IV*: Pl. 74: 670-671, pg. 187). Most of these are red slipped and burnished, and indeed, traces of red slip may be seen on the exterior of the Gezer jug.

-**Pl. 5:3 (No. 213)**: a large jug with a round body, straight neck whose flaring top is rounded, with a trefoil mouth. A thick handle extends from rim to below neck; the base is pointed, with a small thick button on its exterior. This jug was found in Tomb I.

Parallels and Discussion
Gezer: *Macalister III*: Pl. LXV: 33, squatter, Tomb 7 (LB IB-LB IIB).

Lachish: *Lachish II*: Pl. LIB: 277, less globular body, Fosse Temple I; *Lachish IV*: Pl. 75:696, less globular body, wider base, Locus 6027(MB IIC).

Beth Shemesh: *Ain Shems IV*: Pl. LVII: 3, wider base, Stratum IV.

Tel Batash-Timnah: Kelm and Mazar 1995: Fig. 4.28: Stratum VII (LB IIA).

Tel Miqne-Ekron: Killebrew 1996: Pl. 6:10, Stratum IX (LB IIA-early LB IIB).

This jug, which is the only one to lack the typical convex disc base of the period, is an exclusively LB type, though note the earlier comparison from a late MB IIC context at Lachish.

-**Pl. 5:4 (No. 21)**: a large, asymmetric biconical jug with a sharp carination at the lower third of the body and concave walls above, rising to a shelf-like horizontal rim top, protruding both in and out. A wide handle extends from rim to middle of sloping upper stance. The base is a slightly convex disc. The body above the carination is painted with red vertical bands that enclose wavy lines, and the rim top has groups of vertical red hatches. This jug was found in Tomb 1.

Parallels and Discussion:
Lachish: *Lachish IV*: Pl. 84:963, squatter, similar rim, handle from rim, Locus 503 (LB IIB).

---

[11] Nevertheless, it should be noted that one of the tombs from Gezer (Tomb 27-I) was used during the EB IV/MB I period (Dever 1993: 498).

Beth Shemesh: *Ain Shems IV*: Pl. LV: 6,7, handle on shoulder, Stratum IVa).

Tell Beit Mirsim: *TBM I*: Pl. 47:15, similar decoration, Stratum C.

Tel Batash-Timnah: Kelm and Mazar 1995: Fig. 4.28, Stratum VII (LB IIA).

Tel Miqne-Ekron: Killebrew 1996: Pl. 3:1, not decorated, angled in rim; Stratum X (LB I-LB IIA); Pl. 4:18, flaring rim and upper body only, Stratum IX (LB IIA-early LB IIB).

Many variations of this jug type are known throughout the Late Bronze Age, with one or two handles, low or high bases, and if decorated, only above the carination (Amiran 1969: 147). The published jugs of this general type found in the excavations at Gezer differed from the Tomb I jug in their much squatter proportions and handles which were placed on the shoulders (e.g. *Gezer V*: Pl.14:1, Cave I.10A, Upper Tomb Phase, LB IIA), so that the vessel found in the Gezer tombs appears to be quite unique at the site in terms of proportion and handle placement. Close analogies from other adjacent sites set the date of this jug to LB IIA-B. Compared to the more elaborate designs found on some of the parallels, it may be suggested, following Amiran (1969: 162) in her description of the process of degradation of the LB motifs, that our jug is late in the series. Accordingly, this can be argued, in light of its rather sloppy and schematic design, as well as the handle extending from the rim rather than the shoulder.

-Pls. 5:5; 21:3 (No. 65): a small jug with a sharp carination at the lower third of its body, above which the walls are concave, rising to a tapering rim top with a wide trefoil mouth. A loop handle extends from rim to carination. The thick disc base is slightly convex. Red lines are painted outside in a lattice pattern above the carination, and the rim is decorated with an applied red line.

Parallels and Discussion:
Lachish: *Lachish IV*: Pl. 84:959, similar decoration and proportions, smaller handle just under rim, Tomb 216, LB IIA-B; Pl. 84: 967-968, undecorated, Tombs 561 and 543, LB IIA-B (other variations: ibid: Pl. 84: 960, 961-962, 966, 969, all LB II).

Tel Miqne-Ekron: Killebrew 1996: Pl. 2:16, red painted decoration of vertical metopes with zigzag lines above carination; Stratum X (LB IIA-B); this vessel is different in its upper shape - with straight rather than concave sides. However, the analogy is to a small biconical cup with red decoration on its upper part.

This vessel, sometimes termed a mug, suits the common biconical body shape of LB II jugs, goblets and chalices. Some of these were made in small sizes and though handleless, may be compared to our vessel in shape (e.g. *Gezer IV*: Pl. 14:7, Stratum XIV). Its small size implies that it was either made as part of a 'set', along with larger versions of such 'mugs', or was a local imitation of similarly shaped imports popular during the Late Bronze Age. Tufnell suggested that the shape reflects that of the White Slip tankard (*Lachish IV*: 217-218), which might have been the inspiration for the generic biconical body shape of this period as well. An interesting analogy to the shape of this vessel might be seen in a Mycenaean cup at Beth Shemesh, Stratum IV (*Ain Shems IV*: Pl. XXXIV).

It seems that our vessel can be related to Furumark's "cylindrical cups" (Furumark 1941: 54-56, Fig. 15:230-231 of metallic prototypes, dated by him to LHIIA). For another comparison, see also the "bell cups" in Mountjoy 1986: 33, Fig. 33, especially 33:1 (LHIIA) and the "carinated conical cup" in ibid: Fig. 51 (LHIIB). Although the handles of the latter examples are placed below the rim, and the lower part is shallower, some relationship might be suggested which influenced the general shape of this vessel. Amiran, discussing a somewhat similarly-shaped, locally made red-slipped vessel from an LB IIA tomb in Jerusalem, suggested to compare it to "Cypriot mugs or tankards" (Amiran 1960:29; Fig. 3:52).

The very close parallels found in the Lachish tombs, dating to LB IIA-B, set the date for our vessel.

-Pls. 5:6; 21:4 (No. 182): a small squat jug with a wide globular body and medium narrow straight neck and everted rim. The handle extends from the rim to the shoulder, rising above the line of the rim. The base is a narrow thick disc base. Faint traces of painted decoration can be made out to be a design of groups of partially intersecting diagonal lines in brown. This design is similar to that of some of the imitation 'bilbils' (see for example Pl. 9:5-6, 10), although the light colored ware and brown lines recall the typical linear design on imports of the Cypriote "White Painted Cross-Lined" family as well, suggesting that this was an imitation of that ware or at least its decorative motifs (Prag 1985: 162). This jug is similar in concept to the following two small jugs.

-Pl. 5:7 (No. 179): a small squat jug, with a wide globular body and short narrow, straight neck, joined to the body with a ridge. The rim top is everted. A handle extends from rim to shoulder, rising above the rim. The base is a flat disc base. The jug is decorated outside with two horizontal black bands and covered with a self-slip that is highly burnished. At the join of the handle to the body, there are two round pellets, apparently imitating metal rivets. These features lend a metallic quality to this nicely made jug. Although metal parallels to this exact shape are unknown, such vessels may have in fact existed, and mutual influences between these two mediums may have existed (what has been termed "skeuomorphism"; see, e.g., McGovern 1989; for a similar phenomenon in Late Bronze Cypriote vessels, see, e.g., Buchholz 1995).

Similar pellets may be found placed on the top and bottom of single and double strand handles, e.g. a jug from Megiddo Stratum XII (in Amiran 1969: Pl. 34:7) and cylindrical juglets from the tomb at Dominus Flevit, Jerusalem, dated typologically to the transitional MB IIB-LB I period (Saller 1964: Fig. 30:2,3,10,12).

Very few parallels were found for this jug. See *Lachish IV*: Pl. 76:722,723, with a longer neck and a less globular body, dated to LB IIB.

-**Pls. 5:8; 21:5 (No. 183)**: This is a small jug with a wide round body, and short flaring narrow neck. A slightly raised handle extends from rim to shoulder. The base is an everted disc base. Note should be made of the post-firing drilled hole in the mid-body, indicating that this jug served for some special function during its use-life. The exterior is decorated with horizontal and vertical alternating black and red lines, with horizontal lines on the handle. This jug was found in Tomb 1.

This jug too did not have many comparisons. It may be compared to the base and bottom of a small globular jug painted with red and brown horizontal bands from Beth Shemesh, Stratum IV: *Ain Shems IV*: Pl. LVII: 12. See also the neck, body and handle fragment of a small globular jug decorated with in red and black from the Fosse Temple I at Lachish: *Lachish II*: Pl. LIB: 272; the alternating red and black horizontal line decoration on the handle is identical to ours.

-**Pls. 5:9; 21:64 (No. 216)**: A small round bodied jug with a strainer and spout just above mid-body. The short narrow neck is slightly flaring; the rim interior is somewhat concave. A round handle extends from rim to shoulder. The base is a thick ring base. Faint traces of red slip and burnish can be detected. The comparison to a similar jug from Gezer (*Macalister III*: Pl. LXXXVII: 2, Tomb 85, Iron Age IIA), as well as the surface treatment and the strainer, suggest an Iron Age IIA date for this jug.

-**Pls. 5:10; 21:7 (No. 177)**: This is a medium sized jug with an ovoid body, and a long narrow slightly curving neck and concave rim interior, thickened on the outside, with a trefoil mouth. The base is a convex ring base. A very thick handle extends from rim to shoulder. The parallels suggest that this jug should be dated to the late Iron Age I and early Iron Age II, e.g. *Ain Shems IV*: Pl. LX:1, similar shape, not shown if trefoil rim, Stratum III; *Lachish III*: Pl. 86:251, 10th century.

-**Pls. 5:11; 21:8 (No. 188)**: This is a small handleless bottle, with a round body and base, and a short neck. The rim has a triangular exterior and angled interior. The ware of this jug differs from the others; it is light yellow and has a chalky-sandy consistency. A comparison to this shape, though wider, may be seen at Gezer (*Macalister II*: 198, Fig. 353). Though the general shape appears reminiscent of Egyptian forms, no viable parallels could be found among assemblages of Egyptian pottery.

-**Pls. 5:12; 21:9 (No. 215)**: This is a large jug with a high rounded shoulder, straight medium size neck and everted, thickened rounded rim top. The flat base is convex, dipping down in the center. A wide handle extends from the rim top, slightly rising and joining the sloping shoulder. The ware is light buff in color and contains many tiny black and gray inclusions. It may be compared to several jugs typical of the Hellenistic period, such as a very similar shape from Gezer (*Macalister III*: Pl. CLXX:2, "Fourth Semitic Pottery"); see also *Beth Zur*: Pl. XI:1 and a similar, though squatter jug from the Upper City of Jerusalem: Avigad 1983: 78, Fig. 55.

As mentioned above, the possibility also exists that this jug was mistakenly included with the Gezer tomb group.

2.2.5.2. JUDEAN DECANTER

-**SG 77.211H4 (Pl. 26:1**; *Saint Germain-en-Laye*: 149): This is a jug with a cylindrical body that is carinated above the ring base and has a carinated shoulder. The neck is narrow and ridged at the center; a handle extends from the ridge to the shoulder carination. The rim is everted and rounded. The jug was heavily encrusted, but showed traces of burnish and light red or self slip.

This jug is a typical Judean 'decanter', which was one of the most characteristic forms in the the Southern Levant from the 8th century until the end of the Iron Age. This jug type demonstrates some regional variations and the rim of the Gezer jug is typical of the south of Israel (Amiran 1969: Pl. 89:1-4, pg. 262; Gitin in *Gezer III*: 154). At Lachish, the decanter did not become common until after the destruction of Level III; while prototypes did appear in the latter stratum, it predominates in Lachish Level II (*Lachish III*: 292-293). At Beth Shemesh too, the decanter is rare in Stratum IIb and becomes frequent in Stratum IIc (*Ain Shems V*: 140-141). Thus, our decanter should be dated to the 8th-7th centuries, indicating the latest period of use of the Gezer tombs.

2.2.5.3. "COOKING JUGS"

Pl. 26:2-5. SG 77.211G1, SG 77.211G2, SG 77.211G3, SG 77.211G4.

-**SG 77.211G1 (Pl. 26:2**; *Saint Germain-en-Laye*: 149): This is a small jug (13 cm high; rim diameter: 8 cm) with a globular body and round base. It has a short wide vertical neck and a thickened rounded rim; the handle extends from the rim to the short sloping shoulder. The fabric is dark red with many small and medium white inclusions. The exterior is red slipped.

-**SG 77.211G2 (Pl. 26:3**, *Saint Germain-en-Laye*: 149): This is a small jug with a rounded base, round body and wide neck; the rim is slightly everted and plain and a handle extends from the rim to the sloping shoulder. It was heavily encrusted.

-**SG 77.211G3 (Pl. 26:4**, *Saint Germain-en-Laye*: 149): This is a small jug (11.2 cm high; rim diameter: 6.5 cm). It has a rounded base and body, with a wide, slightly inverted neck. The rim is everted and a handle extends from the rim to the bottom of the neck. The vessel has prominent wheel marks outside and light encrustation. The ware is not typical of cooking pots and its neck is somewhat narrower; thus, it is possible that this is a regular jug.

-**SG 77.211G4 (Pl. 26:5**, *Saint Germain-en-Laye*: 149): This jug is squatter than the others (10 cm high, rim diameter: 7.2

Gezer - Tombs

cm). It has a rounded base and globular body with a wide slightly everted neck. The rim is very slightly thickened, with an incised line below its exterior. A handle extends from the rim to the sloping shoulder. There are two lines incised on the shoulder as well. The fabric is dark red with many small and medium sized white inclusions; there are traces of soot on the base.

Parallels:
Lachish: *Lachish III*: Pl. 84:177, Level III.

Tell Beit Mirsim: *TBM I*: Pl. 57:14, Stratum A.

Discussion
These jugs are well known in Iron Age II, sometimes called "cooking jugs" because of the rounded base and the fact that they are sometimes made of typical cooking pot ware. These jugs can be found in northern and southern contexts during all of Iron Age II, though the very common Judean examples are mainly found in 8th and 7th century strata (Amiran 1969: 259). The presence of such 'cooking jugs' (if indeed this was their function), in the Gezer tombs might indicate their use in food preparation, perhaps related to the funerary ceremony (e.g. Bloch-Smith 1992:107).

2.2.6. JUGLETS
The considerable number of juglets from the Gezer tombs consist of various shapes which are well known from MB II until LB IIB: dipper, cylindrical and piriform juglets. Several shapes continue into the Iron Age as well.

2.2.6.1. DIPPER JUGLETS
Pls. 6:1-10; Nos. 59, 67, 75, 66, 98, 99, 89, 171, 187,91; Pl. 10: Nos. 97, 181; 22:1-7.

Pl. 25:6, 9-10; 26:5; SG 77.211E1, SG 77.211E4, SG 77.211E3, AO7002.

NOT ILLUSTRATED IN PLATES:
SG 72.356d, SG 77.211E2

2.2.6.1.1. MB II DIPPER JUGLETS:
These juglets have ovoid bodies, often elongated, with sloping shoulders; the bases are tapered to a point or sometimes to a tiny 'button', which is probably the result of its final cut off from the clay 'foot' on which had been set during manufacture (Price-Williams 1977:9). The long narrow neck is usually flaring, and the rim top is rounded or tapered; the mouth is often pinched. The handle is round-sectioned and extends from rim to shoulder.

-**Pls. 6:1; 22:1 (No. 59)**: the largest juglet of its type in the tombs. Most of its rim is missing.

-**Pls. 6:2; 22:2 (No. 67)**: a medium-sized juglet with a 'button' base. Light colored slip and fine vertical burnish.

-**Pls. 6:3; 22:3 (No. 75)**: a medium sized juglet with broader shoulders and straighter sides, with a button base. The neck is straight and the rim interior is slightly thickened. Most of the rim is missing.

-**Pls. 6:4; 22:4 (No. 66)**: a medium-sized juglet with a pinched rim.

-**Pl. 6:5-6 (Nos. 98, 99)**: base and body of two juglets; No. 99 also has the beginning of its handle. The bodies are relatively straight-walled with broad, rounded shoulders. Note that both vessels were used after their necks and rims had been broken off, a fact strengthened by the relatively uniform break lines at the base of both vessels' neck. In addition, No. 98 has a post-firing drilled hole in the vicinity of the original handle, perhaps indicating that after this vessel was altered, a string was attached through this hole to serve as a handle.

-**SG 77.211E1 (Pl. 22:6**; *Saint Germain-en-Laye*: 149): This is a medium sized dipper juglet). The body is slightly rounded, similar to Pl. 6:5. It is heavily encrusted.

-**SG 72356d** (not illustrated in plates; *Saint Germain-en-Laye*: 149): This is a medium sized dipper juglet, similar to Pl. 6:4, with a narrow elongated body.

-**SG 77.211E2** (not illustrated in plates; *Saint Germain-en-Laye*: 149): This juglet is somewhat stouter than the others (15.8 cm high); the base tip is missing. The fabric is reddish yellow with many small white, black and red inclusions. It is covered with red slip and vertical burnish. It possibly comes from Tomb III.

-**Pl. 10: Nos. 97, 100**: The miniature drawings make it difficult to determine the exact proportions of these juglets; however it appears that they belong with the short bodied juglets. No. 181 shows vertical lines that might represent knife paring, similar to the treatment of the Cypriote White Shaved juglets (see below).

Parallels:
Gezer: *Gezer I*: Pl. 30:16, convex upper neck, Stratum XVIII (MB IIC\LB IA); *Gezer IV*: Pl. 3:15, red slip and burnish, squatter and thicker, Stratum XXII.

Lachish: *Lachish II*: Pl. LIIB: 297-298, Fosse Temple I, Pl. LIIB:303, Fosse Temple II; *Lachish IV*: Pl. 78: 780, Locus 1502, 'Dipper Class A', which was the most common MB II dipper juglet in the tombs at Lachish (ibid: 193).

Beth Shemesh: *Ain Shems II*: Pl. XXIX: 216, 225, Tomb 17, MB IIA (see our No. 59); Pl. XXXVIII:1 (see our No. 66); *Ain Shems IV*: Pl. XXXV: 11, Tomb 11, MB IIB.

Tell Beit Mirsim: *TBM I*: Pl. 42:12-13, Stratum D.

2.2.6.1.2. LB AND IRON AGE II DIPPER JUGLETS
The following vessels are shorter and somewhat wider dipper juglets that represent the development of this type in LB II, when the neck becomes shorter and wider, and the body squat (Amiran 1969: 146). This shape can be found in early Iron Age I contexts as well.

-**Pls. 6:7; 22:5 (No. 89)**: a straight body tapering to a button base; short rounded shoulders. The neck is short; though most of its is missing, a trefoil mouth may be assumed. The handle rises above the rim.

Parallels:
Gezer: *Macalister III*: Pl. CXXII:12, Tomb 252 (late 15th-13th/12th centuries); *Gezer IV*: Pl. 35:8, Stratum XII.

Jerusalem: Amiran 1960: Fig. 2:32, Nahlat Ahim tomb (LB IIA).

-Pls. 6:8; 22:6 (No. 171): a stout, thick-walled juglet with slightly rounded sides and a carinated sloping shoulder. The neck is quite wide, with a trefoil rim. The button base is thick. The handle and part of the rim are missing.

-SG 77.211E4 (Pl. 25:9; *Saint Germain-en-Laye*: 149): This is a small juglet (14.3 cm high), very similar to Pl. 6:8 in general shape. It has a cylindrical body with sloping carinated shoulders. There is a soft carination above the tapering button base. The neck is wide and short; the rim is trefoil. The juglet is lightly encrusted.

Parallels:
Gezer: *Macalister III*: Pl. LXIV: 21, Tomb No. 7 (LB IB-LB IIB\Iron Age I); *Gezer V*: Pl. 16:12, Cave I.10A (LB IIA).

Lachish: *Lachish II*: Pl. LIIB: 300, Fosse Temples I and II; *Lachish IV*: Pl. 78: 787, Locus 542; Tufnell calls these 'Dipper Class B'; the base is often knife-pared to a point and the shape was attributed to the latter part of the Late Bronze Age, 14th-12th centuries (ibid: 194).

Tel Batash-Timnah: Kelm and Mazar 1995: Fig. 4.28, juglet, Stratum VII (LB IIA).

Beth Shemesh: *Ain Shems IV*: Pl. LV: 9, slightly longer neck, Stratum IVa.

-Pl. 6:9 (No. 187): a body of a squat, thick-walled juglet, whose neck, rim and handle are missing. The ovoid body is wider than the other dipper juglets, and the base is rounded. This juglet was found in Tomb I.

Parallels:
Gezer: *Macalister III*: Pl. LXIV: 15, 20-21, Tomb 7, LB IB-LB IIB (see our No. 89).

-Pls. 6:10; 22:7 (No. 91): a small juglet with very different proportions than the others. The squat rounded body is wide with its widest point above mid-body, tapering down to a pointed base. The short wide neck is straight and the rim is missing; the top has been filed down, probably following the breakage of the rim. A thick handle extends from mid-neck to shoulder.

Parallels:
Gezer: *Macalister III*: Pl. LXIV: 14, with thickened rim, Tomb No. 7 (LB IB-LB IIB\Iron Age I).

-AO7002 (Pl. 27:5): A small round bodied juglet (10.3 cm high) with a rounded, somewhat bulbous base. The neck is short and slightly flaring and a loop handle extends from the rim to the sloping shoulder. The fabric is light pink with many small and medium white inclusions. Faint traces of vertical burnish lines can be seen.

-SG 77.211E3 (Pl. 25:10; *Saint Germain-en-Laye*: 149):[12] A round-bodied juglet, with a rounded base, a short, slightly flaring neck and a handle extending from rim to sloping shoulder. The exterior is covered with light red slip and prominent vertical burnish lines.

The commonly known shape and surface treatment of these juglets point to an Iron Age II date. Selected parallels: *TBM III*: Pl. 17:1 (Stratum A); Amiran 1969: 263, Photo 267, unknown provenience, Iron Age II.

Discussion
The dipper juglet begins to appear in the MB IIA becomes popular in the MB IIB and continues through the LB IIB (though note their absence in Fosse Temple III at Lachish). Though the general tendency is that the earlier dippers were longer, it appears that both long and short versions may be found in MB II contexts (Saller 1964:125; see as well Kopetzki 2002), while the LB I-II juglets generaly tend to be shorter and more baggy, with a rounder base (*Lachish IV*: 192). This development continues into the Iron Age as well. The appearance of red slip and polished, vertical burnish is usually an early MB II characteristic (Saller 1964: 125; Maeir 1997: 113). Our No. 67 (Pl. 6:2) is the only juglet to be so treated and may thus considered relatively early in the developmental sequence, as its 'button' base seems to indicate as well (*Lachish IV*: 192). Thus, it may be summarized that our dipper juglets can be placed in the sequence from early MB IIB until LB IIB. Juglets AO7002 and 77.211E3 apparently belong to Iron Age II and thus represent the only dipper juglets of this period in the Gezer tombs, since all the other Iron Age II juglets are 'black juglets' (see below).

The phenomenon of dipper juglets found in tombs together with storage jars (e.g. Tel el-Far'ah South: Price-William 1977: 9) apparently did not exist in the Gezer tombs under discussion, and our juglets apparently were placed as offerings on their own.

2.2.6.2. CYLINDRICAL JUGLETS
Pls. 6:11-12; 22:8. Nos. 63,64

These juglets have straight walls and a carinated shoulder; the cylindrical body is squat. The narrow neck is topped by a ring-like, everted rim. The handle, thick or thin ribbon-sectioned, extends from just below the rim to the shoulder. The wide base is rounded or almost flat.

---

[12] Included under the inventory number 77.211E, four juglets are mentioned in the Saint Germain-en-Laye catalogue. The only one that is photographed, 77.211E3 (Pl. 25:10), is Iron Age II. Another juglet in this series, 77.211E2, was examined and found to be an MB II dipper juglet (see pp. 22 above). Thus, since it is not clear what periods the two missing juglets of this number belong to, they will be disregarded in the summary of our assemblage.

-**Pls. 6:11; 22:8 (No. 63):** The shoulder of this juglet is sharply carinated; it stands 11 cm high and has traces of a buff slip and burnish.

-**Pl. 6:12 (No. 64):** This juglet is stouter than No. 63 (8 cm high), with a rounded shoulder and almost flat base. The thin ribbon-sectioned handle rises slightly above the rim.

Parallels and Discussion:
Gezer: *Gezer I*: Pl. 30:18-19, Stratum XVIII.

Lachish: *Lachish II*: Pl. LIIB: 288, Fosse Temple I; *Lachish IV*: Pl. 77: 751-758, 760-761, Tufnell's Cylindrical Class E, though the ribbon handle of our jug is more similar to that of Cylindrical Class F, which is dated slightly later than Class E (*Lachish IV*: 190-191).

Tell Beit Mirsim: *TBMIa*: Pl. 15, Stratum D.

The cylindrical juglet appears as early as MB IIA but is common in MB IIB. This type does not continue past LB I (Amiran 1969: 107, 146; Saller 1964: 102-105); the latest one to be found at Lachish came from Fosse Temple I (*Lachish IV*: 191). The cylindrical juglets replaced the piriform juglets in the south in late MB II (e.g. Kempinski 1983: 189).

2.2.6.3. PIRIFORM JUGLETS
Pls. 6:13-14; 22:9-10. Nos. 62,61

These juglets have piriform bodies with a high, wide sloping shoulder tapering down to a very narrow base. The short neck is narrow and flaring on top. A handle extends from just below the rim to the shoulder.

Despite the morphological similarity between the two, they are differentiated by the Tell el-Yehudiyeh ware of No. 61.

-**Pls. 6:13; 22:9 (No. 62):** a slightly thickened rim exterior. Thin ribbon-sectioned handle. Small, thick convex disc base. Covered with a brownish-gray slip and vertical burnish.

Parallels:
Gezer: *Macalister III*: Pl. CXLII:26, more concave shoulders, Pl. CLIII:8; *Gezer I*: Pl. 31:24, reddish brown slip and burnished, similar body shape, with ring-like rim and 'button' base, Stratum XIX.

-**Pls. 6:14; 22:10 (No. 61):** Tell el-Yehudiyeh ware with punctured design of two bordered bands of slightly diagonal lines; double-strand handle; button base.

Parallels:
Gezer: *Macalister III*: Pl. XXIII: 16, Cave 15 I; Pl. LX: 12, Tomb i.

Lachish: *Lachish IV*: Pl. 77: 729, Locus 1552 (MB IIB).

2.2.6.4. DERIVATIVE PIRIFORM JUGLETS
Pls. 6:15; 22:11. No. 60

Pl. 25:7. SG 77.211I1

-**Pls. 6:15; 22:11 (No. 60):** a juglet with biconical body proportions, whose widest diameter is at mid-body, rather than above it. The narrow neck is flaring on top, with a thin ribbon-sectioned handle extending from under the rim to the shoulder. The base was a small disc base.

-**SG 77.211I1 (Pl. 25:7;** *Saint Germain-en-Laye*: 149): a juglet (11.7 cm high) very similar to Pl. 6:15; heavy encrustation.

Parallels:
Lachish: *Lachish IV*: Pl. 77: 744, Locus 1508, Tufnell's 'Piriform Class C' (ibid: 189); see also a juglet from Menahat with a squat biconical body shape (Amiran 1969: 112, Photo 109). For comparisons to this body shape among the Tell el-Yehudiyeh juglets, see Kaplan's Biconical Types 1 and 2 (Kaplan 1980: 24-26).

Discussion
The piriform juglet, which first appeared in MB IIA, was a popular MB IIB form that did not continue past LB I (Amiran 1969: 112). Following Kempinski (1983:184-185) and Price-Williams (1977:), Maeir (1997:114) has demonstrated that this shape was more dominant at northern sites, where it co-existed with the cylindrical juglets (see above); this is in contrast to southern sites, where the cylindrical juglets eventually replaced the rarer piriform shapes. The relatively small amount of piriform (n=3) and cylindrical (n=2) juglets in the Gezer tombs does not enable this contention to be checked, although the parallels to our cylindrical juglets point to a somewhat later (LB I) date than the piriform juglets.

The punctured design on No. 61 places it with the family of Tell el-Yehudiyeh ware,[13] which becomes progressively rarer towards the end of MB II (Maeir 1997: 134). No. 61 is Kaplan's Piriform Type 3 and this very juglet is published by her (Kaplan 1980: 23-24, Fig. 80:c). The geographic range of this type is restricted to the Southern Levant (ibid: 63) and it falls mainly in the chronological range of MB IIB and apparently does not reach MB IIC (ibid: 72). According to Bietak's classification (Bietak 1989: A66.15), this juglet belongs to the "späten palästinensischen gruppe", which likewise only appears in the southern Levant in the late MB IIB. The motif appearing on the only Tell el-Yehudiyeh juglet in the tombs is relatively simple compared to the intricate designs found on various Tell el-Yehudiyeh juglets, and in fact, the few parallels that could be found to our specific design all came from the Jericho tombs, where this type of juglet is especially common (see Kaplan 1980: 72, Fig. 63:f, from Jericho, Tomb A; Fig. 66:a, Jericho, Tomb D,

---

[13] Following Kaplan's definition of this ware (Kaplan 1980:5).

squatter body). This juglet is one of the few vessels in the Gezer tombs with a relatively limited range - purely MB IIB.

The brownish-gray burnished slip on our No. 62 may suggest an attempt to imitate the Tell-el-Yehudiyeh ware, without the punctured decoration.

From the published material, it appears that the piriform juglet was not a common shape at Gezer, nor was it at Lachish, in accordance with its general scarcity in the south. Tufnell's 'Piriform Juglet Class A', which included three examples of Tell el-Yehudiyeh juglets, was generally scarce at Lachish (*Lachish IV*: 189).

2.2.6.5. "BLACK JUGLETS"
The following juglets belong to the so-called Iron Age II-III "black juglets" (Amiran 1969: 256).

-Pls. 6:17; 22:13 (No. 180; Pl. 10: 100): a juglet with a stout body, wide sloping shoulders and a soft body carination above a 'button' base; the neck is straight and narrow. A handle extends from rim to shoulder. The pinkish clay is rough outside and shows no traces of slip or burnish. The phenomenon of the 'black' juglets being slipped red or remaining non-slipped, is well known throughout the entire duration of the existence of this type. The position of the handle and general proportion of these juglets are a certain indicator of their chronology. The relatively short proportions of Pl. 6:17 and the handle extending from the rim date it to a later part of the Iron Age II (Amiran 1969: 259).

An additional example of this type appears to be Pl. 10: No. 100, but the schematic drawing makes it difficult to ascribe it with certainty to this type.

"BLACK JUGLETS" - NOT DRAWN:
Louvre:
-AO 7003[14] (Pl. 27:3-4) two juglets, each ca. 8.5 cm high; both of black fabric with many small white inclusions; traces of burnishing. One juglet has a sack-shaped body, while the other is rounded.

-AO 6999: a medium sized juglet (ca. 11.8 cm high); handle extending from below rim to shoulder; round body; light pink fabric with few small white and black inclusions; traces of red slip; light encrustation.

-AO 7000 (Pl. 27:2): a small squat juglet (ca. 8.4 cm high); handle extending from rim to shoulder; pink fabric with many small white, gray and red inclusions; traces of red slip and vertical burnishing.

-AO 7001 (Pl. 27:1): a small squat juglet (ca. 6.9 cm high); handle extending from rim to shoulder; pink fabric with many small white, gray and red inclusions.

Saint Germain-en-Laye:
-SG 77.211I2 (Pl. 25:8): a medium sized juglet (ca. 10.9 cm high); handle extending from below rim to shoulder; fabric exterior peeling.

-SG 77.211I3: a small juglet (6.9 cm high), handle extending from below rim to shoulder; black fabric; traces of black slip outside.

-SG 72.356g: a small juglet (7.4 cm high); handle extending from below rim to shoulder; black fabric and polished black slip outside.

Discussion
The position of the handle and general proportions of most of the above black juglets point to a somewhat late date in the Iron Age II sequence, probably continuing down to the very end of this period. These juglets augment the other late Iron Age II vessels from the Gezer tombs, stressing the use of the tombs as late as the end of Iron Age II. The inclusion of such juglets in funerary contexts is well known at other sites as well (e.g. Bloch-Smith 1992:72-81).

2.2.6.6. JUGLET VARIA
-Pls. 6:16; 22:12 (No. 80): a sloping shoulder and round body fragment; the neck, rim and lower body are missing. It was decorated outside with rather irregularly spaced and uneven horizontal red lines, two of which enclose vertical red lines on the lower shoulder. A brown line is found at the neck and near the break on the bottom. It was self slipped and burnished to a polish.

Discussion
The mode of decoration and general shape indicate that it possibly was an imitation of an import, such as a small Mycenaean stirrup jar (e.g. Amiran 1969: 186, Pl. 57:10-11). The typical decoration of such jars included horizontal bands, but also occasionally some vertical hatching on or below the shoulder (e.g. Stubbings 1951: Pl. XVI:17).

2.2.7. FLASKS
Pls. 7:1-3; 20:5-7. Nos. 178, 116, 122

The three flasks (excluding the Mycenaean jug-flask that is discussed below with the other Aegean material) found in the tombs are of different types and will be described individually.

-Pls. 7:1; 20:5 (No. 178):[15] a wide, lentoid body and a narrow, slightly convex neck. The rim exterior is truncated with a sharp edge. The two handles extend from below this edge to the shoulder with a smear that forms arched 'petals'. The body is decorated with red concentric circles, with horizontal lines below and on the handle. This flask was found in Tomb 1.

---

[14] Four juglets were listed as belonging to this registration number; however, only two were photographed (Pl. 27:3-4) and 2 are missing.

[15] This flask has already been published in Amiran 1969: 166, Photo 167.

Gezer - Tombs

Parallels:
Gezer: *Macalister III*: Pl. LXV: 23, Tomb 7, different rim (LB IB-LB IIB\Iron Age I); Pl. LXXXIV: 14 (LB IB-LB IIB).

Lachish: *Lachish II*: Pl. LIVB: 349, Fosse Temple III.

Tell Beit Mirsim: *TBM Ia:* Pl. 18:11, Stratum C.

Discussion
The characteristic handle attachment forming 'petals' relegates this flask to LB II (Amiran 1969: 166); the parallels support this date.

-Pls. 7:2; 20:6 (No. 116): a globular, swollen body with prominent wheel marks and a pinched center. The long neck is concave, flaring out on top to a thickened round rim. The two ribbon-sectioned handles extend from below the rim to the shoulder. The flask is undecorated.

Parallels:
Lachish: *Lachish IV*: Pl. 84: 958, concentric circles, Locus 523 (LB IIB-10th cent.); Pl. 84: 953, concentric circles, Locus 556 (transitional LB IIB\Iron Age I).

Discussion
The shape of this flask and the method in which the handle was attached, as well as the parallels mentioned above, indicate that it should be dated to the transitional LB\Iron Age I horizon.

-Pls. 7:3; 20:7 (No. 122): This lentoid flask has a spoon with a narrow aperture attached to its short neck. Two high, perforated lug handles are placed on the shoulders. The flask is red slipped outside with no traces of burnishing.

Parallels:
Gezer: *Macalister III*: Pl. LXV: 25, Tomb 7 (LB IB-LB IIB\Iron Age I); Pl. LXX:8, Tomb 9 (Iron Age I, early 10th cent.).

Lachish: *Lachish IV*: Pl. 86: 998, Locus 559, dark red slip, irregular burnish, black concentric circles.

Discussion
This "spoon flask" is Mazar's Type FL 4 (Mazar 1985: 74). This type is well-known in Iron Age I and subsequently becomes extremely rare.

2.2.8. PYXIS
Pls. 7:4-5; 20:8. Nos. 173, V1715

Pl. 26:6. SG 72.356f

There are three pyxides in the Gezer assemblage. Two are similar to each other and one is unique in its double neck.

-Pls. 7:4; 20:8 (No. 173): This pyxis is locally produced, with a stout body, a shoulder carination and an additional carination above the wide rounded base. The shoulders are sloping and the short neck is flaring, with a round rim top. Two horizontal handles (one missing) extend from just below the shoulder carination. It is undecorated.

Parallels:
Gezer: *Macalister III*: Pl. CXXII: 8, Tomb 252, late 15th-13th\12th centuries; *Gezer IV*: Pl. 29:18, Stratum XIII; Pl. 38:5, Stratum XII.

Lachish: *Lachish II*: Pl. LIVB: 344, Fosse Temple III.

Beth Shemesh: *Ain Shems IV*: Pl. LIX: 21, with black lines, Stratum III.

Tell Beit Mirsim: *TBM I*: Pl. 44:3, Stratum C.

-Pl. 7:5 (No. V1715; Rockefeller Museum): This pyxis is similar in basic concept to the other two pyxides in the corpus (Pls. 7:4; 20:8; 26:6); its height (12 cm) makes it taller than Pl. 7:4 and more like the pyxis from Saint Germain-en-Laye. It has two horizontal handles on the pronounced shoulder and a ring base. The unique feature is the double neck, which is flaring, with both sides facing opposite directions. The vessel is undecorated. It was found in Tomb IX.

Discussion
Double vessels are known from the Early Bronze Age and onwards and undoubtedly their form follows function, be it domestic or cultic. Though they are not common, many derive from mortuary contexts, suggesting that they might have been manufactured for a specific funerary purpose. This might be true of our vessel as well but would be hard to determine, since no exact parallels to this vessel have been found in either funerary or domestic contexts.

Selected examples of double vessels are: twin bottles, EB I (Tomb 3, Ophel, Jerusalem: Amiran 1969: Pl. 11:12); a double 'bilbil'; LB II (Nahlat Ahim tomb, Jerusalem; Amiran 1960: Fig. 1:13); a double libation vessel, Iron Age I (Tell Qiri: Ben-Tor and Portugali 1987: Fig. 17:8); two composite (double or triple) flasks, Iron Age I (Tell Qasile; Mazar 1985:73-74). Note the double pyxides, joined at the body, from Megiddo: "Jar 143", Stratum VIB (*Megiddo II*: Pl. 73:13) and "Jar 130", Stratum VII, with red and black geometric decoration (ibid: Pl. 68:8). Quadruple joined pyxides ("Jar 150") were found at Megiddo in Stratum VIA, painted in a red geometric design (ibid: Pl. 77:8).

Dothan (1982:130-131) discussed the appearance of "composite pyxides" in Iron Age I contexts. In light of the fact that they do not appear earlier than the Iron Age I and the existence of parallels from the MYC IIIC pottery, Dothan claims that the appearance of this type is to be related to the influx of MYC IIIC pottery and styles during the Iron Age I (associated with the arrival of the Sea Peoples). Further corroboration to this view may be suggested based on Mazar (1985:72), who noted the connection between the composite flasks of the Iron Age I found in Palestine (which are, conceptually, quite similar to the composite pyxides) and those found in contemporary Cypriote contexts. Once again, this might be connected to a "Sea Peoples" cultural influence.

It should be noted that opposed to the other "composite pyxides" known from other Iron Age I contexts (e.g. Dothan 1982:130-131), the example from Gezer is not comprised of two separate vessels that were joined together. Rather, it consists of two partial vessels (each missing about a quarter of its "normal" body) that were joined together (for a discussion of the pottery technology of this vessel, see below, Chapter 6).

-**Pyxis SG 72.356f** (Pl. 26:6; *Saint Germain-en- Laye*: 149; 12.3 cm high; not illustrated): This pyxis is similar to Pl. 7:4, though somewhat taller. It appears to belong to a later phase of Iron Age I. It has two horizontal handles and it is broken at the neck. The ware is reddish yellow with white and red inclusions; it is covered by a peeling red slip outside and is encrusted. This pyxis was found in Tomb IX.

Discussion
The pyxis is one of the shapes adopted into the Canaanite ceramic repertoire from Mycenaean prototypes (Amiran 1969: 277). The squat pyxis with a rounded base was considered by Dothan to be a later development of the original Mycenaean type that had been imported into the country in the Late Bronze Age II. It was adopted by the local potters and continued to appear as late as the 9th century (Dothan 1982: 131). Our pyxides recall Mazar's Pyxis Type 1, though the latter's upper carination is not as emphasized (Mazar 1985: 77; Pl. 27:21). The shape and comparisons suggest an Iron Age I date, though the presence of red slip on two of the vessels may indicate that it can be as late as early Iron Age II.

2.2.9. IMPORTS
The imports that are found in the Gezer tombs are of Mycenaean and Cypriote origin.

2.2.9.1. MYCENAEAN IMPORTS
Pls. 8:1-3; 23:1. Nos. 147,149,150; Pl. 10: No. 148

2.2.9.1.1. PIRIFORM JARS
-**Pls. 8:1; 23:1 (No. 147)**: intact except for two partially broken handles and a chipped away section on the lower body. The short wide neck is splayed and the outer rim is down turned. The base is a slightly convex disc base with everted edges. There are three horizontal handles with a round section, placed on the shoulder. Its decoration is monochrome, in dark reddish-brown paint that is somewhat opaque in places. It includes a thick band on and above the base, with three rather irregular narrow bands painted above it, bordered by a thick band. The upper body below the shoulder is left unpainted, and the zone below the handle has a thin band bordered by two thicker bands. The shoulder is covered with a scale pattern (Furumark's Motif 70 - Furumark 1941:Fig. 70:1; MYC IIA-IIIB), which is the most common design for handle zones on piriform jars from LH I to LH IIIB:1 (Leonard 1994:185). Each handle is painted and has a round painted patch around it on top of the scales. The neck is also monochrome, partially rubbed away on the rim top, with the paint continuing into the inner neck.

-**Pls. 8:2; 23:1 (No. 149)**[16]: intact except for one missing handle.[17] The short wide neck is almost straight, and the everted rim top is horizontal. The three vertical handles, placed on the shoulder, have a flat oval section. The lower foot is somewhat wider than that of No. 147. The base is a thick flat disc with an everted edge. The decoration is monochrome, in a lighter shade of reddish-brown, and is basically similar to No. 147, though the zones of painting differ: one narrow band tops the painted base and an additional band is painted on the middle of the body, where there is a blank zone in No. 147. The upper part of the vessel is decorated just like No. 147, though the shoulder is wider. For a discussion of the pottery technology of this vessel, as seen through Computed Tomography Analysis, see below, Chapter 6.

-**Pl. 10: No. 148**: The miniature drawing shows a shape similar to the two described above, with three horizontal handles. The decorative motif on the shoulder differs and appears to be vertical lines, bordered by a group of four horizontal bands below.

Parallels:
Gezer: *Macalister III*: Pl. LXVI: 44, 49, Tomb 7; LB.

Lachish: *Lachish IV*: Pl. 83:945,946, LB IIA.

Jerusalem: Saller 1964: Fig. 58:4, wider body, Dominus Flevit tomb.

Discussion
These vessels may be compared to the general Furumark's Shape (FS) 'conical-piriform', which include a number of variations (see Furumark 1941: Fig. 4: FS35; FS39; FS44; FS45; all MYC IIIA:2, pictured with both horizontal and vertical handles). An analogy may also be made to FS 46-47 (ibid: 45, Fig. 12:46-47, both with horizontal handles, MYC IIIA:2). Furumark's definition of these as 'Levanto-Mycenaean' types has been contested by Leonard, both on the grounds of provenience and distribution frequency in the East (Leonard 1994: 7-8)[18]. The shape of our jar can be compared both to Mountjoy's 'medium piriform jar' (Mountjoy 1986: 70-71, Fig. 80) and to her 'small piriform jar' (ibid: 70-72, Fig. 81); both are LH IIIA:2. This shape is Form 7 in Leonard's index, with references to the

---

[16] This jar has already been published in Amiran 1969: 180, Photo 180.

[17] It is most likely that the broken-off handle is the result of accidental breakage during it use-life or during its placement in the tomb, or perhaps during the excavation and subsequent handling. Nevertheless, one should note the existence of similar phenomena (in which handles or spouts are purposely broken off prior to burial) -- the ritual "killing of pottery" in contemporary Mycenaean tombs. For a recent discussion of this ritual, see Soles 1999.

[18] Leonard notes that in fact, these so-called 'Levanto-Mycenaean' types are quite rare in the East and are very common on Cyprus. For example, FS 46-47 is represented by only 5 examples in Syria-Palestine known at the time of Leonard's study (Leonard 1994: 19-20).

occurrences of our shape (FS 44-47) in the east (Leonard 1994: 17-22).

Most of these parallels were found at coastal sites in Syria-Palestine, with more limited appearances inland in the Shephelah (Tell Beit Mirsim, Lachish, Beth Shemesh and Gezer), the north (Hazor, Dan, Megiddo, Qiri, Beth Shean) and the east (Jericho, Amman). Thus, this is not a commonly found vessel in the vicinity of Gezer and can be dated to LB IIA.

2.2.9.1.2. FLASK
Pls. 8:3; 23:1. No. 150

This flask has a narrow neck and everted rim, with two handles extending from mid-neck to shoulder. The globular body is symmetrically swollen; the base is a narrow ring base. The flask is self slipped and highly burnished, with a red painted decoration of equidistant dense narrow concentric circles encircling a fully painted small circle ("bull's eye") in the center. The upper neck has dense, thin horizontal lines and the handles and base are covered with a red paint. The side panel is decorated with dense thin horizontal lines with a gap between them in the center.

Parallels:
Gezer: *Macalister III*: Pl. CLI:21.

Discussion
This is Furumark Shape 'globular' (Furumark 1941: Fig. 5:187-189, MYC IIIA:2) and Mountjoy's 'vertical type flask'; see Mountjoy 1986: Fig. 95: 2, late LH IIIA:2, equated with to FS 189). This is Leonard's Form 48, with the division of the variants (FS 187-189) mainly chronological, with FS 187-188 being earlier (MYC IIIA:1-early 2) and rare in the East, and FS 189 being later (MYC IIIA:2-late)[19] and very common in the East (Leonard 1994: 83-87, although note that much of the material cited is fragmentary).

Discussion
It seems that the four Mycenaean imports found in the tombs may be ascribed to LB IIA, the period that witnessed a great influx of Mycenaean imports into Canaan (Amiran 1969: 179). Like the vessels from our tombs, much of the published Mycenaean pottery from Gezer appears to have originated in LH IIIA, though there is a representation of LH IIIB as well in Macalister's Tomb 58 (Stubbings 1951: 63-64,83-84). This is notable in light of the contention that the majority of the Mycenaean wares imported into Canaan are MYC IIIB, and were excavated in LB IIB strata or in tomb deposits (Amiran 1969: 181). This is evidenced at Lachish, where Tufnell claimed that more Mycenaean imports date to LH IIIB than to LH IIIA (*Lachish IV*: 212).[20]

Both the conical-piriform jar and the globular flask are not very common among the Mycenaean imports in the Shephelah and their presence in the Gezer tombs may be an indication of the economic status of the tomb users, perhaps similar to the tomb that was published by the HUC excavations with its rich display of imported wares (see *Gezer V*).

2.2.9.2. CYPRIOTE IMPORTS

2.2.9.2.1. WHITE SHAVED JUGLETS
Pls. 8: 4-6; 23:2-3. Nos. 174,175,176; Pl. 10: Nos. 97,129.

NOT ILLUSTRATED IN PLATES: SG 72.356e (*Saint Germain-en-Laye*:149).

All four juglets have similar characteristics: hand-made, light buff colored fine metallic ware, inserted handle, pinched mouth and the typical smoothed shaved finish on the exterior. The base of No. 176 is slightly more pointed. Part of the rim of No. 175 is missing. It is difficult to determine these characteristics on the miniature drawings appearing in Pl. 10, though it seems that these two juglets do belong to this group.

Selected parallels:
Gezer: *Macalister III*: Pl. LXIV: 5, Tomb 7 (LB IB-LB IIB); *Gezer V*: Pl. 18:1, Cave I.10A, lower burial phase (LB IB-LB IIA); 7:20, Cave I.10A (LB IIA).

Lachish: *Lachish IV*: Pl. 79: 819, Tomb 216; Pl. 79:820, Tomb 501 (LB IIA-B).

Beth Shemesh: *Ain Shems I:* Pl. XXXVIII: 7, LB II.

Jerusalem: Amiran 1960: Fig. 1:20, Nahlat Ahim tomb (LB IIA).

Discussion
These juglets are considered a Cypriote imitation of the Canaanite dipper juglet (Amiran 1969: 173; Bergoffen 1989: 134-135). These imported juglets were handmade, with the handle inserted into the shoulder and the body finished by paring the body and base with a sharp instrument. This group (jugs, juglets and bottles) was imported to the East in large quantities in LB IIA, although earlier examples (late LB I) can be found (*Gezer V*: 79). Gittlen (1981: 51,53-54) claims that the import of these juglets, which had been expressly manufactured for the markets in the east, ceased after LB IIA. The technique of knife paring, especially near the base of the vessel, was adopted for locally made juglets as well (*Lachish IV*: 194; Gittlen 1981: 54).

2.2.9.2.2. WHITE SLIP MILK BOWL
Pl. 10: No. 199.

The only representative in the Gezer tombs of this common imported ware is a milk bowl, of which only a small schematic drawing remains, so that the vessel itself could not be examined. The rendition of the decoration appears to be of

---

[19] Note a very similar flask from Megiddo in Amiran 1969: 180-181, Photo 190, which is attributed to MYC IIIB, LB IIB.

[20] A similar situation is noted regarding the Mycenaean imports at Ugarit. See Hirschfeld 2000:69.

horizontal lines under the rim exterior and a series of three vertical lines extending below these lines to the base. The handle is the typical wishbone shape.

Discussion
The earliest imports of the White Slip family began in LB IA (White Slip I) and peaked in LB IIA (Gittlen 1981: 50-51; for more recent discussions, see the various contributions in Karageorghis 2001), with the typical decorative pattern of ladder and lozenge fillings bordered by horizontal and vertical lines (White Slip I and II). The process of rigidity and schematization in the design is a chronological indicator, and the specimen from the Gezer tombs with a depleted motif of simple lines represents the very end of the series in late LB IIB, (Amiran 1969: 172-173). Thus, our bowl may be dated to late LB IIB and very early Iron Age I. See also *Lachish IV*: Pl. 79:835, Tomb 532 (transitional LB\Iron Age I).

2.2.9.2.3. BASE RING JUGS AND JUGLETS ('BILBILS')
Pls. 8:7-14; 23:4-9. Nos. 161, 157, 155, 164, 165, 158, 162, 154, 163; Pl. 10: Nos. 151, 156, 159.

NOT ILLUSTRATED IN PLATES:
Louvre: AO 6991, AO 6992, AO 6993, AO 6994
Saint Germain-en-Laye: SG 72.356H, SG 72.356H1, SG 72.356I

-**Pls. 8:7; 23:4 (No. 161)**: black ware; plastic decoration; handle missing.

Parallels:
Gezer: *Gezer V*: 18:7, 19:4, 20:1, 24:9, Cave I.10A, lower tomb burial phase, LB IB-LB IIA.

Lachish: *Lachish IV*: Pl. 80: 842, Tomb 501(LB II).

Jerusalem: Amiran 1960: Fig. 1:18, Nahlat Ahim tomb (LB IIA).

-**Pls. 8:8-12; 23:5-8 (Nos. 157, 164, 155, 165, 158)**: black metallic ware; wide ring base; white painted decoration: two groups of horizontal lines on the upper and lower neck; on globular body - variations of groups of four lines: diagonal (No. 157); diagonal intersecting (No. 164); diagonal intersecting, bordered by groups of horizontal bands on shoulder and above base (Nos. 155, 165,158). No. 8 is fired to a reddish hue on its neck and part of the upper shoulder.

NOT ILLUSTRATED IN PLATES (ALL SIMILAR TO NOS. 8-12):
-**AO 6991**: 23.3 cm high; mended.

-**SG 72.356H, SG 72.356H1** (24.7 cm high; rim and neck partly missing; encrusted); **SG 72.356I** (encrusted).

Parallels
Gezer: *Macalister III*: Pl. LXV: 31, Tomb 7 (LB IB-LB IIB); *Gezer V*: Pl. 26:2, Cave I.10A, lower tomb burial phase, LB IB-LB IIA.

Chapter 2 - Pottery

Lachish: *Lachish IV*: 843-846; *Lachish II*: Pl. LIB:279, 283 - Fosse Temples II and III.

Jerusalem: Amiran 1960: Fig. 1:17, Nahlat Ahim Tomb (LB IIA).

-**Pls. 8:13; 23:9 (No. 162)**: juglet (11 cm high); reddish-brown ware; double ridge at mid-neck; narrow high trumpet base; handle missing. No apparent join to the neck is visible and the possibility exists that, although rare, the handle joined to the rim (as reconstructed in the drawing).

-**Pl. 8:14 (No. 154)**: juglet (13 cm high) brownish-black ware; neck tilted; faint traces of horizontal bands on neck.

-**Pls. 8:15; 23:10 (No. 163)**: juglet (ca. 15 cm high); black ware with white horizontal bands painted on neck and above base; narrow high trumpet base; body restored.

NOT ILLUSTRATED IN PLATES:
-**AO 6992** (13.5 cm high);

-**AO 6993** (13 cm high; handle broken);

-**AO 6994** (13.2 cm high; heavily encrusted): similar to Nos. 13-15.

Parallels:
Gezer: *Macalister III*: Pl. LXXIV: 6-7, Tomb 30 (LB IB-LB IIB); *Gezer V*: Pls. 19:2-3; 21:7; 23:1; 24:1,7; 25:2; 30:2, lower burial phase (LB IB-LB IIA); Cave I.10A: Pls. 14:2; 15:3-4, upper tomb phase (LB IIA).

Lachish: *Lachish II:* Pl. LIIB: 301, 302, 312, Fosse Temple II and III; *Lachish IV*: Pl. 80: 857,858, 861, 863, 865, 866 (LB IIA-B).

Beth Shemesh: *Ain Shems I*: Pl. XLII: 7, LB II.

Tell Beit Mirsim: *TBM Ia*: Pl. 18:6, Stratum C.

Jerusalem: Amiran 1960: Fig 1:7-10, Nahlat Ahim tomb (LB IIA).

Discussion
Base Ring ware imports, mainly jugs, juglets and bowls, span most of the Late Bronze Age and are found in both funerary and non-funerary contexts, with the jugs dominating in the tombs (Gittlen 1981: 52-53).

The traditional division of this ware (Amiran 1960: 27; *Lachish IV*: 207; *Gezer V*: 77-78, 82-83) between the earlier Base Ring I (with plastic relief decoration like our Pl. 8:7,13, considered LB I-LB IIA) and the later Base Ring II (with white painted decoration, like our Pl. 8:8-12,14 considered LB IIA) is no longer axiomatic. Currently, more complex considerations, based on multivariate data such as technology, fabric, function and regionalism, serve as the basis for defining the chronological and spatial distribution of this ware (Gittlen 1981: 56-57, note 12; and in particular, see Vaughan 1991a; 1991b).

The chronological range proposed by Gittlen for the importation of this ware to Palestine is LB IA to LB IIA, with a great decline, virtually to the point of unavailability, in LB IIB (Gittlen 1981: 50-51). However, it seems that importation of this ware continued throughout the 13th century, though in reduced quantities (Mazar 1990:293, n. 26; Bergoffen 1989: 225-226). Bergoffen differentiated between the juglets, which, for all intents and purposes, is not to be found in the southern Levant in the 13th century, and the jugs, which did continue at that time. She claimed that the reason for this is related to the assumed contents of precious oils in the juglets whose production ceased (Bergoffen 1989: 313-314). Thus, it seems that the Base Ring jugs and juglets found in the Gezer tombs indicate a date of LB I-LB IIA, though the possibility that the jugs date to LB IIB cannot be ruled out.

2.2.9.2.4. WHITE PAINTED JUGLET
-Pl. 8:16 (No. V1713; Rockefeller Museum):

Discussion
This juglet belongs to family of imports termed White Painted III-IV, which was initially imported into Palestine from Cyprus in MB IIB/C and continuing into LB I (for general discussion, see, e.g., Johnson 1982). The vessel has a buff slip and is painted in dark red in the White Painted Pendant Line style. This vessel was found in Tomb VI and has been previously published (Pythian- Adams 1926:Pl. 7, No. 5; note that it was overlooked by Johnson [1982] in her survey of Middle Cypriote pottery from Palestine). For a discussion of the pottery technology of this vessel, see below, Chapter 6.

Parallels:
Gezer: *Macalister III*: pl. LXII:51.

Beth Shemesh: Amiran 1969: Pl. 37:10, Tomb 3 (see also larger juglet from Megiddo, Stratum XII in ibid: Pl. 37:9).

2.2.9.2.5. IMITATION BASE RING JUGS
Pls. 9; 24. Nos. 167,169,123,124,168,170,84,110, 166,160; Pl. 10: No. 151?

Pl. 26:7-8. SG 77.211H2 (rim missing), SG 77.211H3

Pl. 27:6-9. AO 6995, AO 6996, AO 6997 (rim top missing), AO 6998 (rim broken)

Discussion and Parallels
Most of the imitation bilbils from the Gezer tombs include shapes which are quite similar to the imports with straight narrow necks, flaring rim tops, globular bodies, ridge at join of neck to body, handles from mid-neck and flaring ring bases, often high (e.g. Pl. 9:1-2). The fabric is generally reddish-yellow or light pink, with small white, black and red inclusions, similar to the fabric of much of the other vessels in the assemblage. They range from 12.5-21 cm high. The surface treatments differ from jug to jug: some are painted with red diagonal and horizontal line groups imitating the imported Base Ring's white painted designs, though perhaps the design was applied freehand in some cases rather than with a multi-pointed brush as in the original. AO 6997 has alternating diagonal intersecting lines in light and dark red, emulating a typical Late Bronze Age bichrome (red and black) design. AO 6997 has dark painted lines that are almost black (though this might be post-depositional). Others remained undecorated and one was red slipped and burnished, which is rare (Pl. 9:9, No. 166). These may be compared in shape and surface treatment to the large amount of 'Imitation Base Ring Jugs, Class A' from Lachish (*Lachish IV*: 210; Pl. 81:876-884, LB IIB).

Several of the jugs are only vaguely reminiscent of the shape of the imported originals and have shorter, more concave necks, a squatter body of different proportions and a heavier, almost convex disc base (e.g. Pl. 9:4). Some of these still bear a vestigial rendition of the typical linear design, though depleted. The latter imitations may be compared to Tufnell's 'Imitation Base Ring Jugs Class B' (*Lachish IV*: Pl. 81: 885-896); both classes were considered contemporary, dating to the latter half of the 14th century (ibid: 210; Saller 1964: 137). Other comparisons are: Tell Beit Mirsim, Stratum C (*TBM I*: Pl. 47:10); Beth Shemesh (*Ain Shems IV*: PL. LV: 8,12 Stratum IVa); Jerusalem, Dominus Flevit Tomb (Saller 1964: Figs. 50-51).

There are 17 imitation bilbil jugs in the Gezer tombs, as opposed to the 19 imported jugs (both large and small). Although we do not know whether the assemblage under discussion is complete, assuming that this ratio is indeed indicative of our tombs, this in contrast with the finds from the tomb at Dominus Flevit, where there were about 16 imported large-medium Base Ring jugs and 33 small jugs, as opposed to only 9 imitations (Saller 1964: 129). Such was the situation in the Nahlat Ahim tomb in Jerusalem, where there were 27 imports and 4 imitations.[21] At Lachish, Prag noted that there were 210 imported Base Ring vessels from the tombs and Fosse Temple I-III, compared to ca. 71 imitations of this ware from those same contexts (Prag 1985: 160). Needless to say, the fragmentary and ambiguous nature of the Gezer tombs' assemblage must be kept in mind when cautiously making such an analogy.

The imitation Base Ring jugs, wheel made and with a regular, rather than inserted handle attachment, demonstrate a wide range of shapes and decorative patterns (Saller 1964: 137). Tufnell claimed that they began to appear at the time when the imported Base Ring jugs became progressively scarce, probably sometime in the late 14th century (*Lachish IV*: 209-210; *Gezer V*: 77). However, Prag notes that although the decrease in the amount of Base Ring imports in the course of the 13th century is accompanied by a certain increase in imitations, it should be kept in mind that "importation and imitation went side by side" and imports did continue until the end of LB II, alongside the imitations. Notably, the imitation Base Ring ware never attempted to emulate the distinct characteristics of this ware, such as its dark metallic fabric or intricate decorative motifs, but rather

---
[21] This figure pertains to all the imports in the tombs, both Cypriote and Mycenaean.

represented more of an adaptation to fulfill local demands than as a full-blown replacement (Prag 1985: 160-163).

Amiran concluded that a high proportion of imports as opposed to local imitations is a phenomenon common to Late Bronze Age tombs mostly on the Syro-Phoenician coast; she postulated trade links between Jerusalem and this region at the time (Amiran 1960: 25, 31-32).

The ratio of imports to imitation local wares in the Gezer tombs might reflect socio-economic conditions of the tomb users during LB IIB.[22] It might also be explained as being the result of chronological development, with the imitations placed in the tombs at a period when imports decreased and a wide variety of imitations were produced on the local market, perhaps for funerary needs.[23]

2.2.10. SARCOPHAGUS LID (?)
Pl. 10: No. 212

Discussion
Only a miniature drawing remains of what appears to have been a ceramic sarcophagus lid similar to the multi-handled specimen found in Cave I.10A (*Gezer V*: Pl. 17:15). The sarcophagus from the latter tomb was found in the lower tomb deposit of LB I-IIA, and measured 50 m high and ca. 80 m wide. It apparently originally contained two burials but eventually, over time, served as a receptacle for children and infant burials (ibid: 66). Note that one of the two burial artifacts associated with the sarcophagus was a bronze bracelet similar to the one in Pl. 11:14 (see below).

Seger related sarcophagi of this type to the Minoan larnax and posits that it may indicate the existence of a population of Minoan origin at Gezer (*Gezer V*:114; also Gonen 1992:28).[24]

---

[22] Bergoffen concluded that the mere presence of Cypriote imports in tombs is not an indicator of elevated social status; the same was found to be true of such imports in Egyptian tombs (Bergoffen 1989: 249-250, 260-261).

[23] The lack of any examples of the Cypiote "Red Lustrous Wheel-Made Ware" (particularly the so-called "spindle bottles/Syrian bottle"), an import quite common at many sites in Late Bronze Age Canaan, is worth noting. Although this lack might be fortuitous, at least one such vessel is known from other Late Bronze contexts at Gezer (e.g. *Gezer V*: 80, pl. 19:1; An additional vessel, possibly from Gezer [which was obtained though on the antiquities market] is kept in the collections room at the Institute of Archaeology, Hebrew University [registration #2211], previously noted by Åström 1972:743 and Eriksson 1993:257 [although with mistaken registration number!]). The lack of this type in these tombs might have some significance, in light of the distinct chronological and spatial distribution of this ware (e.g. Eriksson 1993:149-153).

[24] The supposed lack of larnakes from contemporary Late Minoan contexts (that would serve as parallels to the larnax from Cave I.10A) that Seger noted (*Gezer V*:114) is uncalled for. As Gonen (1992:142) has stressed, there are ample

Although there may be some basis to such a claim,[25] it should be noted that the appearance of Larnakes does not necessarily imply a Minoan connection (particularly in light of the lack of Minoan or Minoan-style objects from Gezer specifically, as well as the relative paucity of such objects from LB Canaan in general - see, e.g., Leonard 1994; Hankey and Leonard 1998).[26] In addition, it has also been noted in the past (Gilmour 1991:186-187; Gonen 1992:28,142), that larnakes appear in the Mycenaean culture as well, albeit from a later, LH III context (for a list, see e.g. Gilmour 1991:186), and thus, even if this object is in fact part of a larnax, it does not have to be of Minoan origin.[27]

It can also be added that the Larnakes may have also been used by the Sea Peoples during the Iron Age I. Karageorghis (2000:266-274) suggested that the appearance of stone and ceramic bathtubs in Late Cypriote III contexts may be connected to the appearance of the Sea Peoples in Cyprus. He has noted the connections between these bathtubs and the larnakes. Although only one, bona fide, Philistine vessel was found in the tombs excavated by Weill (e.g. the krater in Fig. 3:1, but other vessels dating to the Iron Age I were found),

---

parallels from the Minoan culture dating to just the time frame of Cave I.10A. For more recent discussion of Larnakes, see, e.g., Marinatos 1997; Tsipopoulou and Vagnetti 1999.

[25] See though Gilmour's (1991:191-194) reservations about this suggestion. Gonen (1992: 146-147) has suggested that the finds from another tomb at Gezer (Cave 30, *Macalister I*: 312-314) may indicate that was also used by non-Canaanite elements at Gezer.

[26] Connections (even if indirect and somewhat limited) between Crete and Canaan during the LB II did, nonetheless, exist. Note for example the Syro-Palestinian jars found in several LM IIIA:1 Cretan sites (discussed by Watrous 1992:175), some of which reportedly have a fabric typical of the Levantine southern coastal plain ("from Jaffa to Gaza"). For comparison, it can be noted that during the earlier MB IIB, the connections between these two regions, particularly on the basis of the currently available evidence from the Levant, appear to have been of a more extensive nature (see, e.g., Kislev et al. 1993; Oren et al. 1996; Betancourt 1998; Niemeier and Niemeier 1998; Day et al. 1999; Dothan et al. 2000). Note the recently reported Linear A inscription from Lachish (Finkelberg et al. 1996).

[27] It should be noted that in addition to the two well-known larnakes from Israel mentioned above (Gezer, Cave I.10A and Acre), a possible additional "non-Minoan" larnax may exist (albeit not mentioned by Gilmour 1991 or Gonen 1992). At Ashdod, Area G, Stratum XII, M. Dothan (1993:97) reported a "larnax (coffin) in secondary use" from an Iron Age I context. One should stress though that in the final report of Area G (Dothan and Porath 1993:72, pl. 22:2-3) this "coffin" is defined solely as a "well-fired pottery basin" found in a building with various work-related installations. For "chest-like" objects besides larnakes from the LH Aegean, see, e.g., Rethmiotakis 1997. Although hard to accept (due to a lack of any known corroborating evidence), one should note Morris' (1992:151) suggestion that the larnax is of Near Eastern origin.

both this vessel and other Philistine pottery found in the other excavations at Gezer,[28] indicate that one must at least take into consideration the possibility that if this lost fragment is in fact part of a larnake, it might just date to the Iron Age I, and might be related to the Philistine presence in Gezer.

Nevertheless, the possible existence of an additional larnax lid may indicate that one of the presently discussed tombs could have contained such a sarcophagus as well, linking it, both temporally and typologically, to Cave I.10A. If one accepts Seger's suggested association with the Aegean Larnax, an additional example of such a coffin might strengthen the claim that there were people of Aegean origin at Gezer during the LB.

2.3. PROVENIENCE OF THE VESSELS FROM THE TOMBS

Of the 186 vessels composing our assemblage, only 25 had some indication of provenience marked on them: 18 ceramic vessels and three stone vessels – came from Tomb I (see Table 4); these are presented together in Pls. 12-14:1. Another three were marked as belonging to Tomb III (see Table 5): Jug No. 179 (Pl. 5:7), Milk Bowl No. 199 (Pl. 10- miniature drawing) and possibly dipper juglet 77.211E2. Four vessels are marked as originating in Tomb IX: chalice 77.211F1, lamp 77.211D, double pyxis V.1715 (Pl. 7:5) and pyxis 72.356f (see Table 6). This would imply that there were at least nine tombs from which the finds came, if indeed the designation 'Tomb IX' is consecutive.

There is no way of knowing whether the marked contents comprise the entire assemblage of these tombs and thus no chronological or typological conclusions can be drawn. Based on the extant information, the chronological range Tomb I is LB IIA to Iron Age I, covering the main period of use of the ceramic groups as identified from the typological examination of the corpus (see Table 1).

The unknown provenience of most of the tomb material makes it impossible to determine whether the proportions of vessels from Tomb I (from which the largest amount of provenanced materials is available, see Tables 4-6) are indicative of the other Gezer tombs as well. It seems that percentage-wise, this does not reflect the proportions obtained from the entire assemblage as a whole (see Table 2) and thus we may assume that indeed Tomb I originally included more material than what was recorded. The same conclusion can obviously be reached for Tombs III and IX, in light of the very small amount of vessels related to them (Tables 5-6).

2.4. SUMMARY

The assemblage of 186 vessels discussed above suits tomb groups known from Gezer itself, as well as other sites, with mostly bowls, lamps, juglets and jugs and a limited selection of other vessels (i.e. krater, pyxis, flasks, etc.), along with some small finds. The proportions of vessel classes are on the whole typical of funerary contexts, as seen in Table 2 (though of course these numbers are calculated according to the entire group, without knowing the specific tomb assignations). Bowls are dominant, comprising 31.7%, with jugs and juglets equally composing the second most common class (18.2%), followed by imports (16.7%) and lamps (9.1%). Flasks, chalices and kraters represent only 0.5-2% each. These ratios are very different from those in the Nahlat Ahim tomb (Amiran 1960), where imports consisted of 46.4% of the entire group, imitations of imports were 8.9%, bowls a mere 10.7% and lamps - 3.5%. Tomb 216 at Lachish (*Lachish IV*: 232-235) also shows different proportions: of the ca. 200 vessels found in the tomb, 44% were imports and 2.5% were imitations of imports; 54% were bowls and 10.5% were lamps, which is more like the Gezer tombs under discussion. These differences, mainly in the proportions of imports, might be due to chronological, regional or socio-economic factors, or merely the incomplete nature of the Gezer assemblage.

The chronological range spans the MB IIB and the entire LB, with a fair representation of Iron Age I and II. The main bulk of finds date to LB IIA-B (see Table 1). It seems that there was continuous use of the tombs, though with a decline in LB I and Iron Age I-II. The one earlier vessel (dated to EB IV/MB I) and the one later vessel (Hellenistic period) are temporally extraordinary (the EB IV/MB I jug is regionally out of place as well). Thus, the possibility should be considered that during the course of the handling of these finds over the years, these two latter vessels were mistakenly included with the finds from Gezer (see n. 1).

Most of the shapes are common in Late Bronze Age deposits throughout the country, such as the platter bowls and dipper juglets, and the ubiquitous imported Mycenaean and Cypriote vessels (Table 3). The few types that are more specific to the Shephelah and southern Canaan are some of the types of the carinated bowls and the cylindrical juglets and the Iron Age I, bichrome Philistine krater. This appears to reflect the relatively uniform nature of the Late Bronze Age pottery repertoire in Palestine. The few Egyptian objects (possibly jug 188 [Pl. 5:11], although primarily among the small objects discussed in Chapters 3 and 4 below) may be considered part of the international character of the Late Bronze Age, where Mycenaean, Cypriote, Anatolian and Egyptian objects were traded throughout the Mediterranean basin (e.g. Gale 1991; Knapp and Cherry 1994: 123-155; Knapp 1998). Egyptian influence was especially strong in southern Canaan during the main period of use of the tombs (e.g. Weinstein 1989; 1998).

---

[28] For general comments on the Philistine materials from Gezer, see Dothan 1982:51-54. Note that Dothan (ibid:51) states that Gezer "yielded an unusual wealth of Philistine pottery."

Since there is no way of knowing whether the tombs were robbed prior to the excavations, and if the assemblage reflects only what the plunderers had left behind, or whether other factors (such as various "post-depositional processes") affected the totality of the finds, it is virtually impossible to draw conclusions concerning the standard of living and social relations of the population who used these tombs. As is, the assemblage on the whole is quite utilitarian, with a relative scarcity of luxury items, though the few objects that are included are of a high standard.

The cultural phases represented by the pottery from the Gezer tombs that have been described above (see Table 1), appear to correlate nicely with the occupation strata that have been identified in the various excavations (below, p. 63, Table 7). Although occupation levels dating to the late MB IIA were discovered, it is very scanty and it is only during the MB IIB/C that the town expanded and prospered, as evidenced by major fortifications, structures and tombs – Strata XXI-XVIII (Dever 1993: 499-500; Dever 1998: 69-109). The LB IA presence is scant, and LB IB is also very minimal in the excavated occupation levels, and it is represented primarily by the finds from Cave I.10A (Stratum XVII). Despite this apparent paucity, a number of imported luxury items that belong to this level were discovered (ibid: 501-502). The town witnesses a reflourishing in LB IIA (Stratum XVI) with a slight decline in LB IIB (Stratum XV) (Dever 1998: 110-129). The Iron Age I levels (Strata XIII-XI) are preceded by a short gap at the end of the 13th century BCE (end of the LB) and is well represented on the tell, as is the later Iron Age II, up until the end of the 7th century BCE (ibid: 131-155).

Table 1: Chronological Range of Pottery Types[1]

Vessel Type	MB IIA[2]	MB II B/C	LB IA	LB IB	LB IIA	LB IIB	Iron Age I	Iron Age II
Large Shallow Bowls With Slightly Molded Rim		+	+	+	+			
Small-Medium Shallow Bowls With Thickened Inner Rims				+	+	+		
Large Shallow Bowls With Thickened Inner Rims		+	+	+	+	+		
Large Round Bowl With Shelf Rim								+
Deep Bowl with Molded Rim					+	+		
Deep Rounded Bowl With Plain Rim				+	+	+	+	
Hemispherical Bowl							+	+
Round Bowl With Soft Carination					+	+	+	
Carinated Bowl		+	+	+				
Chalice		+	+	+		+	+	+
Krater							+	
Lamp – straight rim		+	+	+	+	+		
Lamp – everted rim					+	+	+	
Lamp – high disc base								+
Jugs (excluding one EB IV/MB I and one Hellenistic)	+	+			+	+	+	
Decanter								+
Cooking Jugs								+
Bottle (unknown periodization)								
Dipper Juglets		+	+		+	+	+	+
Cylindrical Juglets	+	+						
Piriform Juglets	+	+						
Black Juglet								+
Flasks					+	+	+	+
Pyxides							+	+
Mycenean imports					+			
Cypriote imports					+	+		
Imitation Base Ring Jugs					+	+		

1. This table does not include the few fragmentary vessels to which we were unable to find clear parallels for, nor does it include the vessels drawn in miniature in Pl. 10. The data here also pertains only to those vessels found in the Rockefeller, Louvre and the Saint-Germain-en-Laye Museums that were photographed and/or drawn, omitting those that were mentioned in the various catalogues but were not actually found.
2. None of these are exclusively MB IIA types, but have parallels that span MB IIA-B, so MB IIA was marked here as well.

Table 2: Distribution of Pottery Classes

	Bowls	Kraters	Chalices	Lamps	Jugs*	Juglets	Flasks	Pyxides	Imports	Total
N =	59	1	4	17	34	34	3	3	31	186
%	31.7%	0.5%	2.2%	9.1%	18.2%	18.2%	1.6%	1.6%	16.7%	100%

* Includes imitation Base Ring jugs and 'cooking jugs'.

Table 3: Distribution of Imported Pottery

	Mycenaean	Cypriote White Shaved	Cypriote White Slip	Cypriote Base Ring	Cypriote White Painted	Total imports
N =	4	6	1	19	1	31
%	12.9%	19.4%	3.2%	61.3%	3.2%	100%

Table 4: Distribution of Objects in Tomb I (Late Bronze Age/Iron Age I)

Bowls	Kraters	Chalices	Jugs	Juglets	Flasks	Imports	Imitation Imports	Stone Vessels	Total
1	1	1	3	1	1	7	3	3	21

Table 5: Distribution of Objects in Tomb III (Late Bronze Age)

Jugs	Juglets	Imports (Cypriote Milk Bowl)	Total
1	1	1	3

Table 6. Distribution of Objects in Tomb IX (Iron Age I)

Chalices	Pyxides	Lamps	Total
1	2	1	4

REFERENCES

Aharoni, M., and Aharoni, Y.
1976 The Stratification of Judahite Sites in the 8th and 7th Centuries BCE. *Bulletin of the American Schools of Oriental Research* 224: 73-90.

Amiran, R.
1960 A Late Bronze Age II Pottery Group from a Tomb in Jerusalem. *Eretz Israel* VI: 25-37 (Hebrew).

Amiran, R.
1969 *Ancient Pottery of the Holy Land.* Jerusalem and Ramat Gan: Massada Press.

Ain Shems I = Grant, E.
1931 *Ain Shems Excavations, 1928-1931, Part I-II.* Haver- ford: Haverford College.

Ain Shems III = Grant, E.
1934 *Ain Shems Excavations, Part III.* Haverford: Haverford College.

Ain Shems IV = Grant, E., and Wright, G.E.
1934 *Ain Shems Excavations, Part IV.* Haverford: Haverford College.

Ain Shems V = Grant, E., and Wright, G.E.
1939 *Ain Shems Excavations, Part V.* Haverford: Haverford College.

Åströms, P.
1972 *The Late Cypriote Bronze Age: Architecture and Pottery.* Swedish Cyprus Expedition IV:1C. Lund: Swedish Cyprus Expedition.

Avigad, N.
1983 *Discovering Jerusalem.* Nashville: Thomas Nelson.

Ben-Tor, A. and Portugali, Y.
1987 *Tell Qiri: A Village in the Jezreel Valley.* Qedem 24. Jerusalem: Hebrew University of Jerusalem.

Bergoffen, C.
1989 *Comparative Study of the Regional Distribution of Cypriot Pottery in Canaan and Egypt in the Late Bronze Age.* Unpublished Ph.D. Dissertation. New York: New York University.

Betancourt, P.P.
1998 Middle Minoan Objects in the Near East. Pp. 5-12 in *The Aegean and the Orient in the Second Millennium: Proceedings of the 50th Anniversary Symposium, Cincinnati, 18-20 April 1997*, eds. E.H. Cline and D. Harris-Cline. Aegaeum 18. Liège: Université de Liège.

Beth Shemesh 1913 = Mackenzie, D.
1913 *Excavations at Ain Shems.*, Palestine Exploration Fund Annual 1912-1913. London: Palestine Exploration Fund.

Beth Zur = Sallers, O.R.
1933 *The Citadel of Beth Zur.* Philadelphia: Westminster Press.

Bietak, M.
1989 Archäologischer befund und historische interpretation am beispeil der Tell el Yahudiyehware. Pp. 7-34 in *Akten des vierten Internationalen Ägyptologischen-Kongresses, München, 1985, Band 2*, ed. S. Schoske. Studien zur Altägyptische Kultur, Behiefte 2. Hamburg: H. Buske.

Bietak, M.
1991 Egypt and Canaan during the Middle Bronze Age. *Bulletin of the American Schools of Oriental Research* 284: 27-72.

Bloch-Smith, E.
1992 *Judahite Burial Practices and Beliefs About the Dead.* Journal for the Study of the Old Testament Supplement Series 123, JSOT/ASOR Monograph Series 7. Sheffield: Sheffield Academic Press.

Buchholz, H.-G.
1995 Tönere metallimitationen uner den geffästypen aus Tamassos, Zypern. *Archäologischer Anzeiger* 2: 185-94.

Day, P., Oren, E.D., Joyner, L. and Quinn, P.S.
1999 Petrographic Analysis of the Tel Haror Inscribed Sherd: Seeking Provenance within Crete. Pp. 191-196 in *Meletemata: Studies in Aegean Archaeology Presented to Malcolm H. Wiener, Volume I*, eds. P.P. Betancourt, V. Karageorghis, R. Laffineur and W.-D. Niemeier. Aegaeum 20. Liège: Université de Liège.

Dever, W.G.
1993 Gezer. Pp. 496-506 in *The New Encyclopedia of Archaeological Excavations in the Holy Land, Vol. 2*, eds. E. Stern and A. Gilboa. Jerusalem: Exploration Society (Hebrew).

Dever, W.G.
1998 *Gezer: A Crossroad in Ancient Israel.* Jerusalem: HaKibbutz HaMeuhad (Hebrew).

Dothan, M.
1993 Ashdod. Pp. 93-102 in *The New Encyclopedia of Archaeological Excavations in the Holy Land, Vol. 1* eds. E. Stern and A. Gilboa. Jerusalem: Exploration Society.

Dothan, M., and Porath, Y.
1993 *Ashdod V: Excavations of Area G. The Fourth-Sixth Seasons of Excavations 1968-1970.* `Atiqot 23. Jerusalem: Israel Antiquities Authority.

Dothan, T.
1982 *The Philistines and Their Material Culture.* Jerusalem: Israel Exploration Society.

Dothan, T.
2000 Reflections on the Initial Phase of Philistine Settlement. Pp. 145-158 in *The Sea Peoples and their World: A Reassessment*, ed. E.D. Oren. University Museum Monographs 108. Philadelphia: University Museum.

Dothan, T., Zuckerman, S., and Goren, Y.
2000 Kamares Ware from Hazor. *Israel Exploration Journal* 50: 1-15.

Edelstein, G., and Aurant, S.
1992 The 'Philistine' Tomb at Tell 'Eitun. *'Atiqot* 21: 23-41.

Eriksson, K.O.
1993 *Red Lustrous Wheel-Made Ware.* Studies in Mediterranean Archaeology, Vol. CIII. Jonsered: P. Åström.

Finkelberg, M., Uchitel, A., and Ussishkin, D.
1996 A Linear A Inscription from Tel Lachish (Lach ZA 1). *Tel Aviv* 23: 195-207.

Finkelstein, I.
1995 The Date of the Settlement of the Philistines in Canaan. *Tel Aviv* 22: 213-239.

Furumark, A.
1941 *The Mycenaean Pottery: Analysis and Classification.* Stockholm: Svenska Institutet I Athen.

Gale, N.H. (ed.)
1991 *Bronze Age Trade in the Mediterranean.* Studies in Mediterranean Archaeology 90. Goteborg: P. Åström.

Gezer I = Dever, W.G., Lance, H.D., and Wright G.E.
1970 *Gezer I: Preliminary Report of the 1964-1966 Seasons.* Jerusalem: Hebrew Union College Biblical and Archaeological School in Jerusalem.

Gezer II = Dever, W.G. (ed)
1974 *Gezer II: Preliminary Report of the 1967-70 Seasons in Fields I and II.* Jerusalem: Nelson Glueck School of Biblical Archaeology.

Gezer III = Gitin, S.
1990 *Gezer III: A Ceramic Typology of the Late Iron II, Persian and Hellenistic Periods at Tell Gezer.* Jerusalem: Nelson Glueck School of Biblical Archaeology.

Gezer IV = Dever, W.G., et al.
1986 *Gezer IV: The 1969-71 Seasons in Field VI, the "Acropolis".* Jerusalem: Nelson Glueck School of Biblical Archaeology.

Gezer V = Seger, J.D., and Lance, H.D. (eds.)
1988 *Gezer V: The Field I Caves.* Jerusalem: Nelson Glueck School of Biblical Archaeology. Jerusalem.

Gilmour, G.H.
1991 *Mycenaeans in the East? An Assessment of the Contacts between the Mycenaean World and the Southern Levant in the Late Bronze Age.* Unpublished Master's Thesis. Jerusalem: Hebrew University.

Gittlen, B.M.
1981 The Cultural and Chronological Implications of the Cypro-Palestinian Trade during the Late Bronze Age. *Bulletin of the American Schools of Oriental Research* 241: 49-60.

Gonen, R.
1992 *Burial Patterns and Cultural Diversity in Late Bronze Age Canaan.* ASOR Dissertation Series 7. Winona Lake: Eisenbrauns.

Hankey, V. and Leonard, A., Jr.
1998 Aegean LH I-II Pottery in the East: "Who is the Potter, Pray, and Who is the Pot?" Pp. 29-36 *The Aegean and the Orient in the Second Millennium: Proceedings of the 50th Anniversary Symposium, Cincinnati, 18-20 April 1997*, eds. E.H. Cline and D. Harris-Cline. Aegaeum 18. Liège: Université de Liège.

Hirschfeld, N.
2000 Introduction to the Catalogue. Pp. 67-73 in *Ras Shamra-Ougarit XIII: Céramiques mycéniennes*, by M. Yon, V. Karageorghis and N. Hirschfeld. Paris: Éditions Recherche sur les Civilisations.

Holladay, J.S., Jr.
1990 Red Slip, Burnish and the Solomonic Gateway at Gezer. *Bulletin of the American Schools of Oriental Research* 277/278: 23-70.

Holladay, J.S., Jr.
1995 The Kingdoms of Israel and Judah: Political and Economic Centralization in the Iron Age IIA-B (ca. 1000-750 B.C.E.). Pp. 368-398 in *The Archaeology of Society in the Holy Land*, ed. T.E. Levy. New York: Facts on File.

Johnson, P.
1982 The Middle Cypriote Pottery Found in Palestine. *Opuscula Atheniensia* 14: 49-72.

Kaplan, M.F.
1980 *The Origin and Distribution of Tell el Yahudiyeh Ware*. Studies in Mediterranean Archaeology 72. Goteborg: P. Åström.

Karageorghis, V.
2000 Cultural Innovations in Cyprus Relating to the Sea Peoples. Pp. 255-279 in *The Sea Peoples and their World: A Reassessment*, ed. E.D. Oren. University Museum Monographs 108. Philadelphia: University Museum.

Karageorghis, V.
2001 *The White Slip Ware of Late Bronze Age Cyprus. Proceedings of an International Conference Organized by the Anastasios G. Leventis Foundation, Nicosia, in Honour of Malcolm Wiener*. Contributions to the Chronology of the Eastern Mediterranean. Vienna: Verlag der Österreichischen Akademie der Wissenschaften.

Keel, O.
1998 *Goddesses and Trees, New Moon and Yahweh: Ancient Near Eastern Art and the Hebrew Bible*. Supplement of the Journal for the Study of the Old Testament 261. Sheffield: Sheffield Academic Press.

Kelm, G.L., and Mazar, A.
1995 *Timnah, A Biblical City in the Sorek Valley*. Winona Lake, IN.: Eisenbrauns.

Kempinski, A.
1983 *Syrien und Palästina (Kanaan) in der letzten phase der Mittlebronze IIB-zeit (1650-1570 v. Chr.)*. Ägypten und Altes Testament 4. Wiesbaden: Otto Harrassowitz.

Killebrew, A.E.
1996 *Tel Miqne-Ekron, Report of the 1985-1987 Excavations in Field INE: Areas 5,6,7, The Bronze and Iron Ages*. Jerusalem: The Tel Miqne-Ekron Limited Edition Series.

Killebrew, A.E.
1998 Ceramic Typology and Technology of Late Bronze II and Iron I". Pp. 379-405 in *Mediterranean Peoples in Transition*, eds. S. Gitin, A. Mazar and E. Stern. Jerusalem: Israel Exploration Society.

Kislev, M., Artzy, M., and Marcus, E.
1993 Import of an Aegean Food Plant to a Middle Bronze IIA Coastal Site in Israel. *Levant* 25:145-154.

Knapp, A.B.
1998 Mediterranean Bronze Age Trade: Distance, Power and Place. Pp. 193-207 in *The Aegean and the Orient in the Second Millennium: Proceedings of the 50th Anniversary Symposium, Cincinnati, 18-20 April 1997*, eds. E.H. Cline and D. Harris-Cline. Aegaeum 18. Liège: Université de Liège.

Knapp, A.B., and Cherry, J.F.
1994 *Provenience Studies and Bronze Age Cyprus: Production, Exchange and Politico-Economic Change*. Monographs in World Archaeology 21. Madison: Prehistory Press.

Kopetzki, K.
2002 The Dipper Juglets of Tell el-Dab`a. A Typological and Chronological Approach. Pp. 227-244 in *The Middle Bronze Age in the Levant: Proceedings of an International conference on MB IIA ceramic material, Vienna, 24th-26th of January 2001*, ed. M. Bietak. Contributions to the Chronology of the Eastern Mediterranean III. Vienna: Österreichischen Akademie der Wissenschaften.

Lachish II = Tufnell, O., Inge, C.H., and Harding, L.
1940 *Lachish II: The Fosse Temple*. London: Oxford University Press.

Lachish III = Tufnell, O.
1953 *Lachish III: The Iron Age*. London: Oxford University Press.

Lachish IV = Tufnell, O.
1958 *Lachish IV: The Bronze Age, Plates and Text*. London: Oxford University Press.

Lachish V = Aharoni, Y.
1975 *Investigations at Lachish, The Sanctuary and the Residency (Lachish V)*. Tel Aviv: Gateway Publishers.

Leonard, A.
1994 *An Index to the Late Bronze Age Aegean Pottery from Syria-Palestine*. Studies in Mediterranean Archaeology 114. Jonsered: P. Åströms.

Macalister I = Macalister, R.A.S.
1912 *The Excavation of Gezer, Volume I*. London: John Murray.

Macalister II = Macalister, R.A.S.
1912 *The Excavation of Gezer, Volume II*. London: John Murray.

Macalister III = Macalister, R.A.S.
1912 *The Excavation of Gezer, Volume III*. London: John Murray.

Maeir, A.
1997 *The Material Culture of the Central Jordan Valley during the Middle Bronze II Period: Pottery and Settlement Pattern*. Unpublished Ph.D. dissertation. Jerusalem: Hebrew University of Jerusalem.

Marinatos, N.
1997 Minoan and Mycenaean Lanakes: A Comparison. Pp. 281-92 in *La Crète Mycénienne*, ed. J. Driessen, A. Farnoux. Supplément Bulletin du

Correspondance Hellénique 30. Athens: École Française d'Athènes.

Mazar, A.
1985 *Excavations at Tell Qasile, Part Two, The Philistine Sanctuary: Various Finds, the Pottery, Conclusions, Appendixes*. Qedem 20. Jerusalem: Hebrew University of Jerusalem.

Mazar, A.
1990 *Archaeology of the Land of the Bible, 10,000-586 B.C.E.* New York: Doubleday.

Mazar, A.
1997 Iron Age Chronology: A Reply to I. Finkelstein. *Levant* XXIX: 157-167.

Mazar, A.
1998 On the Appearance of Red Slip in the Iron Age I Period in Israel. Pp. 368-378 in *Mediterranean Peoples in Transition*, eds. S. Gitin, A. Mazar and E. Stern. Jerusalem: Israel Exploration Society.

McGovern, P.E. (ed.)
1989 *Cross-Craft and Cross-Cultural Interactions in Ceramics*. Ceramics and Civilization IV. Westerville, OH: American Ceramic Society.

McNicoll, A.W., Edwards, P.C., Hanbury-Tenison, J., Hennessy, J.B., Potts, T.F., Smith, R.H., Walmsley, A., and Watson, P.
1992 *Pella in Jordan 2*. Mediterranean Archaeology Supplement 2. Sydney: Mediterranean Archaeology.

Megiddo II = Loud, G.
1948 *Megiddo II, Seasons of 1935-39*. Chicago: University of Chicago.

Morris, S.P.
1992 *Daidalos and the Origins of Greek Art*. Princeton: Princeton University.

Mountjoy, P.A.
1986 *Mycenaean Decorated Pottery, A Guide to Identification*. Goteborg: P. Åströms.

Niemeier, W.-D., and Niemeier, B.
1998 Minoan Frescoes in the Eastern Mediterranean. Pp. 69-98 in *The Aegean and the Orient in the Second Millennium: Proceedings of the 50th Anniversary Symposium, Cincinnati, 18-20 April 1997*, eds. E.H. Cline and D. Harris-Cline. Aegaeum 18. Liège: Université de Liège.

Oren, E.D.
1973 *The Northern Cemetery of Beth Shean*. Leiden: E.J. Brill.

Oren, E.D., Olivier, J.P., Goren, Y., Betancourt, P.P., Myer, G.H., and Yellin, J.
1996 A Minoan Graffito from Tel Haror (Negev, Israel). *Cretan Studies* 5:91-118.

Palumbo, G., and Peterman, G.
1993 Early Bronze Age IV Ceramic Regionalism in Central Jordan. *Bulletin of the American Schools of Oriental Research* 289: 23-32.

Pythian-Adams, W.J.
1929 Selected Types of Bronze Age Pottery. *Palestine Museum Bulletin* 3:1-19

Prag, K.
1985 The Imitation of Cypriot Wares in Late Bronze Age Palestine. Pp. 154-166 in *Palestine in the Bronze and Iron Ages: Papers in Honour of Olga Tufnell*, ed. J.N. Tubb. Occasional Publication 11. London: Institute of Archaeology.

Price-Williams, D.
1977 *The Tombs of the Middle Bronze Age II Period From the '500' Cemetery at Tell Fara (South)*. Occasional Publication 1. London: Institute of Archaeology.

Rethmiotakis, G.
1997 A Chest-Shaped Vessel and Other LM IIIC Pottery from Katelli Pediaka. Pp. 407-21 in *La Crète Mycénienne*, ed. J. Driessen, A. Farnoux. Supplément Bulletin du Correspondance Hellénique 30. Athens: École Française d'Athènes.

Saint-Germain-en-Laye = Anonymous
1989 *Catalogue sommaire illustré des collections du musée des antiquités nationales de Saint-Germain-en-Laye, 2. Archéologie comparée: Europe orientale - Asie - Océanie - Amérique. Ouvrage collectif établi par la conservation du musée des antiquités nationales*. Paris: Éditions de la Réunion de musées nationaux.

Saller, S.J.
1964 *The Excavations at Dominus Flevit (Mount Olivet, Jerusalem), Part II, The Jebusite Burial Place*. Jerusalem: Franciscan Press.

Soles, J.F.
1999 The Ritual "Killing" of Pottery and the Discovery of a Mycenaean Telestos at Mochlos. Pp. 787-792 in *Meletemata: Studies in Aegean Archaeology Presented to Malcolm H. Wiener, Volume III*, eds. P.P. Betancourt, V. Karageorghis, R. Laffineur and W.-D. Niemeier. Aegaeum 20. Liège: Université de Liège.

Stubbings, F.H.
1951 *Mycenean Pottery from the Levant.* Cambridge: Cambridge University Press.

TBM I = Albright, W.F.
1932 *The Excavation of Tell Beit Mirsim, Vol. 1, The Pottery of the First Three Campaigns.* Annual of the American Schools of Oriental Research XII. New Haven: American Schools of Oriental Research.

TBM Ia = Albright, W.F.
1933 The Excavation of Tell Beit Mirsim, Vol. IA, The Bronze Age Pottery of the Fourth Campaign. *Annual of the American Schools of Oriental Research* XIII: 55-127.

TBM II = Albright, W.F.
1938 *The Excavation of Tell Beit Mirsim, Vol. II, The Bronze Age.* Annual of the American Schools of Oriental Research XVII. New Haven: American Schools of Oriental Research.

TBM III = Albright, W.F.
1943 *The Excavation of Tell Beit Mirsim, Vol. III, The Iron Age.* Annual of the American Schools of Oriental Research XXI-XXII. New Haven: American Schools of Oriental Research.

Tsipopoulou, M., and Vagnetti, L.
1997 Workshop Attributions for Some Late Minoan III East Cretan Larnakes. Pp. 473-479 in *TEXNH: Craftsmen, Craftswomen and Craftsmanship in the Aegean Bronze Age,* eds. R. Laffineur and P.P. Betancourt. Aegaeum 16. Liège: Université de Liège.

Ussishkin, D. and Wright, G.E.
1970 Gezer. Pp. 111-117 in Mazar, B. et al. (eds.), *The Encyplopedia of Archaeological Excavations in the Holy Land, Volume I.* Jerusalem: Israel Exploration Society (in Hebrew).

Vaughan, S.J.
1991a Material and Technical Classification of Base Ring Ware: A New Fabric Typology. Pp. 119-130 in *Cypriot Ceramics: Reading the Prehistoric Record,* eds. J.A. Barlow, D.J. Bolger and B. Kling. University Museum Monographs 74. Philadelphia: The University Museum.

Vaughan, S.J.
1991b Late Cypriot Base Ring Ware: Studies in Raw Materials and Technology. Pp. 337-368 in *Recent Developments in Ceramic Petrology,* eds. A. Middleton and I. Freestone. British Museum Occasional Paper 81. London: British Museum.

Watrous, L.V.
1992 *Kommos III: The Late Bronze Age Pottery.* Princeton: Princeton University Press.

Weinstein, J.
1989 The Collapse of the Egyptian Empire in the Southern Levant. Pp. 142-150 in *The Crisis Years: The 12th Century B.C.. From Beyond the Danube to the Tigris,* eds. W.A. Ward and M.S. Joukowsky. Dubuque: Kendall/Hunt.

Weinstein, J.
1998 Egyptian Relations with the Eastern Mediterranean World at the End of the Second Millennium BCE. Pp. 188-196 in *Mediterranean Peoples in Transition,* eds. S. Gitin, A. Mazar and E. Stern. Jerusalem: Israel Exploration Society.

Zimhoni, O.
1995 *Studies in the Iron Age Pottery of Israel, Typological, Archaeological and Chronological Aspects.* Tel Aviv: Tel Aviv University.

CHAPTER 3: THE STONE, FAIENCE, BONE AND METAL OBJECTS

Nava Panitz-Cohen and Aren M. Maeir

3.1. INTRODUCTION

In addition to the pottery (which represented the primary material finds in the Gezer tombs -- see discussion, above, Chapter 2), several other objects, made of various materials and typological classes, were discovered. In the present chapter, the majority of the non-ceramic objects will be discussed, save for the glass vessel (see below, Chapter 4) and the glyptics (see below, Chapter 5). The following objects are discussed here: seven stone vessels, one faience vessel, four bone spindle whorls and two bronze objects. The exact provenience within the tombs is only known regarding three of the objects; three of the stone vessels that are marked as originating from Tomb I. Regarding the other objects, it is not known from which tombs they originated.

These non-ceramic objects add an extra dimension to the nature of the tomb assemblage, alongside the pottery repertoire. Most of the objects under discussion should not be considered "luxury goods", as they are quite common in many contexts (domestic, funerary, etc.) throughout the Near East during the Middle and Late Bronze Age. The nature of the objects more or less reflects the standard of the pottery found in the tombs, which is for the most part local and utilitarian. As stated in the discussion of the pottery (and especially vis-a-vis the imports; see above, Chapter 2), the types represented are common throughout the southern Levant during the Late Bronze Age. As such, they do not necessarily indicate a high standard of living, since such vessels were easily obtainable and ubiquitous at this time.

3.2. STONE OBJECTS

The seven stone objects presented below are typical of the repertoire of the so-called alabaster vessels that are commonly found in the Middle Bronze Age II and Late Bronze Age throughout the country in various contexts. The stone from which they are made, as well as the shapes, often imply an Egyptian origin. However, this attribution to Egyptian sources, both of the raw material and the form, is not necessarily the case. It appears that there is a very wide range of possibilities for the origin of such vessels, aside from Egyptian imports. Several possible scenarios can be suggested: 1) The material itself could have been imported and the vessel crafted locally; 2) The material can be local (though visually similar to the Egyptian alabaster) and the vessel was formed to imitate Egyptian shapes; 3) Foreign craftsmen could have been working in Egypt producing these vessels, incorporation non-Egyptian styles; 4) Egyptian workman might have produced them in foreign countries, once again incorporation non-Egyptian styles (see, e.g., Ziffer 1990:45-47; Lilyquist 1996: 134-144; Sparks 1996).

Overall, the chronological framework of these vessel types suits the main horizon of the Gezer tombs - MB IIB to LB II.

3.2.1. JUG
Pls. 11: 1; 28:1. No. 152

This is a small jug (17.5 cm high) with a long narrow neck; the rim is everted and its top is wide and flat. Under the rim are two shallow incisions forming low ridges. The handle extends from below the rim to the shoulder, where it is joined with a protrusion reminiscent of metal attachments; the handle exterior is incised with vertical lines and is banded on top and bottom with horizontal lines. The base is a narrow high flaring ring base with a protrusion on its bottom. The stone from which this vessel was made appears to answer to the definition of 'gypsum' (Ben-Dor 1945; Lilyquist 1996: 137; Sparks 1996:52; Aston, Harrell and Shaw 2000: 21-22, 59-60), though it is covered with a thick layer of encrustation making it difficult to define with certainty. The vessel surface, which is partially chipped away, does not appear to be translucent and lacks the light and dark banding or veins that can occur in the so-called 'Egyptian alabaster' (see below). This jug is recorded as having been found in Tomb I.

The general appearance of this vessel is reminiscent of the Cypriot Base Ring ware 'bilbil' jugs and their local imitations (see, e.g., above, Chapter 2), though the placement of the handle is different.[1] This might be compared to a similar vessel from the Fosse Temple II at Lachish, made of serpentine and though somewhat wider than ours, with a very similar handle attachment. It was dated by comparison to similar forms from the Egyptian 18th Dynasty (e.g., *Lachish II:* 64, Pl. XXV: 6).[2] Lilyquist mentions several vessels similar to ours, though with wider necks (e.g., Lilyquist 1996: Pl. 3: S.2 from Isopata, Royal Tomb, made of 'Egyptian alabaster'; Pl. 20:2-3, from the 'Schatzhaus', Kāmid el-Lōz, made of nummulitic limestone; Pl. 26:1-2, from the 'Schatzhaus', Kāmid el-Lōz made of serpentine, identical handle decoration). Since the possibilities of provenience depend on many factors, such as stone type, vessel shape and combinations thereof, it is difficult to determine with certainty whether our jug was imported or

---

[1] This comparison has been noted in the past. See, e.g., Brovarski et al. 1982:129, #118.

[2] Note a fragmentary vessel, although of slightly different proportions, but made of "Alabaster," which was also reported from the Fosse Temple at Lachish (*Lachish II*:Pl. XXV:11).

locally made (Lilyquist 1996: 139-144). The type of stone, the simplicity of the shape, and its similarity to the local, Palestinian LB imitations of the Cypriot jugs, seem to point to the latter possibility.

3.2.2. 'TAZZE'
Pls. 11:2; 28:2. No. 120

This is a small cup (8.5 cm high; 8.5 cm rim diameter) with thin walls; the upper stance is slightly everted and there is a ridge at mid-body. An additional ridge is placed above the base, which is round and terminates in a small button, which was probably inserted into a pedestal foot (Clamer 1988: 108). This vessel was found in Tomb I.

It is made of a stone similar to that of the above jug, No. 152, a non-translucent surface with no banding or veins and thus, we may deem it gypsum. It was almost entirely covered with encrustation.

This vessel belongs to the category of goblets or 'tazze'. Though such types appear earlier in Egypt, they are common in both Egypt and Palestine during the LB IIA-B, with flat, ring or high bases, and were apparently manufactured both in Egypt and Canaan (Ben-Dor 1945: 105-106). Clamer noted a chronological development. She suggested that the two-ribbed tazze with a separate pedestal foot should be dated to the late 15th-early 14th centuries. The three-ribbed tazze became common during the 14th century. Subsequently, one witnesses the appearance of a flat based tazze and a Palestinian product with the cup and foot made from one piece (Clamer 1988: 108-109; see though Sparks [1996:62] who adds regional distinctions as well). Based on Clamer's definition, it seems that the tazze discussed here belongs to the first, earlier group.

Parallels:
Gezer: *Macalister III*: Pl. CVI:4; *Gezer IV*: Pl. 57:13, Stratum XIII, early-mid 12th century - alabaster, squatter proportions.

Lachish: *Lachish IV*: Pl. 72: 641 - with a high foot; *Beth Shemesh 1913*: 48, Pl. XXII; *Ain Shems II*: Pl. XLVII:5.

3.2.3. JUG
Pls. 11:3; 28:3. No. 121

This is the base and body of a thick-walled alabaster jug with a squat, globular body, and a wide straight neck, which is thinner-walled (broken); the thick base is a convex disc with tapering edges. This vessel was found in Tomb I. The vessel was made of a light-colored stone with a chalky surface that was non-translucent and lacked any veins or banding; its section appears crystalline and it appears to have been made of limestone.

Parallels:
Gezer: *Macalister III*: Pl. CCXII: 10 - alabaster.

Lachish: with a high neck and somewhat larger body (*Lachish II*: Pl. XXV:12).

3.2.4. SHOULDER JAR
Pls. 11:4; 28:4. No. 564

This is a small narrow, 'carrot-shaped' bottle with thick walls (10.5 cm high). It has a short vertical neck with a wide flat-topped rim. The "finish" of the rim-top appears to have been unsuccessful, since one side is narrower than the other, creating an oval effect. The base is thick and solid, consisting of almost a third of the vessel. It is made of light colored stone that suits the description of 'Egyptian alabaster' as it is semi-translucent and has dark and light colored bands concentrated near the base with another light colored band near the shoulder. It has no encrustation at all and is beautifully preserved.

These vessels are termed shoulder jars by Lilyquist (1996: 145, Pl. 4:3-4, from Tell el-Ajjul). Similar vessels, made of alabaster, were imported from Egypt during the late MB II (Saller 1964: 165-166). Ben-Dor differentiated between the Egyptian products, which had sharper shoulders, flared rather than flat-topped rims, and an interior which was drilled straight down (which did not conform to the outer profile of the vessel), while the Palestinian products had rounded shoulders and flat-topped rims (Ben-Dor 1945: 102-103; Ziffer 1990: 47). Based on the shape and the stone type, it seems that our jar could have been an import. This must be cautiously stated, particularly in light of Lilyquist's (1996: 145) reservations about the criteria usually employed for distinguishing *bona fide* Egyptian imported versus local Levantine stone vessels.

Parallels:
Gezer: *Macalister III*: Pl. CCXII:1 - alabaster;

Lachish: *Lachish IV*: Pl. 26:25, Tomb 1552 - calcite, base not as thick (MB IIC/LB I);

Jerusalem: Saller 1964: Fig. 60:1-2,4,6-7 - alabaster, defined as flasks or vases, some with different proportions.

3.2.5. ROUND-BASED JUG
Pls. 11:5; 28:5. No.69

This represents half of the round body of what appears to have been a small jug. It was split neatly down the center, and at what appears to have been a narrow neck. It is made of a light colored stone and the exterior is entirely covered with encrustation. The interior is not encrusted and shows a smooth, lightly and evenly banded surface, apparently answering to the definition of gypsum.

It might be compared to a base from Gezer, Cave I.10A (*Gezer V*: Pl. 13:2), attributed perhaps to a globular vessel, possibly of the 'high necked type' which is dated to the early to mid-18th Dynasty (Clamer 1988:110).

3.2.6. BAGGY JAR
Pls. 11:6; 28:6. No. 565

This is a small jug with an everted neck and bag-shaped body; its wide base is flat. Its rim is wide and flat-topped; it is slightly chipped. The vessel is made of a light colored, slightly translucent stone, and has faint, wide light-colored wavy bands near the base, as well as very light colored 'rippling' on the body. It has no encrustation and is beautifully preserved. It seems to fit the description of Egyptian alabaster, though, as mentioned above, it is difficult to determine whether this vessel was imported or locally made. It has been suggested that the prototype for this shape may possibly be found in Middle Kingdom jars in Egypt (Ziffer 1990: 47), and Ben-Dor (1945) even claimed that these were made in Egypt for the local market.[3] However, Lilyquist contended that the morphological criteria proposed by Ben-Dor to differentiate between local products and imports are untenable. According to Lilyquist's criteria, our vessel should probably be considered a local product, based on morphological and chronological considerations (Lilyquist 1996: 145-146).

Parallel:
Tell el-Ajjul: Lilyquist 1996: Pl. 5:2.

3.2.7. COSMETIC BOWL
Pls. 11:7; 28:7. No. 396

This is a small cosmetic bowl (bowl diameter: 6.5 cm) shaped like a "trussed duck". It has a small round-sided, oval-shaped bowl, with a very low disc base that is oval shaped. A grooved, fan-like appendage protrudes on one end, representing the duck's tail. In the vicinity of the tail, near the narrow diameter of the bowl, are two tiny knobs which suggest the wing tips. The opposite end of the bowl has a narrow loop 'handle', which clearly represents the thin neck and schematic head of a duck facing backwards to join with the bowl's outer rim (representing the duck's head tied to its body).[4] The vessel is made of light, almost white colored stone that was worked very thin, almost to a metallic consistency. It is opaque and has very few slightly darker veins, giving it an almost marble-like effect. It is not encrusted and is beautifully made (though broken and restored). Such cosmetic bowls are very well known at Gezer and other sites.

Parallels:
Gezer: *Macalister II*: 342, Fig. 462 - similar 'tail', but square perforated handle instead of 'neck and head';

Lachish: *Lachish II*: Pl. XX:30 - Fosse Temple II destruction debris, no 'head' or 'tail'.

---

[3] Although it has been suggested that the origin of the baggy jar found in the Middle and Late Bronze Age southern Levant is to be found in Crete or the Aegean, Lilyquist claims that in fact it is a local, southern Levantinian Middle Bronze Age shape (Lilyquist 1996: 145, note 116).
[4] See, e.g., Brovarski et al. 1982:213, #258.

3.3. FAIENCE

3.3.1. FAIENCE BOTTLE
Pls. 11:8; 28:8. No.153

This is a squat tear-shaped faience bottle (8.5 cm high) with an everted neck and small flat base. It is covered with a light blue-turquoise glaze that is painted over with evenly-spaced, dark brown vertical lines on the exterior, running from the neck down to the lower body-carination above the base. The neck also has vertical lines, although not the same as the pattern on the vessel's body.

This is a well-known shape that was initially manufactured in Israel during the MB IIB and is often found in funerary contexts along with scarabs and 'alabaster' vessels (Ziffer 1990: 44). Although the faience vessels, which are found primarily in southern Israel during the late MB IIB, are derived from the Egyptian faience industry, they are certainly local products. Similarly, our bottle is of a type that was not found outside Israel (Sagona 1980: 101-103, 107). These bottles bear geometric or floral designs, divided into three registers: neck, body down to round carination and above the base. Our example is decorated only in the two upper registers and is a rather plain example of its type.

Parallels:
(note that the parallels below have more intricate decorations and somewhat wider bases).

Gezer: *Macalister III*: Pl. CCXI: 13, 26, 28; such bottles appear to have been quite common at Gezer.

Lachish: *Lachish IV*: Pl. 26:13-17, MB IIB-LB II.

Jerusalem: Saller 1964: 166-167, Fig. 61:1.

3.4. BONE

3.4.1. BONE SPINDLE WHORLS

Pls. 11:9; 28:9. No. 1647: a loaf-shaped whorl, with a slightly flattened top and a wide, vertical perforation.

Pls. 11:10; 28:9. No. 1648: a plano-convex/conical shaped whorl with a flattened top and a narrow vertical perforation.

Pls. 11:11; 28:9. No. 1648/1: a dome shaped whorl with a narrow vertical perforation.

Pls. 11:12; 28:9. No. 1648/2: a 'pyramid' shaped whorl with a narrow vertical perforation.

Parallels:
Gezer: *Macalister III*: Pl. LXXI: 24, Tomb 9, dated in *Gezer IV*: Fig. 2 to Strata XIII-IX, Iron I-early 10th century; *Gezer I*: Pl. 36: 8; Stratum XIII, limestone; *Gezer IV*: Pl. 54:3, Stratum XIV, 13th\12th century, ceramic; *Gezer V*: 118-119, Pl. 25:6.

Lachish: *Lachish II*: Pl. XXIX:29-33 - steatite, limestone and bone; *Lachish IV*: Pl. 28:9 - bone, Tomb 216.

Beth Shemesh: *Ain Shems II*: Pl. XLIX: 34; Pl. XLIX: 36.

Jerusalem: Saller 1964: Fig. 63:19-20, 22-23.

Discussion

In sundry discussions, objects that are shaped like the four presented here are described as being of various functions, including buttons, beads, inlays, stoppers, spindle whorls, etc. It seems that the shape of the four bone objects from the Gezer tombs points to their classification as spindle whorls. Bone spindle whorls were common from the MB IIB onwards, becoming particularly popular during the LB, Iron Age II and Roman Periods (although during the latter period, it seems that they served as buttons rather than whorls; Ayalon and Sorek 1999:28).

Various studies have discussed the significance of spindle whorls in burials, generally assuming that the presence of such a burial object is gender associated, with the females usually carrying out the task of spinning. However, there is not enough data to determine this with certainty. Crewe (1998: 36-37) has recently suggested that whorls were placed in burials mainly as a result of their importance to individual spinners rather than as a symbolic act related to a specific belief system.

3.5. BRONZE

3.5.1. TOGGLE PIN
Pls. 11:13; 28:10. No. 1549

This toggle pin is a thin, narrow, round-sectioned solid bronze rod with a perforated swelling (the eyelet) about one third above its apparently pointed end. Both ends are broken and corroded. The rod is slightly bent.

This pin is corroded and fragmentary and thus difficult to categorize according to proposed criteria (see *Lachish IV*: 80). It seems that this is Henschel-Simon's Type 3, which spans the entire MB IIB-LB II, though the tendency is for the pins to be somewhat stouter and the eyelet to be positioned much closer to one end (making them "top heavy"), in the latter part of this time span (Henschel-Simon 1938: 172-174; pl. LXVIII: 14). Due to the state of preservation of our pin it is difficult to determine if in fact it should be placed early or late in the suggested chronological sequence.

Parallel:
Lachish: *Lachish II*: Pl. XXVII: 51, Pit 211, under Fosse Temple II; *Lachish IV*: Pl. 224:3,31.

3.5.2. EARRING?/SCARAB-RING?/ BRACELET?
Pl. 11:14. No. 1650

This is a round ring with a slightly ovoid section, broken at the ends. Near the break on both ends is a narrow ring looped around the circumference. It is impossible to determine whether this was a finger ring, perhaps holding a scarab, a bracelet, or simply an earring.

Parallels:
Gezer: *Gezer V*: 104-105, Pls. 22:10; 30:6.

Lachish: *Lachish II*: Pl. XXVII: 41 - from "Fosse Temple area".

Beth Shemesh: *Ain Shems III*: Plate C - Tomb 13, copper ring with scarab;

Jerusalem: Saller 1964: Fig. 62:18-21.

3.5.3. WEAPON-BLADE
Pls. 11:15; 28:11. No. 107

A tin-bronze tanged, weapon-blade. Dimensions: Overall length 161 mm; maximum width 42 mm; tang length 42.5 mm; maximum tang width 22 mm; maximum thickness of blade 4.1 mm. Weight: 73.12 gr.

The weapon-blade[5] has a single midrib, pronounced, rounded shoulders and a straight, short tapering tang. This blade is not of a type commonly found in Palestine (e.g., Shalev 1986; Philip 1989). The pronounced shoulders and tang are somewhat reminiscent of Maxwell-Hyslop's Type 13 (Maxwell-Hyslop 1946:16-17), although this latter type is typical of 3rd and 2nd millennium BCE Anatolia. Likewise, if one was to assume that the tang is incomplete, some similarity can be seen with the Cypriote "hook-tang weapons," examples of which have also been found at Gezer (Watkins 1981:124-135; Philip 1991). The midrib that is not centered, as well as the fact that both the midrib and tang are aligned in a slightly crescent-shaped manner, indicates the poor production technology of this blade. Despite the lack of exact parallels, the overall typological and technological affinities indicate that the blade should be dated to the 2nd millennium BCE. The fact that this may be a non-local type should be noted as well.

It should be stressed that this is the only metal weapon that was retrieved from the tombs that Weill had excavated. It is hard to determine whether this was in fact the only such object that was discovered in the tombs (and compare the much larger selection of weapons and blades from tomb I.10A at Gezer [*Gezer V*:102-107]), and thus, might have economic and/or social significance, or whether other metal objects from the tombs had been robbed in antiquity (or disappeared since the excavation).

3.6. SUMMARY

As stated in the introduction above, the quantity and types of stone, faience, bone and metal objects that were found in the tombs are not extensive. In fact, these finds appear to indicate that the tombs were not used by people of elevated socio-economic levels. As with other tombs dating to the LB,

---

[5] It is difficult to determine whether this blade served as a dagger-blade or as a projectile-head. The functional definition of such weapons is not always apparent. For a discussion of this problem, see, e.g., Philip 1991:67-69.

both at Gezer and at other sites, it would seem that the existence or non-existence of non-ceramic finds can serve as an excellent gauge for the socio-economic levels (and arguably, their cultural and ethnic affiliations, see, e.g., Parker Pearson 1999) of the populations that utilized these tombs. Thus, for example, at Gezer, the respective LB tombs have varying amounts of these types of finds (for a convenient summary, see Gonen 1992: 62-63; 124-127). In comparison to the finds from these other tombs, the finds from our tombs (save for the glass vessel, see below, Chapter 4), are both quite minimal and not within the realm of distinctly defined "prestige items."

REFERENCES

Ain Shems III
Grant, E. 1934. *Ain Shems Excavations, Part III*. Haverford: Haverford College.

Ain Shems IV
Grant, E. and Wright, G.E. 1934. *Ain Shems Excavations, Part IV*. Haverford: Haverford College.

Ayalon, E. and Sorek, C.
1999 *Bare Bones: Ancient Artifacts from Animal Bones*. Tel Aviv: Eretz Israel Museum (Hebrew and English).

Ben-Dor, I.
1945 Palestinian Alabaster Vases. *Quarterly of the Department of Antiquities of Palestine* XI: 93-112.

Beth Shemesh 1912-1913
Mackenzie, D.1912-1913. *Excavations at Ain Shems*, (Palestine Exploration Fund Annual 1912-1913). London: Palestine Exploration Fund.

Brovarski, E., Doll, S.K., and Freed, R.E.
1982 *Egypt's Golden Age: The Art of Living in the New Kingdom, 1558-1085 B.C.* Boston: Museum of Fine Arts.

Crewe, L.
1998 *Spindle Whorls. A Study of Form, Function and Decoration in Prehistoric Cyprus.* Studies in Mediterranean Archaeology and Literature. Jonsered: Paul Åstrom Forlag.

Clamer, C.
1988 Alabaster Vessels. Pp. 108-115 in *Gezer V: The Field I Caves*, eds. J.D. Seger and H.D. Lance. Jerusalem: Nelson Glueck School of Biblical Archaeology.

Gezer I
Dever, W.G., Lance, H.D., and Wright G.E. 1970. *Preliminary Report of the 1964-1966 Seasons*. Jerusalem: Hebrew Union College, Biblical and Archaeological School in Jerusalem.

Gezer IV
Dever, W.G. et al. 1986. *Gezer IV: The 1969-71 Seasons in Field VI, the "Acropolis"*. Jerusalem: Nelson Glueck School of Biblical Archaeology.

Gezer V
Seger, J.D., and Lance, H.D.(eds.). 1988. *Gezer V: The Field I Caves*. Jerusalem: Nelson Glueck School of Biblical Archaeology.

Gonen, R.
1992 *Burial Patterns and Cultural Diversity in Late Bronze Age Canaan.* ASOR Dissertation Series 7. Winona Lake: Eisenbrauns.

Hankey, V.
1974 A Late Bronze Age Temple at Amman: II. Vases and Objects Made of Stone. *Levant* 6: 160-178.

Henschel-Simon, E.
1938 The 'Toggle-Pins' in the Palestine Archaeological Museum. *Quarterly of the Department of Antiquities of Palestine* VI: 169-209.

Lachish II
Tufnell, O. et al. 1940. *Lachish II: The Fosse Temple*. London: Oxford University Press.

Lachish IV
Tufnell, O. 1958. *Lachish IV: The Bronze Age, Plates and Text.* London: Oxford University Press.

Lilyquist, C.
1995 *Egyptian Stone Vessels: Khian through Thutmosis IV*. New York: Metropolitan Museum of Art.

Lilyquist, C.
1996 Stone Vessels at Kamid el-Loz, Lebanon: Egyptian, Egyptianizing, or Non-Egyptian? Pp. 134-173 in *Kāmid el-Lōz 16. 'Schatzhaus' Studien*, ed. R. Hachmann. Saarbrücker Beiträge zur Altertumskunde 59. Bonn: Rudolph Habelt.

Macalister II
Macalister, R.A.S. 1912. *The Excavation of Gezer, Volume II*. London: John Murray.

Macalister III
Macalister, R.A.S. 1912. *The Excavation of Gezer, Volume III*. London: John Murray.

Parker Pearson, M.
1999 *The Archaeology of Death and Burial*. Phoenix Mill: Sutton.

Saller, S.J.
1964 *The Excavations at Dominus Flevit (Mount Olivet, Jerusalem), Part II, The Jebusite Burial Place.* Jerusalem: Franciscan Press.

Sagona, C.
1980 Middle Bronze Faience Vessels from Palestine. *Zeitschrift des Deutschen Palästina-Vereins* 96: 101-120.

Ziffer, I.
1990 *At That Time the Canaanites Were in the Land*. Tel Aviv: Eretz Israel Museum (Hebrew and English).

CHAPTER 4: AN EGYPTIAN 18TH DYNASTY GLASS VESSEL

Dan Barag

4.1. INTRODUCTION

In this chapter, an Egyptian 18th Dynasty glass vessel that was discovered in one of the tombs excavated by Weill is described and discussed. Unfortunately, no information regarding the context of this find could be retrieved. Nevertheless, due to the character of this find, in addition to the description and discussion of the vessel itself, a brief exposé on its relationship to other glass vessels has been included.

4.2. DESCRIPTION

AMPHORISKOS (Pl. 14:2; HU 214)

The vessels is comprised of two non-joining sections (a,b).

a) Cylindrical neck and tip of a sloping shoulder, decorated by a closely-set festoon pattern in yellow (?). Two concave depressions in diametrical position are situated at the top of the neck (each 11 X 5 mm). The original colour of the vessel is unknown. The glass itself is devitrified, with a blackish surface.

The top of the neck flares slightly outwards and seems to be incomplete, perhaps missing a single thread or a twisted bi-coloured lip.

The preserved dimensions are: H. 57 mm; External diameter 20 mm; Internal diameter 8 mm.

b) Vessel body with a "trumpet base." The central section of the body is decorated by a bi-coloured closely-set festoon. One of the threads might have been in white glass. The lower ends of four ear-handles can be seen at mid-body height. The original colour of the vessel is unknown. The condition of the glass is similar to that of the neck fragment, but the surface has turned partially brown.

The preseved dimensions are: H. 77 mm; Diameter 52 mm; Height of base 14 mm; Diameter of base 34 mm.

Both fragments appear to belong to the same vessel, and thus, the reconstructed height of the entire vessel appears to be c. 150 mm.

4.3. DISCUSSION

Glass amphoriskoi with "trumpet bases" with two, three or even four handles were rather popular in Egypt in the mid-14th cent. BCE ("the el-Amarna period"; Nolte 1968:164-165, amphoriskoi types d-f). The specimen from Gezer belongs to the four-handle type. An excavated parallel to this vessel was discovered in a tomb at Hawaret el-Gurob in the Fayum, dating to the reign of Amenhotep III (Quibell 1901:141-143, pl. I:8; see also Nolte 1968:68, 101,165, pl. XII:1). Additional examples, albeit not from dated contexts, are to be found in various museums (e.g. Nolte 1968:165, pls. V:23; VII:8,9; XI:18,19; XIII:13-14, XIV:19). The amphoriskos from Gezer has an exceptionally long neck. The two oval depressions at the top of the neck are enigmatic, and seem to indicate the existence of two additional elements, elements that are unparalleled in other Egyptian New Kingdom glass vessels.

A footed, two-handled, globular core-formed glass jar ("Krateriskos"), dating to the el-Amarna period was discovered in Cave I.10A at Gezer during the HUC excavations (Barag 1988: 101-102, pls. 15:7; 74:A). The amphoriskos from R. Weill's excavations is contemporary with that vessel and one might even suggest that it could have been among the gifts sent by Amenhotep III or IV to one of the rulers of Gezer. R.A.S. Macalister published the top of an Egyptian core-formed spouted lentoid glass flask, which to judge by its style, dates from the 19th Dynasty (13th cent. BCE) (*Macalister II*:240, fig. 392).

Egyptian core-formed glass vessels have been discovered time and again at sites in the Southern Levant, in contexts dating to the Late Bronze Age.[1] These include sites which were under direct Egyptian control (e.g. Tell el-'Ajjul and Beth Shean) or maintained contacts with the Egyptian authorities (e.g., Gezer, Megiddo and Kumidi/Kāmid el-Lōz). A four-handled amphoriskos dating from the El-Amarna period, similar to the amphoriskos from Gezer

---

[1] For an annotated bibliography of Egyptian New Kingdom glass vessels from Palestine and Syria (including those mentioned in the discussion below), see Barag 1970:185-187, 198. For additional finds, see now: Lehrer-Jacobson 1988:212-223, figs. 85-86, colour plates 7-9, 20; Miron 1990:103-105, fig. 56, pls. 32-33; Schlick-Nolte 1996:183-202, pl. 34:1; Matoïan 2000. It should be noted that the long and narrow tubular glass flasks, several of which have been found in Late Bronze contexts from the Southern Levant, and that have been identified by Harden as being of Cypriote origin, are, in my opinion, Egyptian products. For examples of such vessels from, e.g., Tel Gerisa and Tel Eitun, see Harden 1981:36, pl. I:12, fig. 1:12.

discussed in this chapter, was excavated in Tomb 387 (the so-called "Mycenaean Tomb") at Tel Dan/Laish. That amphoriskos seems to be a rare example of such a vessel from an inland site with little attested contacts with Egypt.[2] Numerous glass vessels were also deposited in Southern Levantine tombs dating to the Late Bronze Age (e.g. Dharat el-Humraiya south of Jaffa; Beth Shemesh; Tel Eitun and Qaraye near Sidon - all areas under Egyptian control).

Temples of local deities, such as the Fosse Temple at Lachish, the Temples at Beth Shean, the Timna temple in Wadi Arabah and the temple at Serabit el-Khadem in Sinai, were furnished with considerably more generous gifts, i.e. larger numbers of Egyptian New Kingdom glass vessels, probably sent by the Pharaohs to propitiate the local deities.[3]

In summary, it appears that based on current finds, the various Egyptian glass vessels from Late Bronze Age contexts in the Southern Levant are found in sites that were occupied by the Egyptians and/or under direct Egyptian control. When found outside areas under direct Egyptian control, they have been discovered in either temples or in the tombs of high level personages. Clearly, this is an indication of both the cultural affiliation and the value of these vessels.

---

[2] This glass vessel from Tel Dan will be published by the current author (forthcoming in the excavation report). Limited evidence for contact between Late Bronze Age Tel Dan and Egypt may possibly be attested in the New Kingdom Egyptian scarab (dating to Rameses II) found in the Late Bronze Age levels at this site (see Biran 1994:120, fig. 85).

[3] It should be noted that the shrine from Tell Deir 'Alla yielded, however, only one glass vessel, a lentoid flask, dating to the 19th Dynasty. Surprisingly, despite the fact that the final publication of the Tell Deir 'Alla shrine and the relevant finds has appeared, save for a brief description and a small-scale line drawing, this very interesting vessel was not deemed worthy of discussion! See Franken 1992:58, fig. 4-19:22.

REFERENCES

Barag, D.
1970 Mesopotamian Core-Formed Glass Vessels (1500-500 B.C.). Pp. 131-199 in *Glass and Glassmaking in Ancient Mesopotamia*, A.L. Oppenheim, R.H. Brill, D. Barag, and A. von Saldern. Corning: The Corning Museum of Glass.

Barag, D.
1988 An Egyptian Glass Jar. Pp. 100-101 in *Gezer V: The Field I Caves*, eds. J.D. Seger and H.D. Lance. Jerusalem: Nelson Glueck School of Biblical Archaeology.

Biran, A.
1994 *Biblical Dan*. Jerusalem: The Israel Exploration Society.

Franken, H.J.
1992 *Excavations at Tell Deir 'Alla: The Late Bronze Age Sanctuary*. Louvain: Peeters.

Harden, D.B.
1981 *Catalogue of Greek and Roman Glass in the British Museum*. London: British Museum.

Lehrer-Jacobson, G.
1988 Egyptian Glass. Pp. 212-217 in *The Egyptian Mining Temple at Timna*, ed. B. Rothenberg. Researches in the Arabah 1959-1984, Volume I. London: Institute for Archaeo-Metallurgical Studies.

Macalister II = Macalister, R.A.S.
1912 *The Excavation of Gezer, Volume II*. London: John Murray.

Matoïan, V.
2000 Données nouvelles sur le verre en Syrie au IIe millénaire av. V.C.: le cas de Ras Shamra-Ougarit. Pp. 23-47 in *La route du Verre*, ed. M.D. Nenna. Travaux de la Maison de l'Orient Méditerranéen, 33. Lyon: Maison de l'Orient Méditerranéan.

Miron, R.
1990 *Kāmid el-Lōz 10: Das "Schatzhaus" im Palastbereich*. Bonn: R. Habelt.

Nolte, B.
1968 *Die Glasgefässe im alten Ägypten*. Münchener Ägyptologische Studien 14. Berlin: B. Hessling.

Quibell, E.
1901 A Tomb at Hawaret el Gurob. *Annales du service des antiquités de l'Égypte* 2:141-143.

Schlick-Nolte, B.
1996 Kostbare Glasgefässe aus dem "Schatzhaus". Pp. 183-202 in *Kāmid el-Lōz 16* ed. R. Hachmann. Bonn: R. Habelt.

CHAPTER 5: THE GLYPTIC FINDS: STAMP-SEAL AMULETS

Othmar Keel

5.1. INTRODUCTION

In this chapter, the glyptic finds from the tombs excavated by Weill at Gezer are discussed. Four stamp-seal amulets were recovered among the finds from these tombs in the Hebrew University Collections, including three scarabs and one square-shaped seal (Figs. 15-16). Unfortunately, no information regarding the original find-context of these objects could be obtained from the available documentation. Thus, these finds can provide only a very general idea of the date and cultural contexts during which these tombs were in use.

The catalogue, description and discussion of these items are based on the system used in the *Corpus der Stempelsiegel-Amulette aus Palästina/Israel* (Keel 1995a; 1997). In fact, these very items will be included in one of the forthcoming volumes of this catalogue, along with the stamp-seal amulets from the other excavations at Gezer.

As in the above *Corpus*, the following conventions are used:

The description of the heads, backs, and sides of the scarabs (e.g., B2/0/e9) follows the classification system of Tufnell 1984: 31-38 and Keel 1995a: § 74-114.

§ + number (e.g., § 128) refer to the corresponding paragraph in Keel 1995a.

Place name + number (e.g., Afek no. 45) refer to the corresponding entry in Keel 1997.

5.2. CATALOGUE

5.2.1. OBJECT (Fig. 15:1): Scarab, A6/0?/d8, the back is missing, linear engraving (§ 326-327), enstatite (§ 386-391, yellowish-white, 15.2 x 10 x 5 mm.

Base: A horizontal bar divides two mirror-image fountain-like arrangements, each consisting of two vertical lines that end in two round interlocking spirals. The fountain-like arrangement has close parallels, for instance, on impressions from Kahun (Petrie 1890: pl. X:42) and Uronarti (Dunham 1967: 70, Seal Impressions 7, nos. 123 and 125). It would appear that this scarab is imported.

Date: Late 12th or 13th Dynasties.

Context: Unknown

Collection: Institute of Archaeology, Hebrew University of Jerusalem, Excavations of R. Weill, no. 111.

Bibliography: Previously unpublished.

5.2.2. OBJECT (Fig. 15:2): Scarab, A2/vIv/d5, partly linear (spirals), partly hollowed out engraving (§ 326-328.333), enstatite (§ 386-390), yellowish-white, 20.1 x 15 x 9.5 mm.

Base: Cross pattern with spirals in the four corners. The spirals are turned towards the horizontal bar. At the end of each vertical bar is a small rectangle, from which two uraei emerge, turning outward. Close parallels are Tell el-ʿAǧul no. 275 (cf. also Tell el-ʿAǧul no. 185) and Randall-Maciver and Mace 1902: pl. 53:5 = Jaeger 1982: 323, n. 613, ill. 815. The latter is a double-sided oval piece with the throne-name of Thutmosis III. It is probably contemporaneous with this king, but in any case, is 18th Dynasty. This also applies to two additional, albeit less close parallels: Petrie 1917: pl. XXVII:53 and Matouk no. 1983. Both these parallels are also double-sided oval pieces. The other side of the piece in Petrie 1917 bears a recumbent sphinx and the throne-name of Thutmosis III. Only one side ot the second piece is published, showing a Hathor fetish (Matouk 1977: 376, no. 135). It would appear that this piece is imported.

Date: 18th Dynasty from Thutmosis III and onwards (1479-1292 BCE).

Context: Unknown

Collection: Institute of Archaeology, Hebrew University of Jerusalem, Excavations of R. Weill, no. 112.

Bibliography: Previously unpublished.

5.2.3. OBJECT (Fig. 16:1): Scarab, D2/vIv, the legs are not indicated at all, more than half the plinth is missing, hollowed out engraving (§ 328-330), enstatite (§ 386-390), green tinted composition (§ 394-395), the inside is whitish, 16 x 11.8 x 7 mm.

Base: The remnant of the plinth bears a cross pattern with spirals in the four corners. The spirals are turned towards the vertical bar, which is rather typical of the Middle Bronze Age (e.g. Tufnell 1984: pl. XXIII:2017-2019; 2032-2033). The scarab belongs to the "Beth-Shean Stratum IX group" (see discussion below).

Date: 18th Dynasty from Thutmosis III on (1479-1292 BCE).

Context: Unknown

Collection: Institute of Archaeology, Hebrew University of Jerusalem, Excavations of R. Weill, no. 113.

Bibliography: Previously unpublished.

In light of the parallels to this scarab, and it being seen as belonging to a specific and well-defined group of scarabs, a short discussion of this group is warranted. The scarabs in this group are all made of composite material, with the legs not indicated at all. Consequently, the back of the beetle rests on the plinth. The pronotum and elytra are marked by a single line. The humeral callosities are represented by two V. The average length ranges between 14-16 mm. Since the early Late Bronze Age at Beth-Shean, Stratum IX (and, to a lesser extent, Stratum VIII and VII) produced several scarabs with these particular features, I defined this clear group as the "Beth-Shean Stratum IX group." It should be noted that McGovern, Fleming and Swann found evidence of silica production at Beth-Shean during the 19th Dynasty, limited to the manufacture of small artifacts, such as beads and pendants (1993: 27).

Stratum IX precedes this period, and is characterized by the beginning of Egyptian administration at Beth-Shean, dated to the reign of Thutmosis III. The base of the scarabs of this group display motifs typical of the 18th Dynasty. A peculiarity of the group is that motifs that are normally oriented to the right (§ 415) in this case face left. This may be explained by the fact that the craftsmen and women who manufactured the molds, copied imported Egyptian scarabs, with the result that the scarabs produced in these molds would face in the opposite direction to the original. An example is the recumbent caprid with a twig. On imported enstatite stamp-seal amulets, it looks to the right (Tell el-'Aǧul nos. 135 and 314; Giveon 1985: 126f, no. 48), but on a Stratum VIII composite material scarab from Beth-Shean, it faces left (Rowe 1940: 85 and pl. 39:2). A similar scarab was found at Megiddo (Oriental Institute, University of Chicago, Megiddo 21017, unpublished) and another at Tell Abu Hawam (Abu Hawam no. 10). A Beth-Shean Stratum VIII scarab belonging to the Stratum IX group bears a striding lion, also a typical motif of the 18th Dynasty. Instead of striding to the right, however, the lion marches to the left (Weinstein 1993: fig. 168:3). The same is true of a scarab featuring Ptah from Beth-Shean Stratum IX (University Museum, Philadelphia, UM 29-104-69 = Keel, Keel-Leu and Schroer 1989: 295, fig. 48). On this scarab, as well as on a rectangular piece found at Shechem (Horn 1973: 284 and fig. 1:65), the sign of life and the Djed-pillar appear in front of the Ptah image. Ptah is looking to the right on the imported rectangular enstatite piece found at Shechem and to the left on the composite material scarab from Beth-Shean. A representation of Taweret said to come from 'Atlit (no. 29) also belongs to this group. While on regular enstatite stamp-seal amulets Taweret is turned to the right (Tell el-'Aǧul no. 215), on the scarab from 'Atlit she strides to the left.

On two imported 18th Dynasty stamp-seal amulets the name of Amun is combined with the 'nḫ and s signs, probably to be read *Jmn s 'nḫ*, i.e. "Amun makes live" (Weinstein 1993: 222), is written from right to left (Rowe 1936: no. S. 47; Tufnell et al. 1940: pl. 32A-B:10). On two scarabs from Beth-Shean of the Stratum IX group, found in Stratum VIII and VII, the name of Amun is written from left to right (Weinstein 1993: figs. 167:1, 168:2), although the 'nḫ and s are in the same order as on the imported items.

Two additional scarabs in the Beth-Shean Stratum IX group – found in Stratum IX – bear a subject peculiar to this group, which is not found on imported enstatite scarabs: one enthroned and one striding man, each holding a lotus (University Museum, Philadelphia, UM 29-104-55 and 29-104-59, both unpublished). The parallels from Beth-Shemesh (enthroned; Grant 1932: 26, no. 1395 = University Museum, Philadelphia, UM 61-14-917), Ta'anach (striding; Sellin 1904: 28-29 and fig. 23), and Lachish (striding; Tufnell 1958: pls. 37-38, 308, 311) are also scarabs without legs made of composite material, with the figures engraved on the plinth looking to the left.

Of the 17 items in the "Beth-Shean Stratum IX group", 8 were found at Beth-Shean – 4 in Stratum IX, 3 in Stratum VIII and 1 in Stratum VII. Three examples come from north of the Carmel range (Ta'anach, Megiddo, and Tell Abu Hawam), and the remaining 6 are from 'Atlit, Gezer, Beth-Shemesh, and Lachish. The distribution pattern is the opposite of that of scarabs imported from Egypt, 11 such pieces (65%) found north, 6 (35%) south of the Carmel mountain range.

5.2.4. OBJECT (Fig. 16:2): Double-sided square shaped piece (cf. § 214), the style and subjects of which suggest to class it with the rectangular pieces of type III according to Keel 1995a (§ 216-218, 225-228) although it can not be considered a typical representative of that otherwise well-defined group (cf. also Keel 1995b: 121-126). The engraving is partly linear, partly hollowed out, possibly using a drill (§ 326-327), black stone, 10.4 x 10.4 x 6.8 mm.

Base: Side A: Quadruped with head turned back and raised tail; Side B: vulture with one or possibly two spread wings. Neither the quadruped with its head turned back nor the vulture have exact parallels on other pieces, but similarly stylized wings are typical of this group (cf. Keel 1995b: 12-125, figs. 46, 48, 53-55, 57).

Date: Late Bronze Age IIA (1400-1300 BCE).

Context: Unknown

Collection: Institute of Archaeology, Hebrew University of Jerusalem, Excavations of R. Weill, no. 115.

Bibliography: Previously unpublished.

5.3. CONCLUSION

The four stamp-seal amulets described above constitute too small an assemblage to draw any significant conclusions. It is noteworthy that two of the four items are Egyptian imports and two are typical of the stamp-seal amulet workshops north of the Carmel range. Three objects are characteristic of the Late Bronze Age I or IIA, and No. 1, dated to the Middle Kingdom, may be an heirloom. The fact that all the glyptic finds are not of local production (in fact not even of Southern Palestine) fits in well with the existence of other non-local finds (e.g. imported pottery) in the tomb.

REFERENCES

Dunham, D.
1967 *Uronarti, Shafalk, Mirgissa. Second Cataract Forts II*. Boston: Museum of Fine Arts.

Giveon, R.
1985 *Egyptian Scarabs from Western Asia from the Collections of the British Museum*. Orbis Biblicus et Orientalis Series Archaeologica 3. Fribourg and Göttingen: University Press and Vandenhoeck and Ruprecht.

Grant, E.
1932 *Ain Shems Excavations (Palestine) 1928-1931 II*. Biblical and Kindred Studies 4. Haverford: Elihu Grant.

Horn, S.H.
1973 Scarabs and Scarab Impressions from Shechem – III. *Journal of Near Eastern Studies* 32: 281-289.

Jaeger, B.
1982 *Essai de classification et datation des scarabées Menkhéperrê*. Orbis Biblicus et Orientalis Series Archaeologica 2. Fribourg and Göttingen: University Press and Vandenhoeck and Ruprecht.

Keel, O.
1995a *Corpus der Stempelsiegel-Amulette aus Palästina/Israel. Einleitung*. Orbis Biblicus et Orientalis Series Archaeologica 10. Fribourg and Göttingen: University Press and Vandenhoeck and Ruprecht.

Keel, O.
1995b Stamp Seals – The Problem of Palestinian Workshops in the Second Millennium and Some Remarks on the Preceding and Succeeding Periods. Pp. 93-142 in *Seals and Sealings in the Ancient Near East. Proceedings of the Symposium Held on September 2, 1993, Jerusalem, Israel*, ed. J. G. Westenholz. Bible Lands Museum Jerusalem Publications 1. Jerusalem: Bible Lands Museum.

Keel, O.
1997 *Corpus der Stempelsiegel-Amulette aus Palästina/Israel. 1. Von Tell Abu-Farağ bis 'Atlit*. Orbis Biblicus et Orientalis Series Archaeologica 13. Fribourg and Göttingen: University Press and Vandenhoeck and Ruprecht.

Keel, O., Keel-Leu, H., and Schroer S.
1989 *Studien zu den Stempelsiegeln aus Palästina/Israel II*. Orbis Biblicus et Orientalis 89. Fribourg and Göttingen: University Press and Vandenhoeck and Ruprecht.

Matouk, F.S.
1977 *Corpus du scarabée égyptien. II Analyse thématique*. Beirut: Fouad S. Matouk.

McGovern, P.E., Fleming, S.J., and Swann, C.P.
1993 The Late Bronze Egyptian Garrison at Beth Shan: Glass and Faience Production and Importation in the Late New Kingdom: *Bulletin of the American Schools of Oriental Research* 290-291: 1-27.

Petrie, W.M.F.
1890 *Kahun, Gurob, and Hawara*. London: Kegan Paul, Trench, Trübner and Co.

Petrie, W.M.F.
1917 *Scarabs and Cylinders with Names. Illustrated by the Egyptian Collection in University College, London*. British School of Archaeology in Egypt 29. London: University College (reprinted 1974, Warminster and Encino, CA: Aris and Phillips and Joel L. Malter).

Randall-Maciver, D., and Mace A.C.
1902 *El Amrah and Abydos 1899-1901*. Egypt Exploration Fund. London: Kegan Paul, Trench, Trübner and Co.

Rowe, A.
1936 *A Catalogue of Egyptian Scarabs, Scaraboids, Seals and Amulets in the Palestine Archaeological Museum*. Cairo: Institut Français d'Archéologie Orientale.

Rowe, A.
1940 *The Four Canaanite Temples of Beth-Shan I. The Temples and Cult Objects*. Publications of the Palestine Section of the Museum of the University of Pennsylvania 2. Philadelphia: University of Philadelphia.

Sellin, E.
1904 *Tell Ta'annek*. Denkschrift der kaiserlichen Akademie der Wissenschaften in Wien, Philosophisch- historische Klasse 50/4. Vienna: Gerold.

Starkey, J.L., and Harding, L.
1932 *Beth-Pelet II. Prehistoric Fara. Beth-Pelet Cemetery*. British School of Archaeology in Egypt 52. London: University College and Bernard Quaritch.

Tufnell, O.
1958 *Lachish IV (Tell ed-Duweir). The Bronze Age*. London: Oxford University Press.

Tufnell, O.
1984   *Studies on Scarab Seals. Vol. II: Scarab Seals and their Contribution to History in the Early Second Millennium B.C.* (with contributions by G.T. Martin and W.A. Ward). Warminster: Aris and Phillips.

Tufnell, O., Inge, C.H., and Harding, L.
1940   *Lachish II (Tell ed-Duweir). The Fosse Temple.* London: Oxford University Press.

Weinstein, J.M.
1993   The Scarabs, Plaques, Seals, and Rings. Pp. 221-225, Fig. 165-168 in *The Late Bronze Egyptian Garrison at Beth Shan: A Study of Levels VII and VIII*, eds. F.W. James and P.E. McGovern. University Museum Monograph 85. Philadelphia: The University of Pennsylvania and The University of Mississippi.

CHAPTER 6: MEDICAL COMPUTED TOMOGRAPHY (CT) OF SELECTED POTTERY: PRELIMINARY RESULTS

Nachum Applbaum and Yaakov H. Applbaum

6.1. INTRODUCTION

In this chapter we will present preliminary observations from the analysis of five ceramic vessels from the tombs excavated by R. Weill at Gezer, using Medical Computed Tomography (CT). The vessels were tested at the Institute of Radiology at Haddasah University Medical Center in Jerusalem, Israel, where we first discovered that CT scans might be used to expand our knowledge about ceramic artifacts, their fabric, and the method by which they had been made. The scans, and the techniques subsequently developed to enhance these studies, were conducted at this venue.

6.2. METHODS

For our tests we used a helical multislice CT scanner (Twin Flash CT Scanner - Elscint, Haifa, Israel). The data was stored digitally so as to allow further study and processing after the initial scanning process was completed. Data Processing was performed on an Omnipro Workstation (Elscint, Haifa, Israel).

Medical X-Ray Computed Tomography, commonly known in the medical profession as "CT," is a non-destructive radiographic technique. It is widely used in medical radiology as a diagnostic tool, as it is superior to conventional radiography.

The successful use of CT as an efficient and powerful non-destructive analytical tool for the study of clay and ceramic archaeological artifacts has been reported by us previously (Applbaum et al. 1995; 1999; 2001). This method has also gained recognition among archaeologists and museum curators (Janson et al. 2001; Schreiber 1999; Anderson and Fell 1995; Hershkovitz et al. 1995; Vandiver and Ellingson 1991; Notman 1986).

As demonstrated previously (Applbaum and Applbaum 1999), this process is brief and totally non-destructive. All the data obtained during the scanning is digital and is stored for further study and analysis. Furthermore, these stored digital images can be printed, with fine detail, on film or paper.

In Computed Tomography an X-Ray tube and a series of electronic detectors rotate around an object (Colsher and Pelc 1988; Wiesen and Miraldi 1994). The X-rays pass tangentially through the scanned object. In passing through the object the X-rays are measured by detectors. A digital image is formed from the collected data. Consecutive "slices" through the object allow us to collect a series of images that provide a full picture of the object in cross section. The advantage of CT is that the overlapping parts of the object do not obscure the image as they do in standard X-rays. Furthermore, because the data is acquired as a volumetric data set, it can not only be manipulated to form images in different planes but, if needed, can also generate 3-D images.

The scanning process itself is performed in two stages; followed by post-scanning processing and interpretation of the data collected.

In the first stage we conduct a preliminary scan called a "surview" or "scout scan." In this scan a digital radiograph of the object is produced (e.g., Pl. 29:1,5). The image is a 2 dimensional representation of the 3 dimensional object; similar to those obtained from conventional radiography and xeroradiography. The resolution and clarity of these digital radiographs, however, are of a much higher quality than of those obtained with other conventional radiological techniques. As we will demonstrate, these images are valuable in the study of the objects.

The "surview" also serves us in planning our CT study of the object. We can mark on this image the exact areas we wish to scan. We can plan the exact distances between the scanning slices as well as thickness of these slices. Furthermore, based upon our preliminary observations of these 2 dimensional radiographs we can, if needed, concentrate our "second stage" scanning on specific areas.

Upon completion of the preliminary stage, the object is once again passed through the scanner and the "slices" are obtained, as noted above. In this particular study we scanned thin slices using a high-resolution technique. We used this technique to obtain fine detail and good contrast. Our CT scanning process allows us to observe both qualitative and quantitative differences in the densities of the material of which the artifact was formed.

We can measure different features of the ceramic object, such as the length, width or thickness of specific parts of the object. The contour of objects in different planes can also be viewed. The density of the material at any given point can be measured (Applbaum and Applbaum 1999).

These images are particularly useful in the accurate study of ceramic material (Applbaum and Applbaum 2001). They allow us to observe inclusions and voids inside the body of the clay. We are able to observe their size, nature and distribution. This information is most important as it provides us with highly probable answers to many of the questions that are crucial to the understanding of ceramic technology (Braun 1982; Foster 1985; Carr 1990; Stoltman 2001). The distribution and orientation of inclusions and elongated voids are characteristic and peculiar to each of the different types of forming techniques (Vandiver 1988; Leonard et al. 1993). Micro-cracks can also be observed in the images obtained. The size and angles of these cracks also serve as clues to the nature of the fabric (Carr 1993). The CT images also yield valuable information as to the techniques used to add handles and spouts and other decorative motifs to these artifacts.

6.3. SAMPLE

From the Gezer tomb assemblage we chose five whole vessels for scanning; two bowls, a juglet, a piriform jar and a composite pyxis.

Bowl (HU 136, Pl. 1:11)

This is a shallow bowl with a rounded inner rim. The rim is somewhat distorted in its circumference, a phenomenon quite common in vessels of this type. This distortion has been attributed to, what may have been, mass production techniques, (above, chapter 2, p.11; Killebrew 1998:399). The bowl has a simple disk base.

In analyzing the "surview", the first stage of our scanning process, the digital radiograph of this vessel (Pl. 29:1), we could clearly analyze the fabric used in the forming of this vessel. We determined that the clay is very coarse with multiple inclusions.

This observation was substantiated by the sections obtained during the scanning of this vessel (Pl. 29:2). Xeroradiographic studies have shown that in radiological images we are able to view the temper (i.e. opening material) and non-plastic inclusions added by the potters to the clay material (Rye 1977:208; Braun 1982; Glanzman 1982:166; Carr 1990; Carr and Riddick 1990). The contrasting lighter exposed areas seen in our images indicate particles of greater resistance to the penetration of the radiation, in comparison to their surrounding matrix of fired clay particles (Pl. 29:3) (Glanzman and Fleming 1993; Pierret and Moran 1996).

Although we have not yet studied the exact nature of these particles we can clearly view their quantity and orientation within the fabric. We can also distinguish areas of darker exposure. These darker areas represent either air voids or areas where the temper material had been weathered out. Temper of an organic origin would have burned out during the firing of the vessel, thereby leaving a void in the matrix of the fabric. Crystalline carbonates used as temper, such as crushed shells or limestone, could have also dissolved, leaving holes in the matrix of the fabric, which would show up as a contrasting darker exposure.

McGovern and others have noted (McGovern 1986:193; Vaughan 1991) that heavily tempered fabric is better adapted to coiling than for wheel throwing. In this preliminary study we are not yet prepared to express our view as to whether this bowl was formed from coils or thrown on a wheel, a topic recently addressed by Margil and Middleton (1997; 2001). We would, however, like to point out that, in the sections we have obtained with the CT, in the area of the vessel's base, we are able to view the "behavior" of the voids and inclusions (Pl. 29:4). The voids and inclusions spiral from the center of the base of the bowl, outward, towards its circumference. What exactly this tells us about how the bowl was formed, is one of the questions we are trying to resolve in our current research. Does this observed outwards spiraling from the center mean that this vessel was formed on a fast wheel, or does it, on the contrary, indicate that this bowl was formed with the use of coils?

The distorted rim and rough finish of the bowl, as visually observed, can now be attributed to the coarse quality of the fabric used in its production, as observed and quantified in our scans. Can the quality of the fabric and the forming technique be attributed to its having been mass-produced, in this period? This is another question we hope to address, but only after a series of tests will be conducted on vessels that were commissioned to be produced under controlled conditions. We also plan to test additional samples of vessels from this period, particularly of the types that have already been tested.

Carinated Bowl (HU 85, Pl. 3:1)

In the images obtained for this vessel it is clear that the fabric used by the potter is of a higher quality (Pl. 29:5). Very few inclusions could be observed in the fabric and they are all very small in size. This means that the temper added by the potter to the clay was of very fine particles. It appears that a very small quantity of organic material was added to the clay. The vessel had been restored at some time in the past as the restoration work can be clearly seen through visual examination of the exterior of the bowl, as well as the surview and in the sections obtained during the scanning process. The walls of this bowl are extremely thin and finely executed (Pl. 29:6). Only a highly skilled potter could have created this bowl.

The complexity of the forming process used in the forming of this bowl, and our lack of control data with which to compare it, does not permit us to discuss, in this report, the technique and technology used by the potter.

We would, however, like to point out that in the sections we obtained in scanning across the center of the vessel, we were able to observe that the center of the bowl is very thin. Because the data from the scanning is digital, we were able, during the post-scanning analysis, to analytically measure the thickness of this section in the vessel (Applbaum and Applbaum 1999). In Pl. 29:7 we demonstrate how we were able to enlarge our image and mark and measure the thickness of the center of the bowl. As can be observed in the image, the thickness, or perhaps we might say, the thinness of the center of the bowl is +/- 1 mm. This extraordinary bowl testifies to the outstanding craftsmanship of the potter.

Composite Pyxis (RM V1715, Pl. 7:5)
Inclusions and voids could be observed in the images of this vessel (Pl. 30:1). This means that, either the fabric used in the forming of this vessel was relatively rich in temper, or, the temper that was added to the clay was coarse in nature. The fabric viewed in each half of the vessel is of the same composition and can be attributed to the forming of the whole vessel from the same material.

In the axial sections obtained we can clearly see evidence of the technique that was used by the potter in his forming of this composite vessel (Pl. 30:2). He began by forming a pyxis. He then sliced off one of the walls of the pyxis from the shoulder of the vessel, downward, to the center of the base. As can be observed, the slicing was probably accomplished with a very sharp object, leaving a clean cut. He then formed a second vessel of the same height and size, but not as round in circumference as the first. He cut this vessel as well and removed one wall from the shoulder to half of its base. The potter then joined the two halves.

Our scans also allowed us to determine the potters method of matching the two halves. On one half of the vessel, the potter cut and flattened the lip, in preparation for joining it with the other half (Pl. 30:2). This allowed the potter to match and cover the lip of the other half when joining the two halves. On the second half no such preparation could be observed, possibly because the matching of the second half did not need its lip flattened. After the two halves were joined, the potter covered the joined lips with a layer of clay. This layer of clay both strengthened the join and concealed it.

The complexity of the techniques used in forming this vessel clearly points to careful planning and accurate execution by a highly skilled potter.

Piriform Jar (HU 149, Pl. 8:2)
In the scans we made of this vessel, we found the fabric to be of a fine quality, containing very few inclusions (Pl. 30:3). Also, very few voids could be observed. This indicates that very little organic temper was added to the clay. The walls of the vessel are extremely constant in their thickness from the base to the rim. Such evenness in its thickness is a definite indication that the potter was highly skilled.

Although we do not want to address technological issues in-depth in this preliminary report, we would like to point out one observation. In our scans of the area where the handles are affixed to the vessel, we observed an air void, located between the exterior of the body of the vessel and the handle (Pl. 30:3-4). This indicates that the handle was pasted on to the body after the vessel was formed. A thin layer of clay was then used to cover the join and conceal it from the naked eye. The void may also attest to the stage at which the handle was affixed, apparently when the vessel was partially dry.

White Painted Juglet (RM V1713, Pl. 8:16)
From the images we have obtained for this vessel we can see that the fabric used by the potter was somewhat coarse and contains many inclusions. We can also verify the typological observation that identifies this juglet with the imported "Cypriote White Painted Juglet" family. These vessels have two characteristic technological peculiarities that cannot be observed from their exterior with the unaided eye.

A. They are hand-built and not formed or thrown on a wheel.
B. Cypriote potters did not usually "paste" the handles to the body of the vessel. It was their common practice to insert the handle into the body of the vessel. This has been attested to in studies sundry fragmentary vessels (e.g. Merrillees 1982:157; Ben Tor 1992:236; Leonard et al. 1993:108 n.17).

The juglet we tested is an intact, complete vessel. It is therefore hard to determine, through unaided visual observation, whether it was hand-built or wheel thrown. It is also impossible to determine whether the handle was pasted to the surface of the vessel or inserted into its body.

In the surview image of the juglet we could already observe some information regarding the technology used by the potter during the forming of the juglet.

In Pl. 30:5 one can see a transverse scan of a section of the juglet. From viewing this image we can definitely observe irregularities in the thickness of its walls. These irregularities attest to the fact that this vessel was formed by hand and was not thrown on a wheel.

In the longitudinal section obtained from the area where the handle was connected to the body (Pl. 30:6) we can clearly see that the handle was inserted into the body of the vessel in the traditional Cypriote fashion. The body of the juglet was pierced in the area of its shoulder. One end of the handle was externally pasted the rim of the vessel. An air void can be seen in the section obtained for this area. This internal void was trapped there when the handle was added. The potter covered the join in order to conceal it as well as to strengthen it. The second end of the handle was pushed into the pierced hole. An air void can clearly be seen in the transverse and longitudinal image of this area (Pl. 30:6-7).

In our scanned images we can observe cracks, some of which can also be observed from the exterior of the vessel. In our images, however, we can determine that some of them are severe cracks that call for the restoration of the vessel. Improper handling of this intact, and very fine artifact, could result in being seriously damaged.

6.4. SUMMARY AND CONCLUSIONS

In this preliminary report, we have presented our initial observations from the analysis of five ceramic vessels of the Gezer assemblage using Medical X-Ray Computed Tomography (CT). We have again shown that the CT is an efficient tool for the study of various aspects of ceramic technology. As a non-destructive radiological tool, CT can supply us with spectrums of information; broaden the attainable from any prior used technique. We can view cross-sections of the tested object at any required plane. This allows us to identify inclusions, voids and micro-cracks. This information is important for the classification of ceramic artifacts and for identifying the techniques used in the forming of the sample, whether it was slab built, coil built, hand formed, wheel thrown and wheel shaped. Techniques such as Xeroradiography have been used extensively to collect similar information (Heinemann 1976; Alexander and Johnston 1982; Vandiver and Lacovara 1985-1986). Standards for the interpretation of Xeroradiographic images have been set, based upon intensive testing. Xeroradiography has even been used, in some cases, to replace Petrography as the test of choice (Carr and Komorosky 1995; Stoltman 2001:301).

Not having conducted comparative studies of the artifacts, we are presenting only a preliminary report at this time. We feel that to be able to reach concrete conclusions based upon our interpretations of the CT images, comparative studies using Xeroradiography should be conducted (Meduri et al. 1993). Unfortunately, Xeroradiography is a technique that is currently unavailable in Israel, as it has been replaced, in all of our country's medical radiology departments, by other imaging techniques. To overcome this problem, however, we have proceeded to "put the horse in front of the cart."

We have commissioned an expert potter to form a series of vessels under controlled conditions, using as many of the forming techniques as are currently known to us. After these "control" vessels are scanned, and the resulting images rendered by the CT's are analyzed and studied, we will be able to check the analysis and interpretation of these five Gezer vessels presented above, as well as that of other ceramic artifacts.

At that time, we expect to publish our final report for this group of vessels from Gezer. Furthermore, we will attempt to use these selfsame studies of the "control" group to quantify and classify our results so that they might serve as a "Digital Standard" by which all CT studies of ceramic artifacts could be measured.

REFERENCES

Alexander, R. E., and Johnston, R. H.
1982 Xeroradiography of Ancient Objects: A New Imaging Modality. Pp. 145-154 in *Archaeological Ceramics*, eds. J. S. Olin and A. D. Franklin. Washington D.C.: Smithsonian Institution Press.

Anderson, T., and Fell, C.
1995 Analysis of Roman Cremation Vessels by Computerized Tomography. *Journal of Archaeological Science* 22:609-617.

Applbaum, N., and Applbaum, Y. H.
1999 The Use of Medical Computed Tomography (CT) in the Study of Ceramic Archaeological Finds. Pp. 42-53 in *Computer Applications in Archaeology*. Tel Aviv: Tel Aviv University, Department of Archaoeology and Ancient Near Eastern Studies.

Applbaum, N., and Applbaum, Y. H.
2002 The Use of Medical Computed Tomography (CT) in the Study of the Ceramic Technology of Figurines. Pp. 214-220 in *Sha'ar Hagolan 1: Neolithic Art in Context*, eds. Y. Garfinkel and M. Miller. Oxford: Oxbow.

Applbaum, N., Applbaum, Y., and Horowitz, W.
1995 Imaging with the Aid of Computed Tomography of Sealed Documents from the Ur III Period. *Archaeology and Science Bulletin* 3:8-12 (Hebrew).

Ben Tor, A.
1992 *The Archaeology of Ancient Israel*. New Haven: Yale University Press

Braun, D. P.
1982 Radiographic Analysis of Temper in Ceramic Vessels: Goals and Initial Methods. *Journal of Field Archaeology* 9: 183-192.

Carr, C.
1990 Advances in Ceramic Radiography and Analysis: Applications and Potentials. *Journal of Archaeological Science* 17:13-34.

Carr, C.
1993 Identifying individual vessels with X-radiography. *American Antiquity* 58: 96-117.

Carr, C., and Komorowsky, J.
1995 Identifying the Mineralogy of Rock Temper in Ceramics using Xerodiography. *American Antiquity* 60:723–749.

Carr, C., and Riddick, E.B.J.
1990 Advances in Ceramic Radiography and Analysis: Laboratory Methods. *Journal of Archaeological Science* 17:35-66.

Colsher, J.C., and Pelc, N.J.
1998 Computerized Tomography Systems and Performance. In *Radiology: Diagnosis, Imaging Intervention*, eds. J.M. Taveras and J. T. Ferrucci. Philadelphia: Lippincot Raven.

Foster, G.V.
1985 Identification of Inclusions in Ceramic Artifacts by Xeroradiography. *Journal of Field Archaeology* 12(3): 373-376.

Glanzman, W.
1982 Xeroradiographic Examination of Pottery Manufacturing Techniques: A Test Case from the Baq'ah Valley, Jordan. *MASCA Journal* 2: 163-169.

Glanzman, W.D., and Fleming, S.J.
1993 Fabrication Methods. Pp. 94-102 in *The Late Bronze Egyptian Garrison at Beth Shan: a Study of Levels VII and VIII*, eds. F.W. James and P.E. McGovern. Philadelphia: The University Museum, University of Pennsylvania.

Heinemann, S.
1976 Xeroradiography: A New Archaeological Tool. *American Antiquity* 41: 106-111.

Hershkovitz, I., et al.
1995 New Remedy for Plastered Skull: Non-Invasive Imaging of a Modeled Cranium from Kfar Hahoresh, Israel. *Journal of Archaeological Science* 22:779-789.

Jansen, R.J., Koens, H.F.W., Neeft, C.W., and Stoker, J.
2001 Scenes from the Past: CT in the Archaeological Study of Ancient Greek Ceramics. *RadioGraphics* 21:315-321.

Killebrew, A.
1998 Ceramic Typology and Technology of the Late Bronze II and Iron I Assemblages from Tel Miqne-Ekron: The Transition from Canaanite to Early Philistine Culture. Pp. 379-405 in *Mediterranean Peoples in Transition, Thirteenth to Early Tenth Centuries* BCE, eds. S. Gitin, A. Mazar and E. Stern. Jerusalem Israel: Israel Exploration Society.

Leonard, A., et al.
1993 The Making of Aegean Stirrup Jars: Technique, Tradition, and Trade. *Annual of the British School in Athens* 88: 105-123.

Magrill, P., and Middleton, A.
1997 A Canaanite Potter's Workshop at Lachish, Israel. Pp. 68-74 in *Pottery in the Making World Ceramic Traditions*, eds. I. Freestone and D. Gaimster. London: British Museum Press.

Magrill, P., and Middleton, A.
2001 Did the Potter's Wheel Go Out of Use in Late Bronze Age Palestine? *Antiquity* 75:137-144.

McGovern, P.E., Habottle, G., and Christopher, W.
1986 Ware Characterization: Petrography, Chemical Sourcing and Firing. Pp. 173-193 in *The Late Bronze Age and Early Iron Ages of Central Transjordan: The Beq'ah Valley Project, 1977-1981*, ed. P.E. McGovern. Philadelphia: University of Pennsylvania Museum.

Meduri, A., et al.
1993 Xeroradiography and Digital Luminescence Radiography in the Study of the Techniques of Manufacturing Ancient Ceramics: The Advantages and Limits. *Radiologia Medica (Torino)* 86(1-2): 116-126.

Merrillees, R.S.
1982 Late Cypriote Pottery Making Techniques. Pp. 155-159 in *Archéologie du Levant: Recueil à La mémoire de Roger Saidah*, eds. M. Yon et al. Collection de la Maison de l'Orient Méditerranéen No. 12. Série archéologique, 9. Lyon: Maison de l'Orient.

Notman, D.N.H.
1986 Ancient Scanning: Computer Tomography of Ancient Mummies. Pp. 13-24 in *Science in Egyptology*, ed. R.A. Davis. Manchester: Manchester University Press.

Pierret, A., and Moran, C.J.
1996 Quantification of Orientation of Pore Patterns in X-ray Images of Deformed Clay. *Microscopy Microanalysis Microstructures* 7: 421-431.

Rye, O.S.
1977 Pottery Manufacturing Techniques: X-ray Studies. *Archaeometry* 19: 205-211.

Schreiber, T.
1999 *Athenian Vase Construction: A Potter's Analysis*. Malibu: J.Paul Getty Museum.

Stoltman, J.B.
2001 The Role of Petrography in the Study of Archaeological Ceramics. Pp. 297-326 in *Earth Science and Archaeology*, eds. P. Goldberg, V.T. Holliday and C. Reid Ferring. New York: Kluwer Academic/Plenum Publishers.

Vandiver, P.B.
1988 Radiographic Imaging Technologies for Archaeological Ceramics. Pp. 25-32 in *Materials issues in art and archaeology : symposium held April 6-8, 1988, Reno, Nevada, U.S.A.*, eds. E.V. Sayre, et al. Materials Research Society Symposium Proceedings 123. Pittsburgh: Material Research Society.

Vandiver, P.B., et al.
1991 New Applications of X-radiographic Imaging Technologies for Archaeological Ceramics. *Archaeomaterials* 5:185-207.

Vandiver, P.B., and Lacovara, P.
1985-1986 An Outline of Technological Changes in Egyptian Pottery Manufacture. *Bulletin of the Egyptological Seminar* 7:53-85.

Vaughan, S.J.
1991 Material and Technical Classification of Base Ring Ware: A New Fabric Typology. Pp. 113-119 in *Cypriot Ceramics: Reading the Prehistoric Record*, eds. J.A. Barlow, D.C. Bolger and B. Kling. University Museum Monograph 74, University Museum Symposium Series 2. Philadelphia: University of Pennsylvania.

Wiesen, E.J., and Miraldi, F.
1994 Imaging Principles in Computed Tomography. P. 31 in *Computed Tomography and Magnetic Resonance Imaging of the Whole Body* (3rd Edition), eds. J.R. Haaga and C.F. Lanzieri. Saint Louis: Mosby.

CHAPTER 7: SUMMARY

Aren M. Maeir

7.1. INTRODUCTION

In the preceding chapters, the finds from the tombs that the late Raymond Weill had excavated at Gezer were presented and discussed. These finds represent a cross-section of the material culture of Gezer from the latter parts of the Middle Bronze Age II, through most of the Late Bronze Age, as well as portions of the Iron Age. Despite the limited amount of information that was available on the tombs and the context of the related finds, a close study of the objects themselves, coupled with a comparison with the finds from the other excavations at Gezer (and from other sites), has produced several interesting insights (see Table 7).

All told, the finds from these nine tombs represent a rich collection of finds dating to the Middle Bronze and Late Bronze Ages and to the Iron IIB-IIC period.[1] Among the various types of finds, the well-preserved pottery assemblage offers fine examples of various vessels that were typical of the respective periods, including several that are either rare, or in some cases unique (see above, Chapter 2).

But not only the pottery is of interest. Several of the objects from among the other classes of finds are noteworthy as well, particularly the unique glass vessel (discussed in Chapter 4).

7.2. THE LATE BRONZE AGE

Despite the wide temporal span of the use of these tombs as indicated from the finds, the overall majority of the objects from the tombs date to the Late Bronze Age, and in particular to the Late Bronze Age IIA and IIB (c. 14th and 13th centuries BCE). This correlates nicely with the stratigraphic evidence from the site, where one sees, at this very period, evidence of a flourishing settlement. To a large extent, the finds from the tombs represent a typical assemblage of the southern Land of Israel during the Late Bronze Age II. The local and imported pottery, as well as the other classes of finds, fit in well with the material culture typical of the region during of this period. As at other sites, evidence of extended trade contacts, both local and overseas is seen, as well as objects of diverse technological origins (e.g. McGovern 1985; Leonard 1989; Bunimovitz 1995). Thus, for example, alongside relatively simply-made pottery, one finds imported vessels of high quality (including objects of Aegean, Cypriote and possibly Egyptian origin). Likewise, while one sees evidence of objects of relatively common materials and simple production processes (such as the bone objects), high-level "prestige" items, exhibiting more exotic materials and complicated fabrication technologies, are present as well (e.g. the glass vessel).

The significance of the glass vessel from these tombs can only be stressed (Chapter 4). Very few glass vessels from the Late Bronze Age have been found in Palestine. Of these few, two have been discovered at Gezer: the vessel reported above and the glass vessel from Tomb 10A of the American excavations (Barag 1988). Although this might be just a question of luck, nevertheless, one wonders whether this is an indication of the economic strength and trade connections of the site. Needless to say, these two luxury items of Egyptian origin are somewhat reminiscent of the list of riches that *Milkilu*, the king of Gezer was asked to acquire, by the order of the Pharaoh, in EA 369 (Moran 1992:366).

As noted in Chapter 5, most of the glyptic finds appear to be of Egyptian origin, once again indicating the cosmopolitan nature of Late Bronze Age Gezer. The presence of several "prestige" items may hint to the fact that some of these burials may have been of upper echelon elements of the Late Bronze Age population of Gezer. Due to the available evidence, little more can be said in this regard. Thus, although there is historical and archaeological evidence for a king at Gezer during the period of the El-Amarna letters (mid-14th cent. BCE, e.g. Ross 1967), as well as apparent evidence of Egyptian administrative functions at the site during the Late Bronze Age II (e.g. Pilcher 1923; Singer 1986-1987; Bunimovitz 1988-1989; Maeir 1988-1989; Dever 1998:123-127; Hasel 1998:184-188; *pace* Higginbotham 1999:100-102,136), the evidence that is presently available does not allow us to connect these activities to the tombs described above.

Unfortunately, very little information is known about the specific burial customs that were implemented in these tombs. One may assume, in light of other Late Bronze Age tombs (e.g. Gonen 1992), that these tombs were in fact multiple-interment burial caves, several of which have been excavated and published by the other excavators at Tel Gezer. Although, as stated above, the "prestige" items from the tombs might indicate that high-level personages were connected to these burials, little else can be said on the social dimensions of the tombs (see, e.g., Parker Pearson 1999). Noteworthy is the possible remains of a sarcophagus (larnax) lid (above, Chapter 2, pp. 31-32), particularly in light of the

---

[1] This is if one disregards the two anomalous vessels, dating, respectively, to the Early Bronze IV/Middle Bronze I and the Hellenistic periods, that may very well be intrusive elements, not part of the original contents of the tombs. Alternatively, they may be an indication of very limited activities in the tombs during these two periods. It should be noted that among the tombs that Macalister excavated, one sees tombs that were used from the Late Bronze through the Hellenistic periods. See for example Tomb 58, *Macalister III*:pls. LXXXI-LXXXIII).

larnax discovered by the American excavations (*Gezer V*:114-115). If in fact this is evidence of an Aegean-style burial custom, one wonders whether this might be an indication of either the actual presence of persons of Aegean origin at Gezer, or more likely, of Aegean cultural influences.

The latter option seems to be more reasonable for several reasons. Very few Aegean and Aegean-style objects were found at Late Bronze Age Gezer. All such ceramic vessels can be defined as specialized containers and fine table wares, typical components of the international trade during this period (Leonard 1994). There is no evidence of locally produced Aegean-style (as opposed to locally made or "Aegeanized") pottery and/or various kitchen ware (such as found during the Iron Age I in Philistia, e.g. Killebrew 1998). Likewise, save for the possible fragments of the larnax lid and the other larnax from the American excavations, few other distinctly Aegean objects have been reported. Thus, there is relatively little likelihood that these finds are indicative of the presence of persons of Aegean origin at Gezer.

The radiological examination of selected vessels from the tombs (Chapter 6) provides an important, and, to a large extent, an innovative contribution. To begin with, it would appear that the utility of this avenue of research is clearly demonstrated. The insights revealed through this analysis seem to indicate that this analytic method has come of age, expanding beyond the somewhat limited horizons of many earlier attempts to utilize Medical Radiology for the examination of pottery (e.g, see comments in Rice 1987:403-404). Not only has the current analyses provided important information on the technological background of the vessels, but it has also demonstrated the importance and potential contribution of such studies in future archaeological research (although see Adan-Bayewiz and Wieder 1992 for important reservations on the use of radiologial analyses, particularly regarding suggested applications for determining pottery provenience). This was shown for example through the interesting insights that were obtained on the production methods of the various bowls and of the unique double-pyxis. The information about the surprisingly thin base (less than 1mm thick) of the exceptionally well-made carinated bowl dating to the Middle Bronze Age II, is of interest as well. Such evidence is additional testimony to the outstanding technical proficiency of the Middle Bronze Age II potters, particularly in comparison to the much simpler fabrication methods seen in the local Late Bronze wares of Canaan, the predominant pottery types found in these tombs. Needless to say, the preliminary nature of these analyses requires that further research on additional objects of this type from this and other sites.

7.3. THE OTHER PERIODS

As mentioned above, in addition to the lion's share of the finds that date to the Late Bronze Age, evidence for the use of the tombs during the Middle Bronze Age II, the Iron Age I and the Iron Age II were found. Several comments on these finds are warranted. The Middle Bronze Age II finds all date to a relatively late phase of this period. The pottery types are typical of this region of the southern Levant during this period. Based on the typological discussion of these vessels (above, chapter 2), it can be assumed that these interments were contemporary with Strata XIX and XVIII in the American excavations (e.g. *Gezer IV*: 8-9, fig. 2). The fact that one of the scarabs from the tombs was identified as an Egyptian made scarab, dating to the Middle Kingdom (above, chapter 5), does not imply the use of the tombs during the earlier stages of the Middle Bronze Age. Although there is evidence of earlier Middle Bronze Age phases in the excavations (e.g. *Gezer IV*: 8-9, fig. 2), the lack of other finds dating to the earlier Middle Bronze Age does not support a claim for an earlier use of the tombs as well. Two explanations for its appearance in the tomb can raised (as suggested by Keel, above, chapter 5, p. 51). Either it is an heirloom, or, perchance, it is an example of the well-known phenomenon in which earlier Egyptian objects were traded throughout the entire ancient Near East, and appear in contexts that are much later than their original period of production and initial usage (e.g. Helck 1976).

The few finds dating to the Iron Age I appear to correspond to Strata XIII-XII, the early to middle "Philistine" phases at Gezer. The Philistine style krater as well as several other typical Iron Age I vessels, of types that are commonly found at sites in Philistia, serve as evidence of this cultural phase in the tombs. Although hardly indicative of intense use of the tombs during this period, these finds do add an additional facet to the well-known, and quite impressive list of Philistine material culture from the site (e.g. Dothan 1982:51-54; Singer 1985:116-118; Dever 1998: 137-152; Finkelstein 2002:282-283).

The Iron Age II period is represented by quite a few vessels of various types. These vessels may have originated from tombs that were used solely in the Iron Age II, as well as other, earlier tombs that had been reused. In the typological discussion (above, chapter 2), these vessels were dated to the 8th-7th centuries BCE (particularly to the latter part of that time span) and appear to belong to types that are typical of Judean controlled areas. If so, they may represent the re-use of these tombs during the late 7th century BCE (Stratum VA), when it has been suggested that Gezer was occupied by the Judean kingdom during the reign of Josiah (e.g. *Gezer III*: 38, but see Na'aman 1991; Finkelstein 2002:287). The Judean character of the finds would hardly allow us to date the use of these tombs to earlier stages of the Iron Age II.

If they were to be dated to these earlier stages, one would expect one of two possibilities: 1) If they date prior to the Assyrian conquest of 733 BCE, one would expect to find evidence of Israelite (northern) influences in the pottery, since Gezer was under Israelite control at that time; 2) Alternatively, if they dated subsequent to the Assyrian conquest, one would expect some evidence of Assyrian influences (e.g. Reich and Brandl 1985).

But both such influences are not to be found. Thus, it is much more likely to assume that only subsequent to the waning of the Assyrian control of Gezer could the Judean cultural influences, and related presence, be substantially felt at the site. As stated above, this is most likely due to actual Judean control at Gezer. These Iron Age II finds would be the only evidence of the mortuary customs at Gezer during this ephemeral stage of Judean control of the site. Based on parallels to other Judean sites, the finds do in fact seem appropriate for burials from late Iron Age II Judea (e.g., Bloch-Smith 1992:72-81; Barkay 1994:152-153). It should be noted that save for one burial cave which was apparently re-used in the 8th century BCE (Cave 8I; see *Macalister I*:81-82; *Macalister III*:pl. XVIII:2,16,28; Bloch-Smith 1992:168), all the other Iron Age burials from Gezer are from earlier phases of this period, dating to no later than the late 10th century BCE (for a summary of these tombs, see Bloch-Smith 1992:168, 175-176, 192, 201). Thus, both the unique burial types and the associated pottery strongly support the claim that the site was in fact under Judean control during the latter part of the 7th century BCE. Finkelstein's (2002:187) recent suggestion to minimize this presence, and even suggest that Gezer was controlled by Ekron during this period, does not seem to be supported.

7.4. FINAL COMMENTS

As stated above, the lack of sufficient documentation on the original contexts of the tombs and their respective finds severely hampered the analysis of this excavation. Nevertheless, the richness and diversity of the material remains from these tombs (typologically, chronologically and technologically) has offered a rather fecund ground for the study of the culture at Gezer during the Bronze and Iron Ages, with particular emphasis on the Late Bronze Age. Although additional information would have served us well to deepen and diversify this study, we must thank the original excavators of the tombs, as well as the people and institutions who preserved what had survived over the years, for providing us with the opportunity to rediscover these remains. One can but wonder if some day in the future additional information on these tombs and their excavation will surface. Until then, despite the significant lacunae, what has been written above will have to suffice, perhaps as a *pars pro toto* offering.

Table 7: Stratigraphy of the Excavations at Gezer (e.g., *Gezer V*:6-7; Dever 1998)

Stratum	Period	Period Represented in the Tombs Excavated by Weill
I	Early Roman	
II	Hellenistic	? (single vessel)
III	Hellenistic	
IV	Persian	
V	Iron Age IIC	+
VI	Iron Age IIB	?
VII	Iron Age IIB	
VIII	Iron Age IIA	?
IX	Iron Age IC	?
X	Iron Age IC	?
XI	Iron Age IB	
XII	Iron Age IB	+
XIII	Iron Age IB	+
XIV	LB IIB/Iron Age IA	?
XV	LB IIB	+
XVI	LB IIA	+
XVII	LB IB	?
XVIII	MB IIC/LB IA	+
XIX	MB IIC	+
XX	MB IIB/C	?
XXI	MB IIB	
XXII	MB IIA/B	
---	EB III – MB I	? (single vessel)
XXIII	EB IIB	
XIV	EB IIA	
XXV	EB IB	
XXVI	Late Chalcolithic	

REFERENCES

Adan-Bayewitz, D., and Wieder, M.
1992 Ceramics from Roman Galilee: A Comparison of Several Techniques for Fabric Characterization *Journal of Field Archaeology* 19:189-205.

Barag, D.
1988 An Egyptian Glass Jar. Pp. 100-101 in *Gezer V: The Field I Caves*, eds. J.D. Seger and H.D. Lance. Jerusalem: Nelson Glueck School of Biblical Archaeology.

Barkay, G.
1994 Burial Caves and Burial Practices in Judah in the Iron Age. Pp. 96-164 in *Graves and Burial Practices in Israel in the Ancient Period*, ed. I. Singer. Jerusalem: Yad Izhak Ben-Zvi (Hebrew).

Bloch-Smith, E.
1992 *Judahite Burial Practices and Beliefs About the Dead.* Journal for the Study of the Old Testament Supplement Series 123, JSOT/ASOR Monograph Series 7. Sheffield: Sheffield Academic Press.

Bunimovitz, S.
1988-89 An Egyptian "Governer's Residency" at Gezer? Another Suggestion. *Tel Aviv* 15-16:68-76.

Bunimovitz, S.
1995 On the Edge of Empires - Late Bronze Age (1500-1200 BCE). Pp. 320-331 in *The Archaeology of Society in the Holy Land*, ed. T.E. Levy. London: Leicester University Press.

Dever, W.G.
1998 *Gezer: A Crossroads in Ancient Israel.* Jerusalem: Ha-Kibbutz Ha-Meuchad (Hebrew).

Dothan, T.
1982 *The Philistines and Their Material Culture.* Jerusalem: Israel Exploration Society.

Finkelstein, I.
2002 Gezer Revisited and Revised. *Tel Aviv* 29/2:262-296.

Gezer III = Gitin, S.
1990 *Gezer III: A Ceramic Typology of the Late Iron II, Persian and Hellenistic Periods at Tell Gezer.* Jerusalem: Nelson Glueck School of Biblical Archaeology.

Gezer IV = Dever, W.G., et al.
1986 *Gezer IV: The 1969-71 Seasons in Field VI, the "Acropolis".* Jerusalem: Nelson Glueck School of Biblical Archaeology.

Gezer V = Seger, J.D., and Lance, H.D. (eds.)
1988 *Gezer V: The Field I Caves.* Jerusalem: Nelson Glueck School of Biblical Archaeology.

Gonen, R.
1992 *Burial Patterns and Cultural Diversity in Late Bronze Age Canaan.* American Schools of Oriental Research Dissertation Series 7. Winona Lake, IN: Eisenbrauns.

Hasel, M.
1998 *Domination and Resistance: Egyptian Military Activity in the Southern Levant, 1300-1185 B.C.* Leiden: Brill.

Helck, W.
1976 Ägyptische Statuen im Ausland - ein chronologisches Problem. *Ugarit-forschungen* 8:101-115.

Higginbotham, C.R.
1999 *Egyptianization and Elite Emulation in Ramesside Palestine: Governance and Accomodation on the Imperial Periphery.* Leiden: Brill.

Killebrew, A.
1998 Mycenaean and Aegean-Style Pottery in Canaan during the 14th - 12th Centuries BC. Pp. 159-70 in *The Aegean and the Orient in the Second Millennium: Proceedings of the 50th Anniversary Symposium, Cincinnati, 18-20 April 1997*, eds. E. Cline and D. Harris-Cline. Aegaeum 18. Liège: Université de Liège.

Leonard, A., Jr.
1989 The Late Bronze Age. *Biblical Archaeologist* 52:4-39.

Leonard, A., Jr.
1994 *An Index to the Late Bronze Age Aegean Pottery from Syria-Palestine.* Studies in Mediterranean Archaeology 114. Jonsered: P. Åströms.

Macalister I = Macalister, R.A.S.
1912 *The Excavation of Gezer, Volume I.* London: John Murray.

Macalister III = Macalister, R.A.S.
1912 *The Excavation of Gezer, Volume III.* London: John Murray.

McGovern, P. E.
1985 *Late Bronze Palestinian Pendants: Innovation in a Cosmopolitan Age.* JSOT/ASOR Monograph Series 1. Sheffield: JSOT.

Maeir, A.M.
1988-89 Remarks on a Supposed "Egyptian Residency" at Gezer. *Tel Aviv* 15-16:65-67.

Moran, W.L.
1992 *The Amarna Letters.* Baltimore: Johns Hopkins.

Na'aman, N.
1991 The Kingdom of Judah under Josiah. *Tel Aviv* 18:3-71.

Parker Pearson, M.
1999 *The Archaeology of Death and Burial*. Phoenix Mill: Sutton.

Pilcher, E.J.
1923 Portable Sundial from Gezer. *Palestine Exploration Fund Quarterly Statement* 55:85-89.

Reich, R., and Brandl, B.
1985 Gezer under Assyrian Rule. *Palestine Exploration Quarterly* 117:41-54.

Rice, P.M.
1987 *Pottery Analysis: A Source Book*. Chicago: University of Chicago.

Ross, J.F.
1967 Gezer in the Tell el-Amarna Letters. *Biblical Archaeologist* 30: 62-70.

Singer, I.
1985 The Beginning of Philistine Settlement in Canaan and the Northern Boundary of Philistia. *Tel Aviv* 12:109-122.

Singer, I.
1986-87 An Egyptian "Governer's Residency" at Gezer? *Tel Aviv* 13-14:26-31.

Figures

Fig. 1 - Map of the Southern Levant with the Location of Gezer and Selected Ancient and Modern Sites.

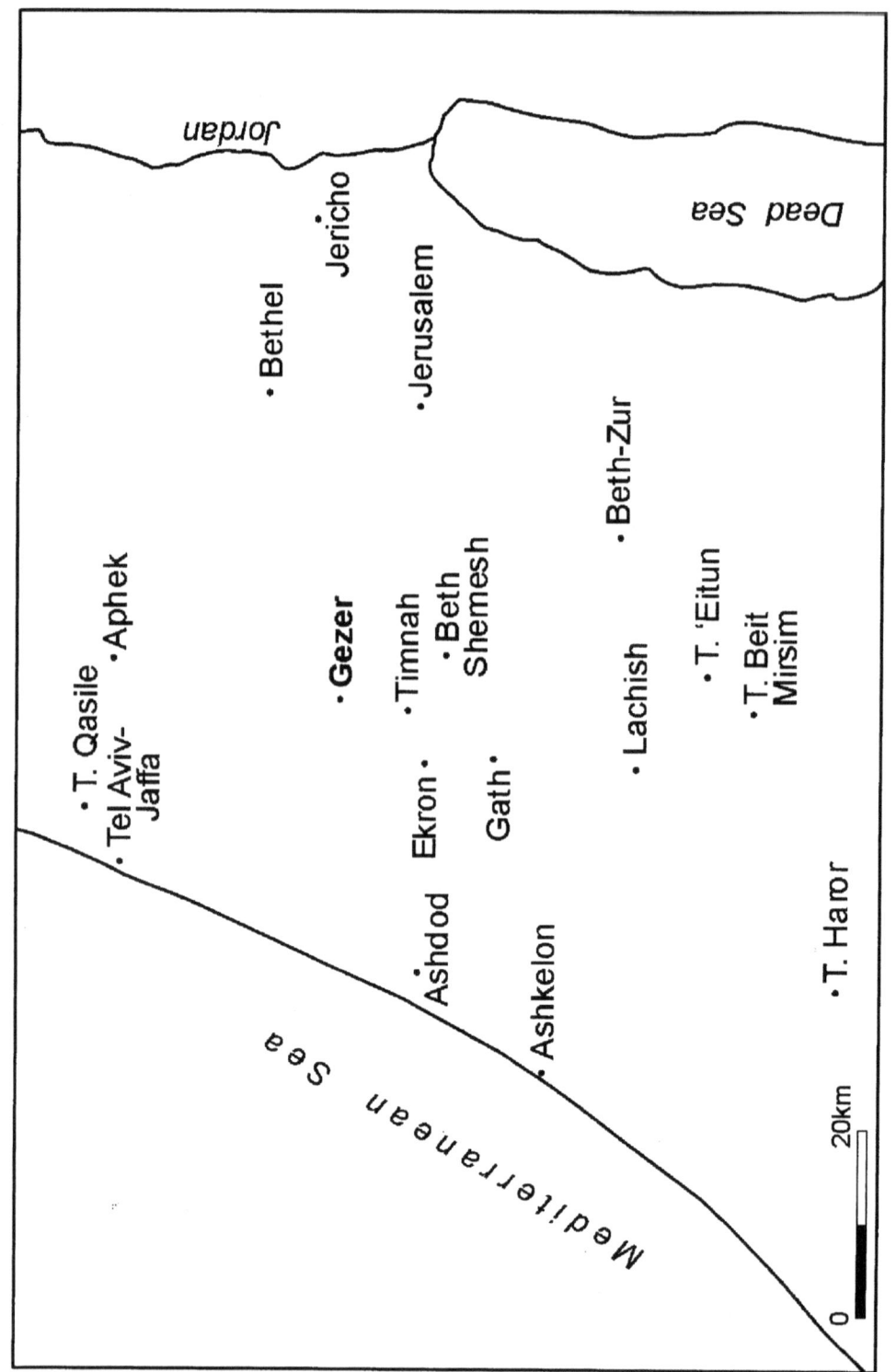

Fig. 2 - Map of Central Israel with the Primary Sites Mentioned in Text.

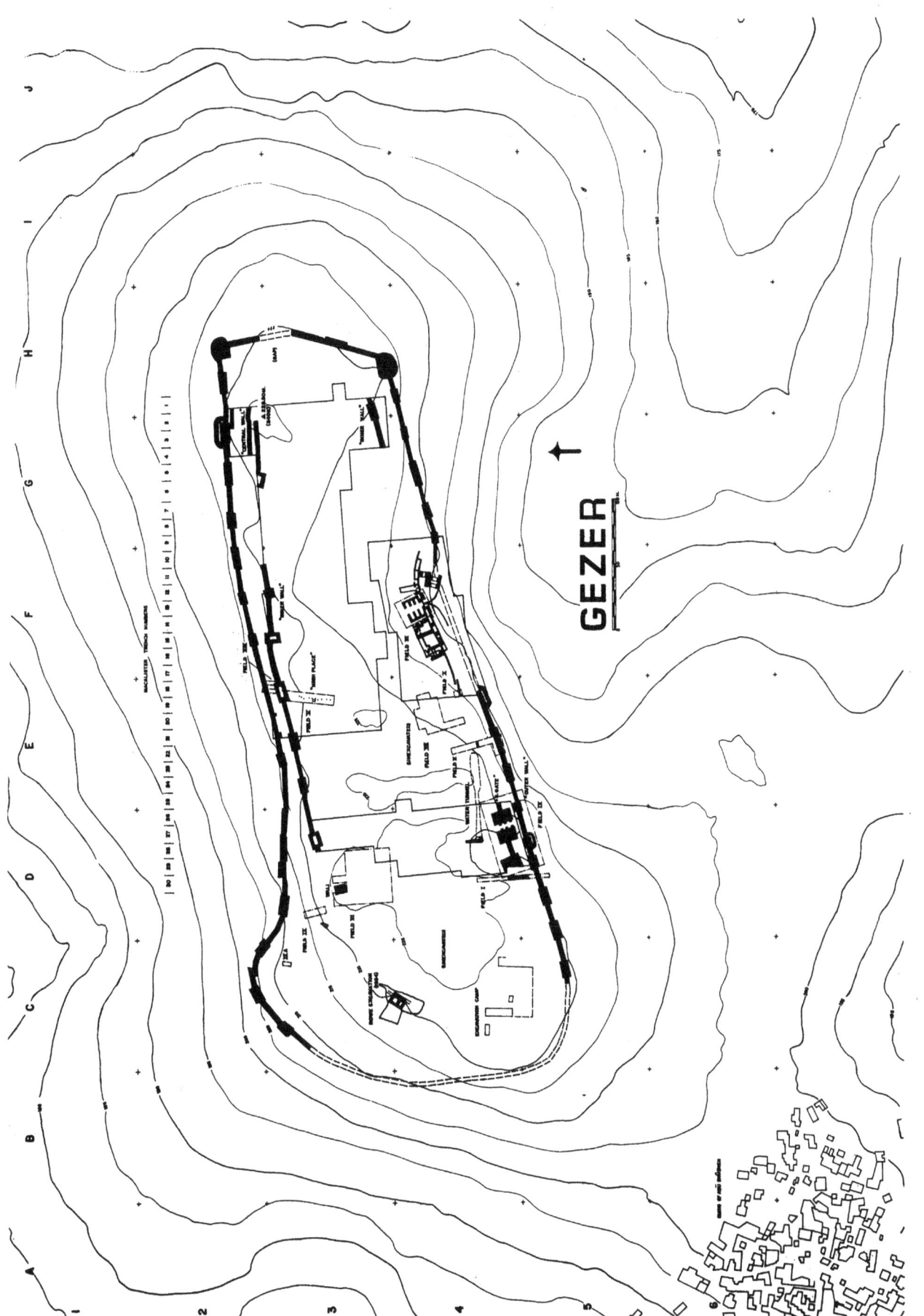

Fig. 3 - Plan of Tel Gezer with the Location of the Excavations by the Various Expeditions. The Location of the Tombs Excavated by R. Weill is not known.

Plates

Plate 1 - Line Drawings of Pottery: Bowls

No.	CRN[1]	Ware Description	Comments
1.	58	Reddish-yellow to light brown, many small white, red and grey, and many large white inclusions.	Possibly buff slip inside; faint traces of red paint on rim; light encrustation inside; mended.
2.	68	Dark to light reddish-yellow with orange tints, gritty surface, few small white and black and few large grey inclusions.	Light encrustation all over.
3.	81	Dark reddish-yellow, some small and large white and black, few large red inclusions.	
4.	80	Reddish-yellow, some small and large white and black, few large red inclusions.	
5.	79		Missing
6.	135	Reddish-yellow, few small and medium white and few small and large red inclusions.	Faint traces of red paint on rim; smooth lines above base.
7.	200	Reddish-yellow, some small black, red and white and few medium white inclusions, few large red and grey pebbles.	
8.	132	Reddish-yellow, some large white and red inclusions, light encrustation inside.	Coarsely finished lower interior and radial smooth lines on upper interior; string cut base.
9.	131	Reddish-yellow, some small white, black and red and few very large white and red inclusions.	Smoothing above base; light encrustation inside.
10.	137	Reddish-yellow, lighter inside, small grey, red and white inclusions and few large reddish pebbles.	Fine smoothing outside; light encrustation all over.
11.	136	Reddish-yellow, some small white and grey and few large white inclusions.	
12.	202	Reddish-yellow, some small and large white and few large red inclusions.	Smoothing on and above base.
13.	139	Reddish-yellow, few small white, black and red inclusions and few large red and grey pebbles.	Fine smooth lines inside and on lower exterior.
14.	211	Reddish-yellow, some medium grey, red and white inclusions and few large grey pebbles.	Smooth lines on and above base; partially burnt on exterior.
15.	207	Reddish-yellow, few small white and few large red inclusions.	Smoothing on base; slightly rippled exterior; encrustation all over.
16.	206	Reddish-yellow, few small white, grey and red, few large grey and white inclusions.	Base chipped along edge; slightly rippled exterior.
17.	209	Reddish-yellow, some small and medium white, grey and red inclusions, few large red and grey pebbles.	Smoothing inside, outside and on base; light encrustation all over.
18.	205	Reddish-yellow to light brown, some small and medium white and red and few large inclusions.	Light encrustation all over.
19.	72	Light brownish-yellow, many very tiny black and few small and large white inclusions.	Smooth lines outside.
20.	208	Reddish-yellow to light brown, some small and medium white and red and few large inclusions.	Red painted band on inner rim; fine smoothing inside and outside; light encrustation all over.
21.	57	Dark reddish-yellow, many small and medium white and grey inclusions.	Partially encrusted.
22.	70		Missing
23.	210	Light brown, many tiny black, some small white and red and few large white inclusions.	Red slip and irregular and horizontal hand burnish lines inside only; slip rubbed off on rim; encrusted inside; mended.

1 - Collection Room Number (Hebrew University)

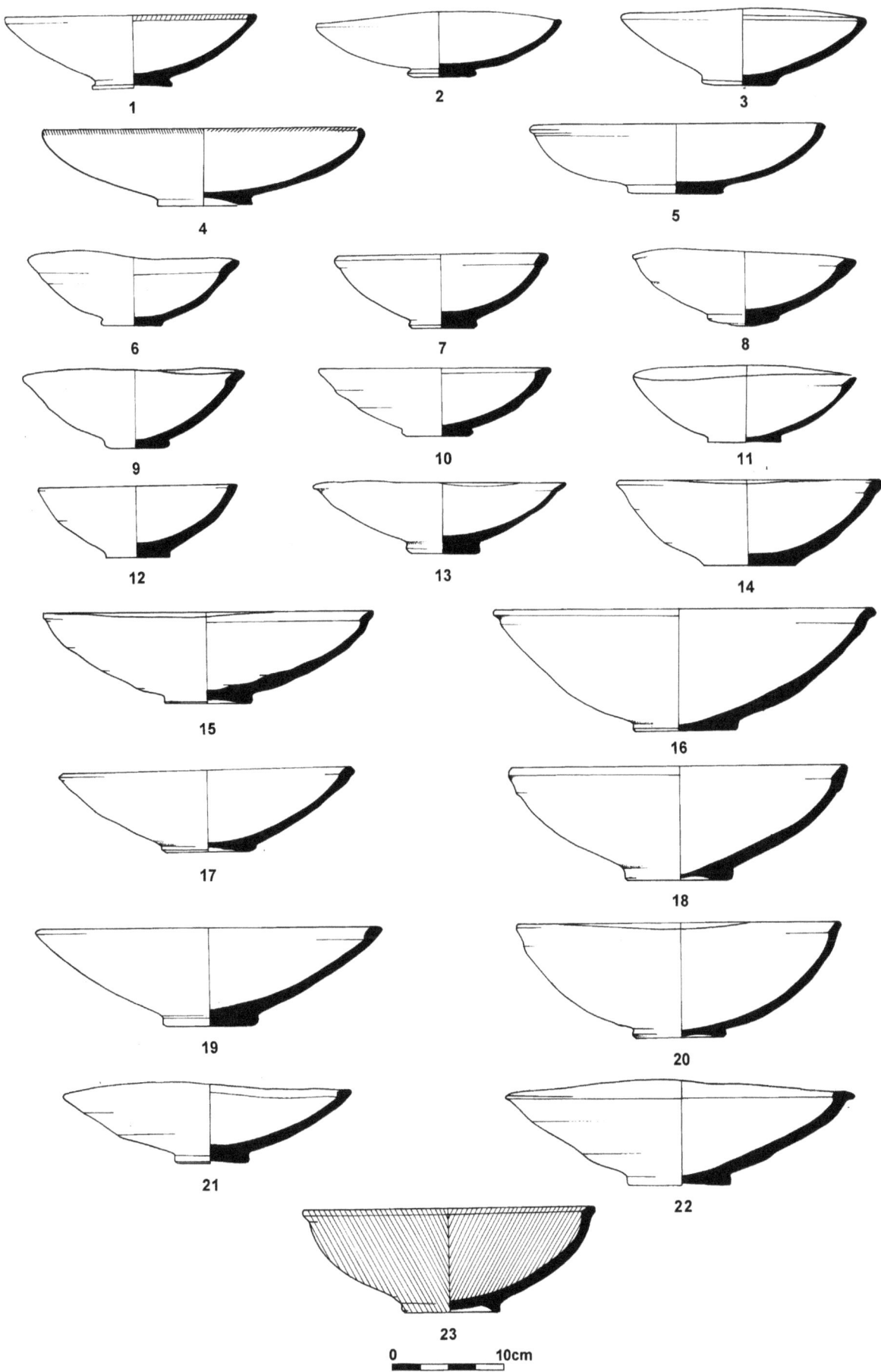

Plate 1

Plate 2 - Line Drawings of Pottery: Bowls

No.	CRN	Ware Description	Comments
1.	87	Reddish-yellow, many tiny black, few small and large white inclusions, gritty surface.	Fine smoothing outside; thick encrustation above base; mended.
2.	96	Reddish-yellow, some small white and black and few medium white and red inclusions.	Fine smoothing outside; thick encrustation outside; mended.
3.	76	Dark reddish-yellow with orange hue, gritty surface, some small white, black and red inclusions.	Smoothing outside; partially encrusted outside; mended.
4.	83	Reddish-yellow, grey core, some small white and few large red inclusions.	Smoothing inside; mended.
5.	203	Light reddish-yellow, some small white, black and red and few large red inclusions.	Smoothing above base; encrustation all over; traces of burning inside.
6.	126	Reddish-yellow, some small black and red inclusions, one very large red pebble.	Red band painted on rim; smoothing on upper exterior; string cut base.
7.	127	Light brown, some small white inclusions, few large grey and red pebbles.	Partially burnt outside.
8.	184	Light brown, few small, medium and large white inclusions.	Red band painted on rim, with drizzles inside; mended.
9.	186	Light brown, many tiny black and some large and small white and black inclusions.	Peeling red slip inside, outside and base; no burnish.
10.	185	Reddish-yellow to light brown, some small white and black inclusions.	Very faint traces of red slip and burnish; string cut base; bulge of untrimmed clay on center interior.
11.	109	Light reddish-yellow, some small grey, black and white and some large white inclusions, few large red and grey pebbles.	Red band painted on rim; red painted design inside; smoothing outside; rim chipped.
12.	86	Light brown to reddish, many small black and white and few large white and red inclusions.	Rim chipped, light encrustation all over.

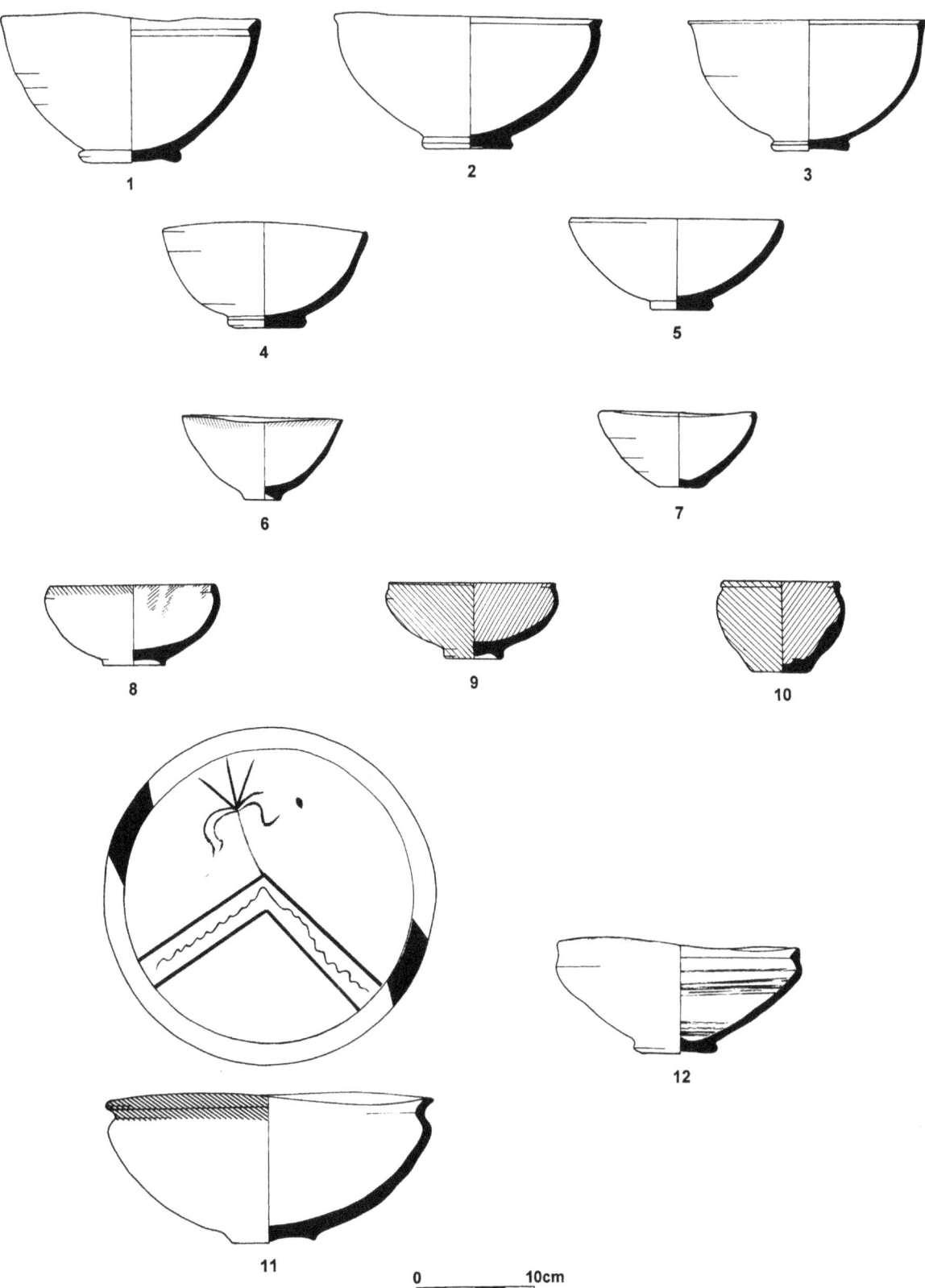

Plate 2

Plate 3 - Line Drawings of Pottery: Bowls, Chalices and Krater

No.	CRN	Ware Description	Comments
1.	85	Buff, metallic, finely levigated.	Self slip and polished continuous burnish; mended.
2.	103	Reddish-yellow, few medium and large white and red inclusions, metallic, gritty surface.	Red painted band on rim exterior and partly on rim interior; smoothing outside; base chipped along edge; mended.
3.	92	Light brown to buff, many tiny and few medium black and white inclusions.	
4.	56	Dark reddish-yellow, many tiny black and few small white inclusions.	Smoothing inside, outside and on base; light encrustation covering part of interior.
5.	141	Reddish-yellow, very many medium and large grey and white, and few large red inclusions, metallic.	Pockmarked, coarse surface; broken.
6.	102	Reddish-yellow, some small and medium white and few large red inclusions.	
7.	101	Light brown to buff, many tiny and a few medium black and white inclusions.	Red paint and burnish lies on rim top and interior; smoothing outside; dark encrustation on one side; base chipped along edge.
8.	105	Reddish-yellow, some small white and black and few large red inclusions.	Red band painted on rim interior and exterior.
9.	93	Reddish-yellow to pink, many small black and grey and some large white inclusions, gritty surface.	Smoothing outside; thick encrustation on rim and part of exterior; mended.
10.	172	Brown, some small white and few large white and grey inclusions.	Fine smoothing inside, partial encrustation outside.
11.	128	Light brown, some small white and grey and few large white inclusions.	Smooth marks outside; mended.
12.	119	Brown, some small and medium white and black inclusions.	Krater; decorated with Philistine bichrome design outside.

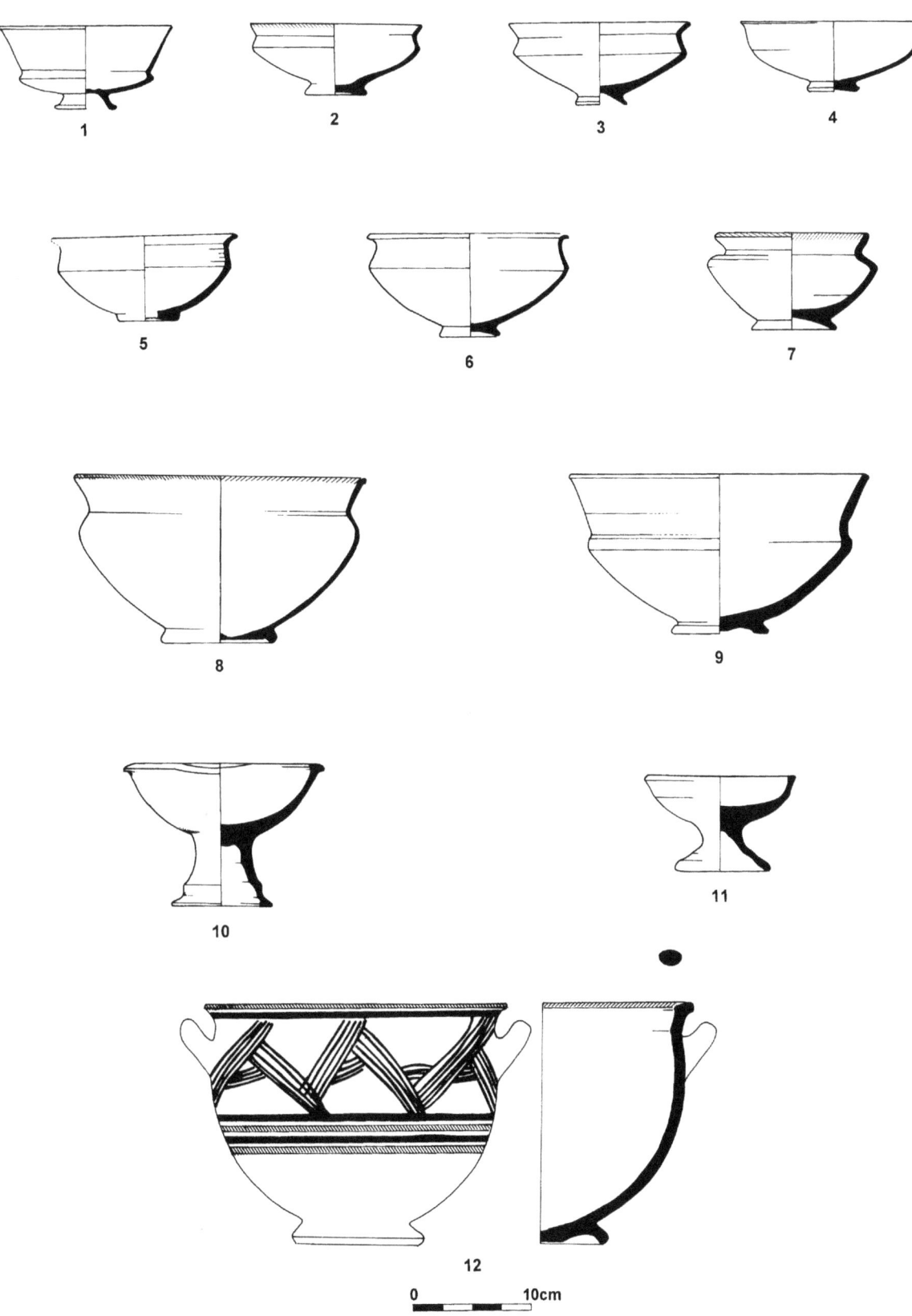

Plate 3

Plate 4 - Line Drawings of Pottery: Lamps

No.	CRN	Ware Description	Comments
1.	95	Light reddish-yellow, some small and medium white inclusions.	
2.	190	Light brown, few small white and few large red inclusions.	No signs of use; heavy encrustation.
3.	94	Light reddish-yellow, few small white, grey and red inclusions.	Partially burnt inside and on wick spout; encrustation all over.
4.	125	Dark to light reddish yellow, some small white and grey inclusions.	Burnt on wick spout; encrustation all over; mended.
5.	196	Light reddish-yellow, some small white and grey inclusions.	Thick encrustation all over; mended.
6.	198	Light reddish-yellow, some small and large white and red inclusions.	Faint traces of burning on wick spout; encrustation all over.
7.	117	Light reddish-yellow, some small and large white and grey inclusions.	
8.	194	Light brown, few large white inclusions.	Traces of red paint on rim; burning on wick spout; thick encrustation all over.
9.	189	Brown, some small grey and black inclusions.	Burnt on wick spout.
10.	197	Brown, some small and large white and few large grey inclusions.	Burnt inside and on wick spout; rim chipped; partial encrustation.
11.	191	Pink to dark reddish-yellow, some small white inclusions.	No signs of use; thick encrustation all over.
12.	195	Light brown, some small and few large white and red inclusions.	Traces of red paint on rim; no signs of use.
13.	118	Light brown to reddish-yellow, few small white and grey and few large white inclusions.	

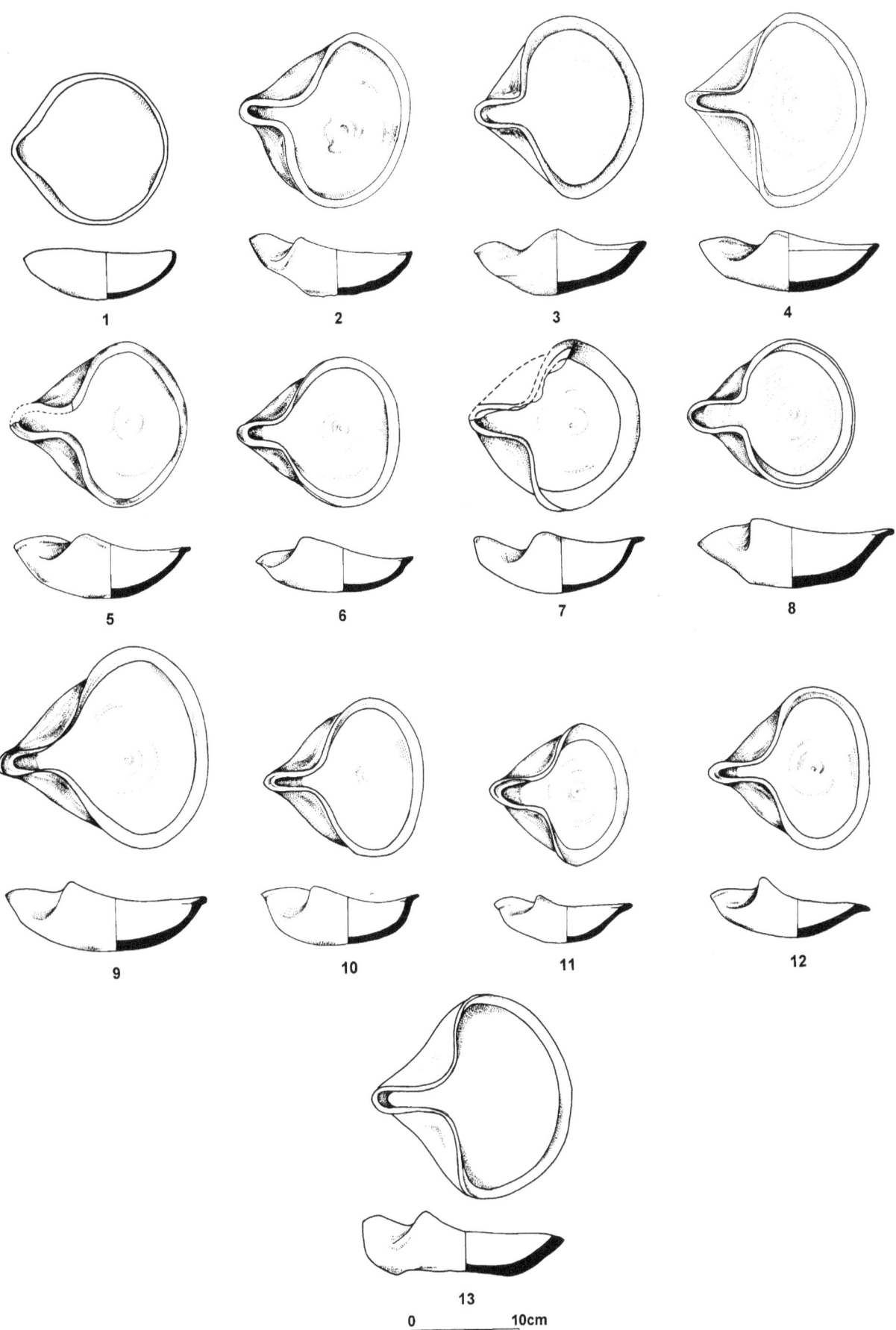

Plate 4

Plate 5 - Line Drawings of Pottery: Jugs and Bottle

No.	CRN	Ware Description	Comments
1.	28	Reddish-orange, many tiny black and small white inclusions.	Faint red painted design outside; rim chipped; light encrustation.
2.	55	Brown, few small white inclusions.	Traces of red slip outside; fine smooth lines above base; chipped on rim; encrustation.
3.	213	Dark reddish-yellow, some small white, black and red and few large red inclusions.	Smooth lines outside; mended.
4.	21	Reddish-brown to pinkish-brown, grey to brown core, many small and some large white inclusions.	Hole drilled under carination after firing; rim chipped.
5.	65	Orange, few small white inclusions.	Faint red painted design outside; traces of red on handle; encrustation; mended.
6.	182	Light brown, some small white and black inclusions.	Diagonal brown lines painted outside, very rubbed away in spots.
7.	179	Brown, few tiny white inclusions.	Highly polished burnish; two black painted horizontal bands on body; mended.
8.	183	Dark reddish-yellow, many small and few large white inclusions.	Red and black painted design; hole drilled at mid-body after firing.
9.	216	Light reddish-yellow, many small white, few small black and few large white inclusions.	Faded red slip outside and on base; partial encrustation; spout broken.
10.	177	Yellowish-brown, many small white and some small black and grey inclusions.	Moderately coarse; two small holes drilled in bottom of neck after firing; rim broken; encrustation.
11.	188	Buff, very few small black inclusions.	Bottle. Partial encrustation.
12.	215	Yellowish-buff, some tiny black inclusions.	Hellenistic.

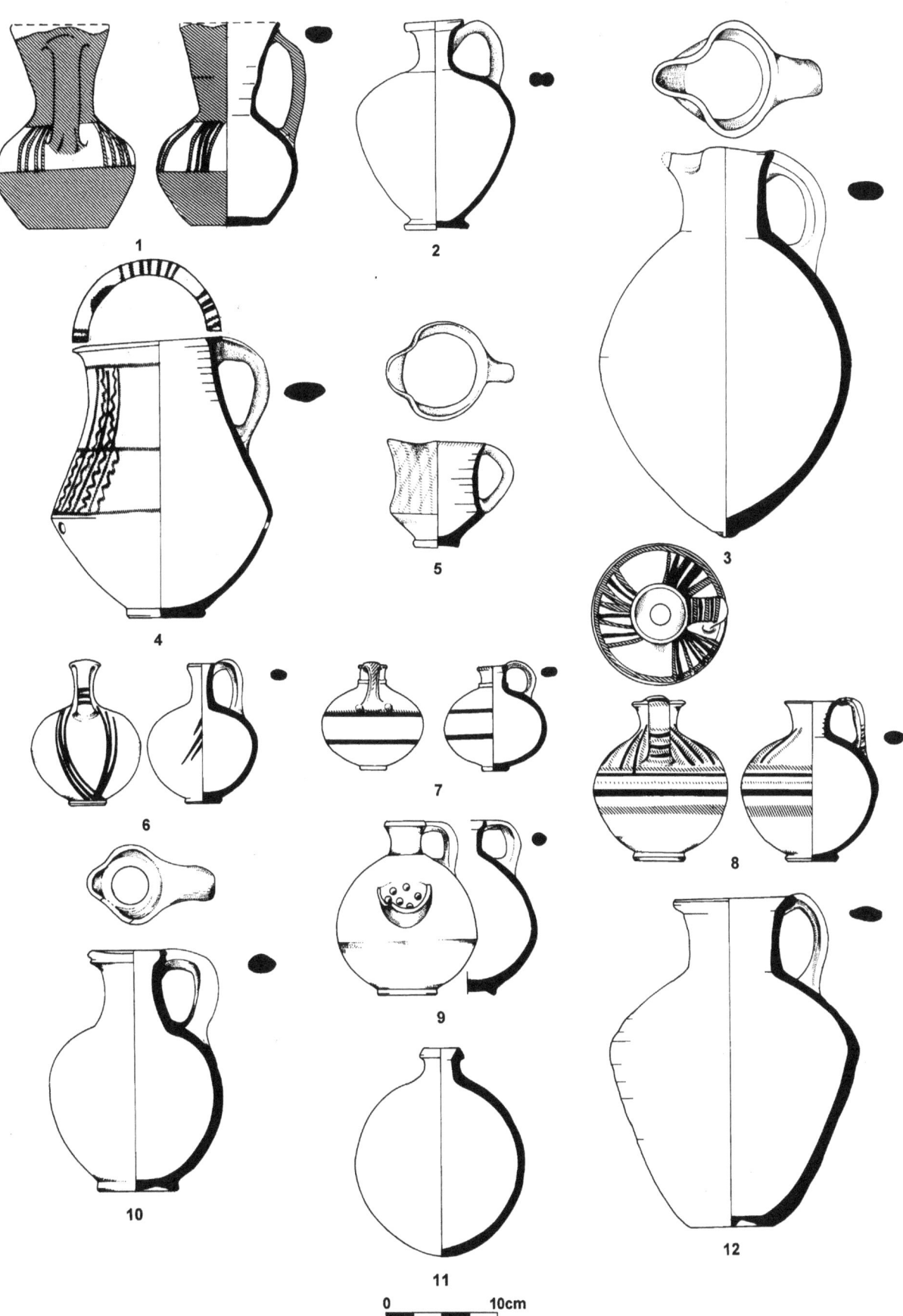

Plate 5

Plate 6 - Line Drawings of Pottery: Juglets

No.	CRN	Ware Description	Comments
1.	59	Reddish yellow ware, light brown core, many small black, some large grey and red inclusions, gritty, pockmarked surface.	Partial encrustation; mended.
2.	67	Brown, many small and few large white inclusions.	Highly polished burnish with vertical burnish lines; light brownish-red slip; rim chipped.
3.	75	Light reddish-yellow, some small white and grey inclusions, gritty surface.	Light encrustation; part of rim and neck missing; cracked.
4.	66	Dark reddish-yellow/orange, few small red and white, few large white inclusions.	Partial encrustation; mended.
5.	98	Pinkish-orange, many small and large white and red inclusions; pockmarked surface.	Crudely made; rim and neck missing; hole drilled after firing near handle.
6.	99	Buff, thick brown core, many small white and few large red and white inclusions, light chalky encrustation.	Uneven vertical lines on exterior (burnishing or scratches?); light chalky encrustation; broken at neck, handle missing.
7.	89	Pinkish-light brown, many small white and few small red and black, some large white inclusions, grey core.	Broken at rim.
8.	171	Yellowish-red, some small and few medium white inclusions.	Handle and part of rim missing.
9.	187	Reddish-yellow, some small white and black and few small red inclusions.	Widely-spaced smoothing; encrustation; neck and handle missing.
10.	91	Reddish-yellow, some small and few large black, white and grey inclusions.	Broken at rim.
11.	63	Brown, some small black and white and large white inclusions, metallic.	Buff slip, burnished.
12.	64	Greyish-brown, some small white and black, few large white inclusions, partial encrustation.	Burnt outside; faint traces of burnish.
13.	62	Grey, few small white and black inclusions, partially encrusted.	Part of rim missing, brownish-grey slip burnt dark, vertical burnish lines.
14.	61	Tell el-Yehudiyeh ware	Faint traces of dark yellowish grey slip and burnish; hole drilled after firing near mid-body; part of rim missing.
15.	60	Brown, many tiny black and white, some large white, and few large red inclusions, sandy exterior, partially encrusted.	Rim and base chipped, mended, faint traces of burnish.
16.	80	Light brown, some small black and white inclusions.	Buff slip; traces of burnish; brown painted decoration; body sherd.
17.	180	Pink, many small white and some small grey and red inclusions.	No traces of slip or burnish; partial encrustation.

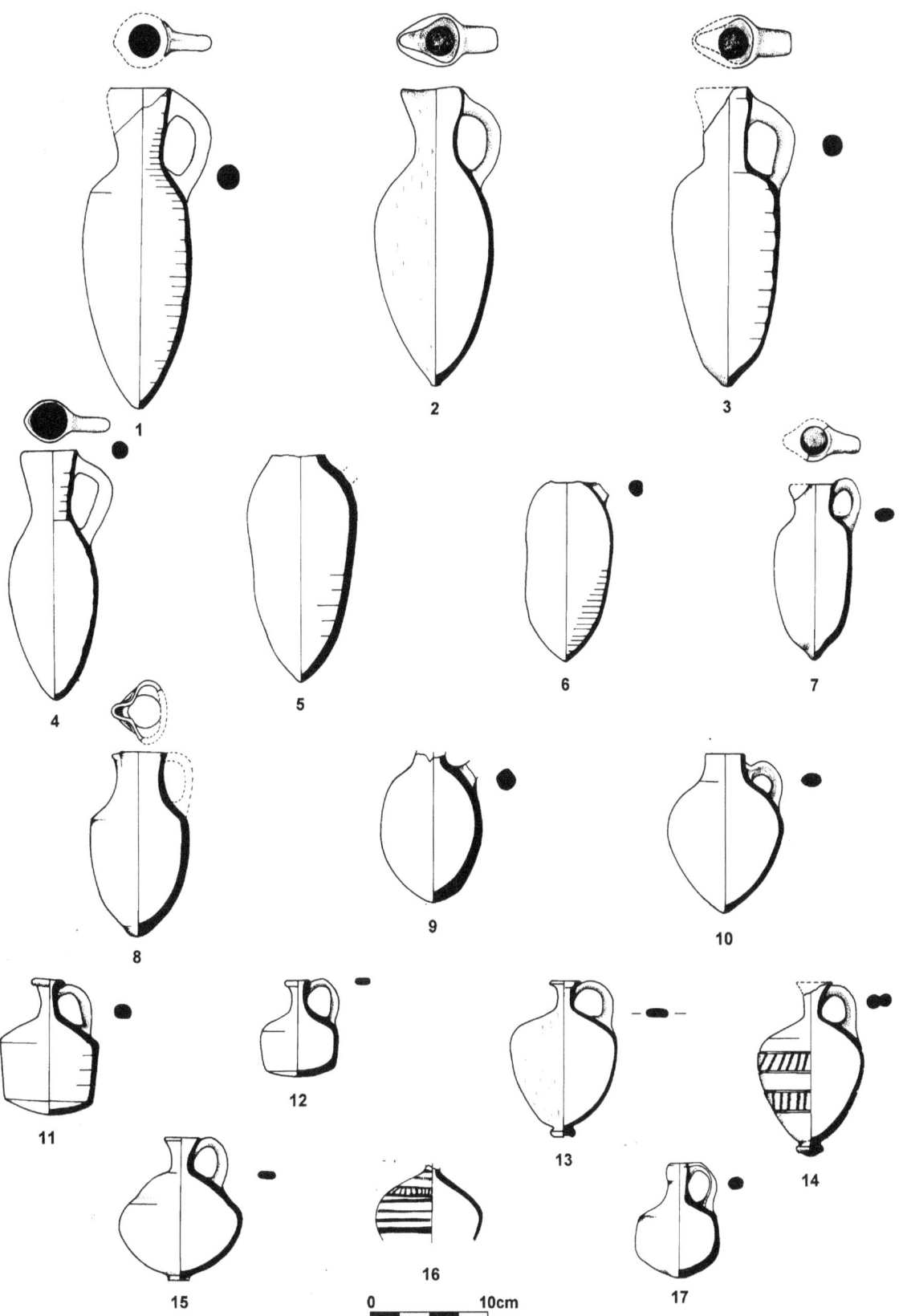

Plate 7 - Line Drawings of Pottery: Flasks and Pyxides

No.	CRN	Ware Description	Comments
1.	178	Light brown, few small and medium white and black inclusions.	Flask; concentric red circles painted outside.
2.	116	Reddish-yellow, some small white and grey and few large white, black and grey inclusions.	Flask.
3.	122	Dark-reddish yellow, some small black and white inclusions.	Flask. Red slip outside, peeling; no traces of burnish.
4.	173	Light brown, few small white and few large grey and red inclusions.	Pyxis. Partial encrustation; part of rim chipped; one handle missing.
5.	V1715*	Reddish yellow, some small white and red inclusions	Double spouted pyxis; broken at neck; red slip outside, peeling; encrusted.

* Rockefeller Museum Inventory Number ("Army Book")

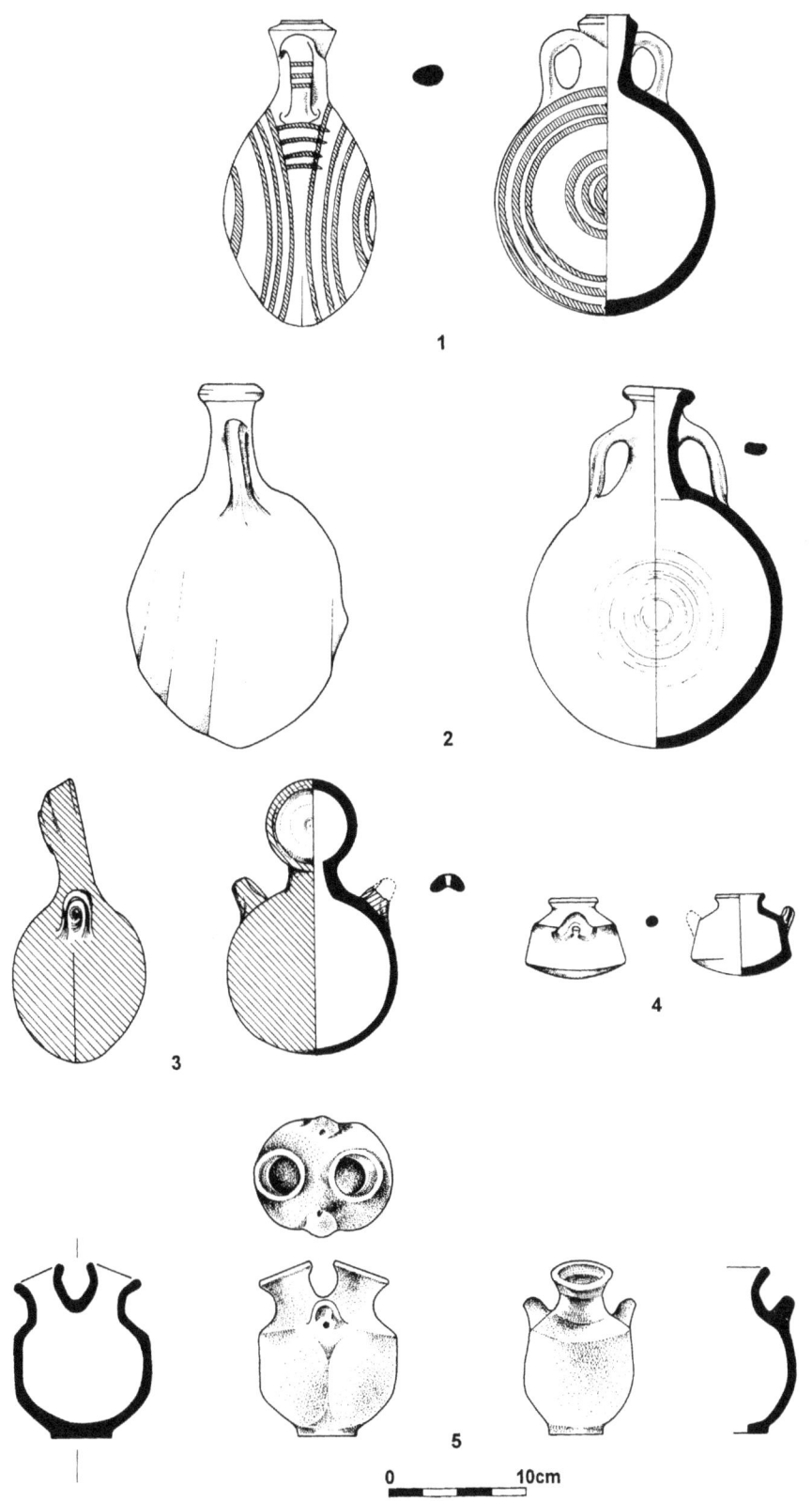

Plate 7

Plate 8 - Line Drawings of Pottery: Imported Vessels*

No.	CRN	Description
1.	147	Mycenaean piriform jar; two partially broken handles; chipped on lower body.
2.	149	Mycenaean piriform jar; one missing handle.
3.	150	Mycenaean flask.
4.	174	White Shaved juglet.
5.	175	White Shaved juglet.
6.	156	White Shaved juglet.
7.	161	Base Ring jug.
8.	157	Base Ring jug.
9.	164	Base Ring jug.
10.	155	Base Ring jug.
11.	165	Base Ring jug.
12.	162	Base Ring jug.
13.	154	Base Ring jug.
14.	163	Base Ring jug.

*See also Pl. 10: Nos. 97, 129, 158,151,159,156,199.

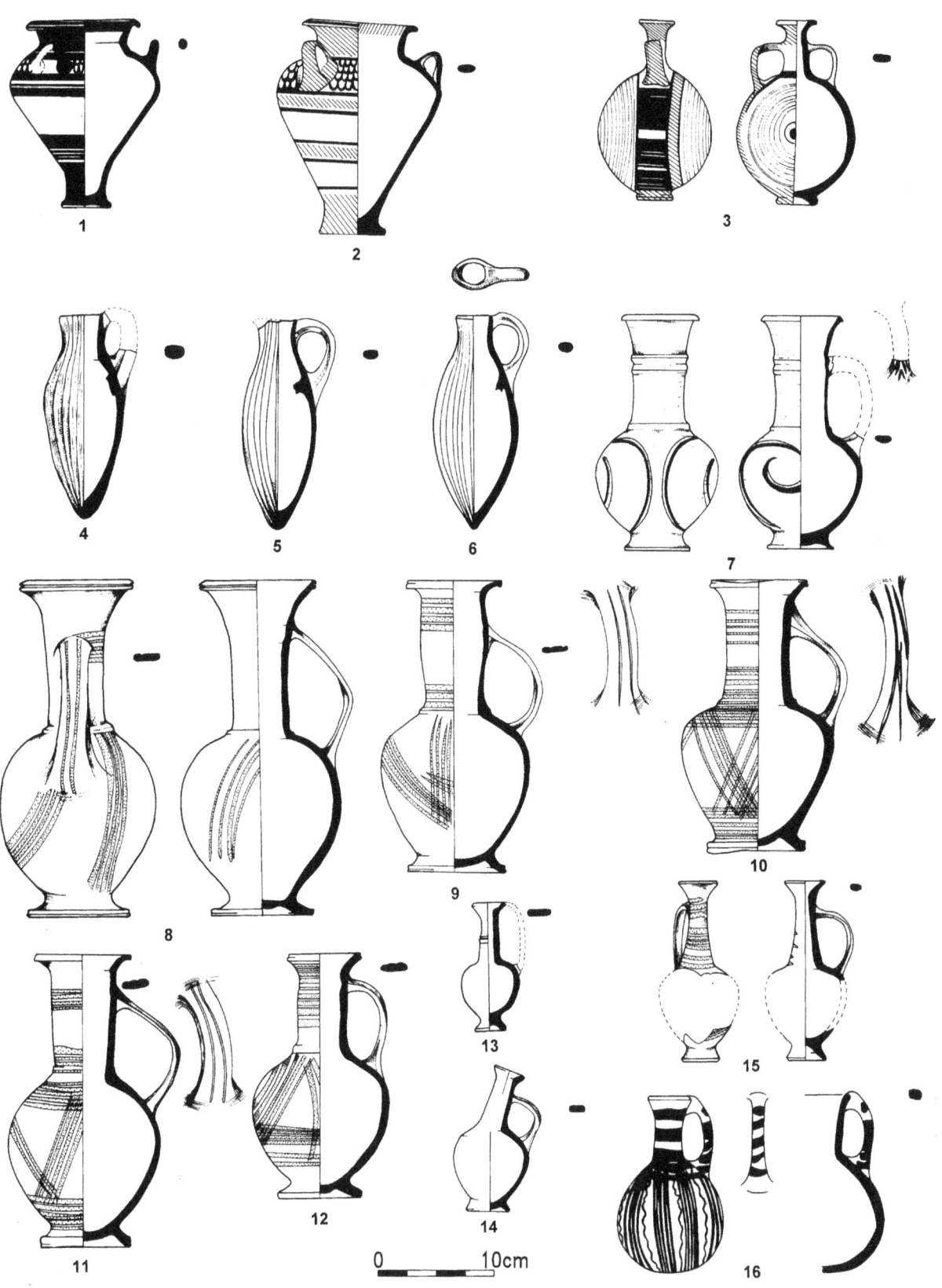

Plate 8

Plate 9 - Line Drawings of Pottery: Imitations of Cypriot Jugs

No.	CRN	Ware Description	Comments
1.	167	Light brownish-pink; some small and medium white, few small and medium red inclusions.	Red painted intersecting diagonal lines on body and horizontal lines at bottom of neck; smoothing; light encrustation.
2.	169	Pinkish-brown; some small and medium white, few large grey and red inclusions.	Red painted irregular intersecting diagonal lines on body and two uneven horizontal lines on neck; horizontal burnish on body and vertical burnish on neck; light encrustation.
3.	123	Light pinkish-brown; some small black and white, few small red inclusions	Red painted diagonal lines, partially intersecting lines on body and horizontal lines on neck and handle; smoothing, light encrustation..
4.	124	Pinkish-brown; few small and medium black and white inclusions.	Few red painted diagonal lines on body; horizontal smoothing on body; light encrustation.
5.	168	Too encrusted to define.	Few diagonal red painted lines on body; heavy encrustation.
6.	170	Light reddish-brown; grey core, some small and few large white, few small and large red inclusions.	Light encrustation.
7.	84	Light brown; some small and medium black and white inclusions.	Heavy encrustation.
8.	110	Pinkish-brown, light brown core; some small and few medium white and black inclusions.	Smoothing on body.
9.	166	Light reddish-yellow; some small white, black and red inclusions.	Red slip outside, irregular and horizontal burnish on body and vertical burnish on neck; body chipped; light encrustation.
10.	160	Light brown, many small and medium white and few small black inclusions; calcification.	Self slip and burnish outside; light "scraping" finish on body; light encrustation.

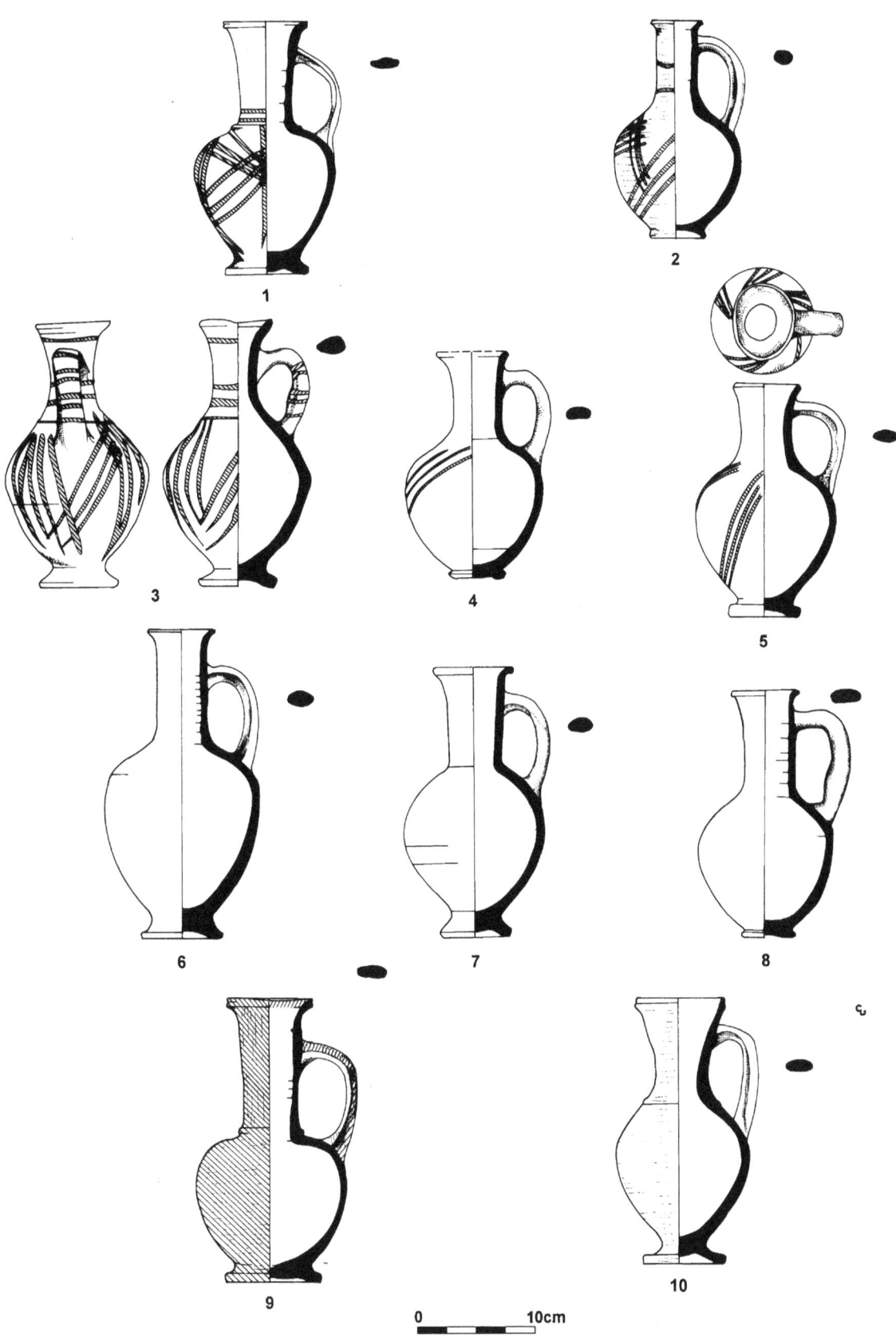

Plate 9

Plate 10 – Schematic Line Drawings of Pottery: Miscellaneous Missing Vessels*

CRN	Vessel	Comments
82	Bowl	See Bowl A
77	Bowl	See Bowl E
78	Bowl	See Bowl E
142	Bowl	See Bowl E
143	Bowl	See Bowl E
204	Bowl	See Bowl E
88	Bowl	See Bowl H
104	Bowl	See Bowl H
144	Bowl	
145	Bowl	
146	Bowl	
97	Juglet	Possibly Cypriot White Shaved.
129	Juglet	Possibly Cypriot White Shaved
100	Juglet	Possibly a "black juglet".
181	Juglet	Possibly with vertical burnish.
148	Mycenaean piriform jar	See Pl. 8:1-2.
151	Cypriot Base Ring jug	See Pl. 8:7-11.
159	Cypriot Base Ring jug	See Pl. 8:7-11
156	Cypriot Base Ring jug	See Pl. 8:7-11.
199	Cypriot White Slip II Milk Bowl	See p. 28-29
212	Clay sarcophagus lid (?)	See pp. 31-32

* The small schematic drawings, executed by Prof. N. Avigad, are the only extant documentation of these vessels.

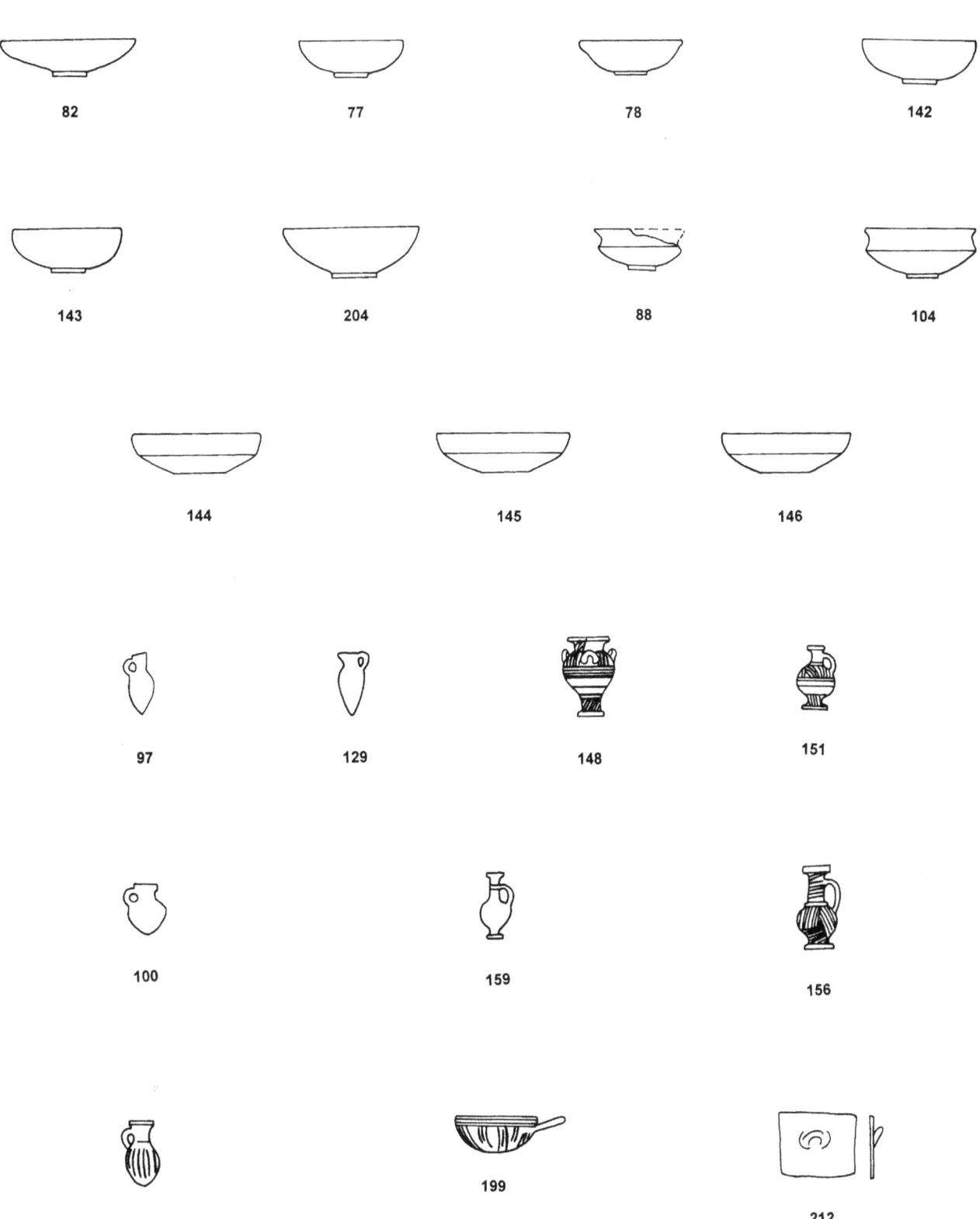

Plate 10

Plate 11 - Line Drawings of Non-Ceramic Objects

No.	CRN	Object	Comments
1.	152	Jug	Stone
2.	120	'Tazze'	Stone
3.	121	Jug	Stone
4.	564	Bottle	Stone
5.	69(?)	Juglet	Stone
6.	565	Bottle	Stone
7.	153	Bottle	Faience
8.	396	Cosmetic bowl	Stone
9.	1647	Spindle whorl*	Bone
10.	1648	Spindle whorl*	Bone
11.	1648/1	Spindle whorl*	Bone
12.	1648/2	Spindle whorl*	Bone
13.	1649	Toggle pin	Bronze
14.	1650	Earring*	Bronze
15.	107	Weapon blade	Bronze

*missing

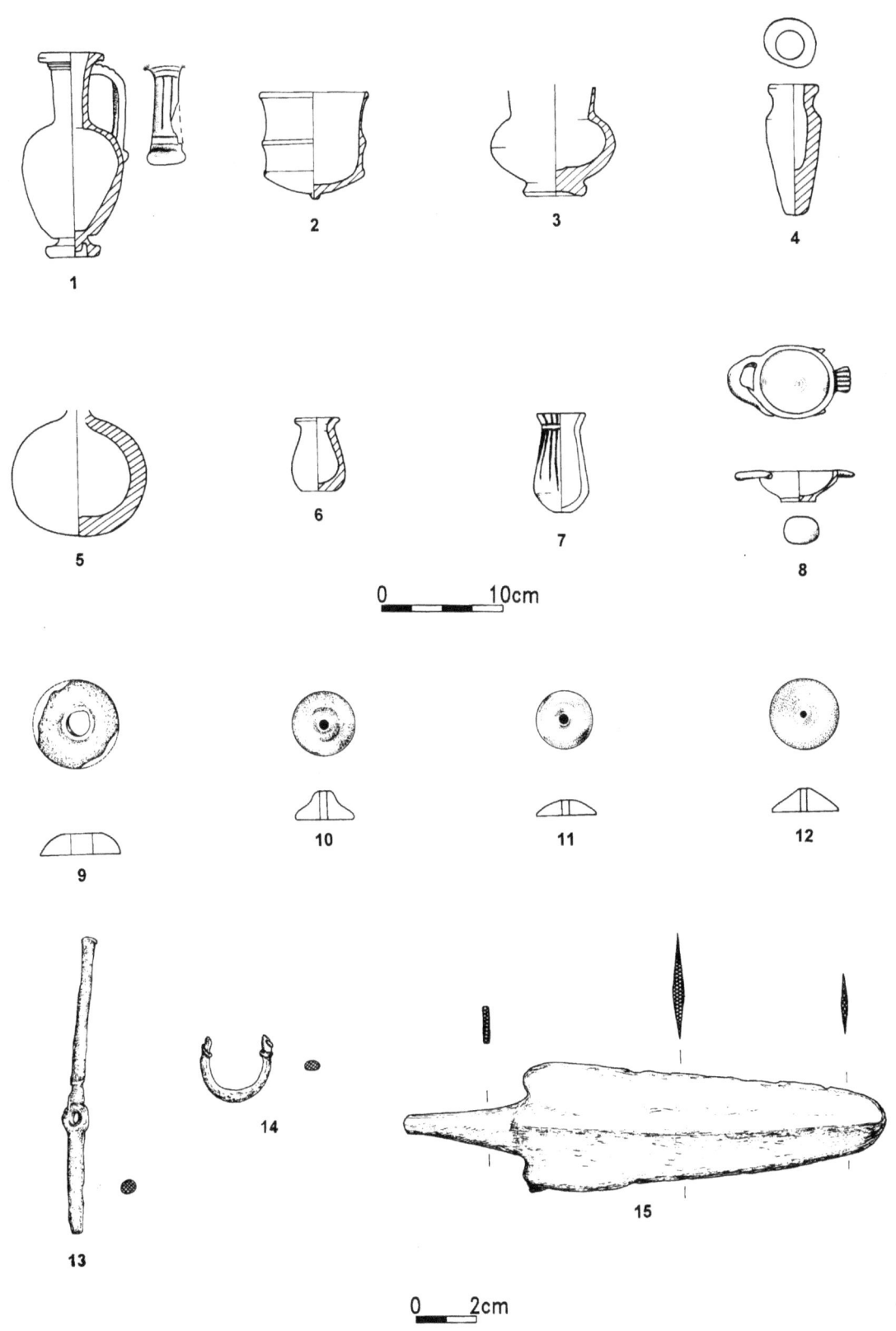

Plate 11

Plate 12 - Line Drawings of the Local Pottery Attributed to Tomb I

No.	CRN	Vessel	Plate
1.	109	Bowl	2:11
2.	119	Krater	3:12
3.	172	Chalice	3:10
4.	21	Jug	5:4
5.	213	Jug	5:3
6.	183	Jug	5:8
7.	187	Juglet	6:9
8.	178	Flask	7:1

Plate 12

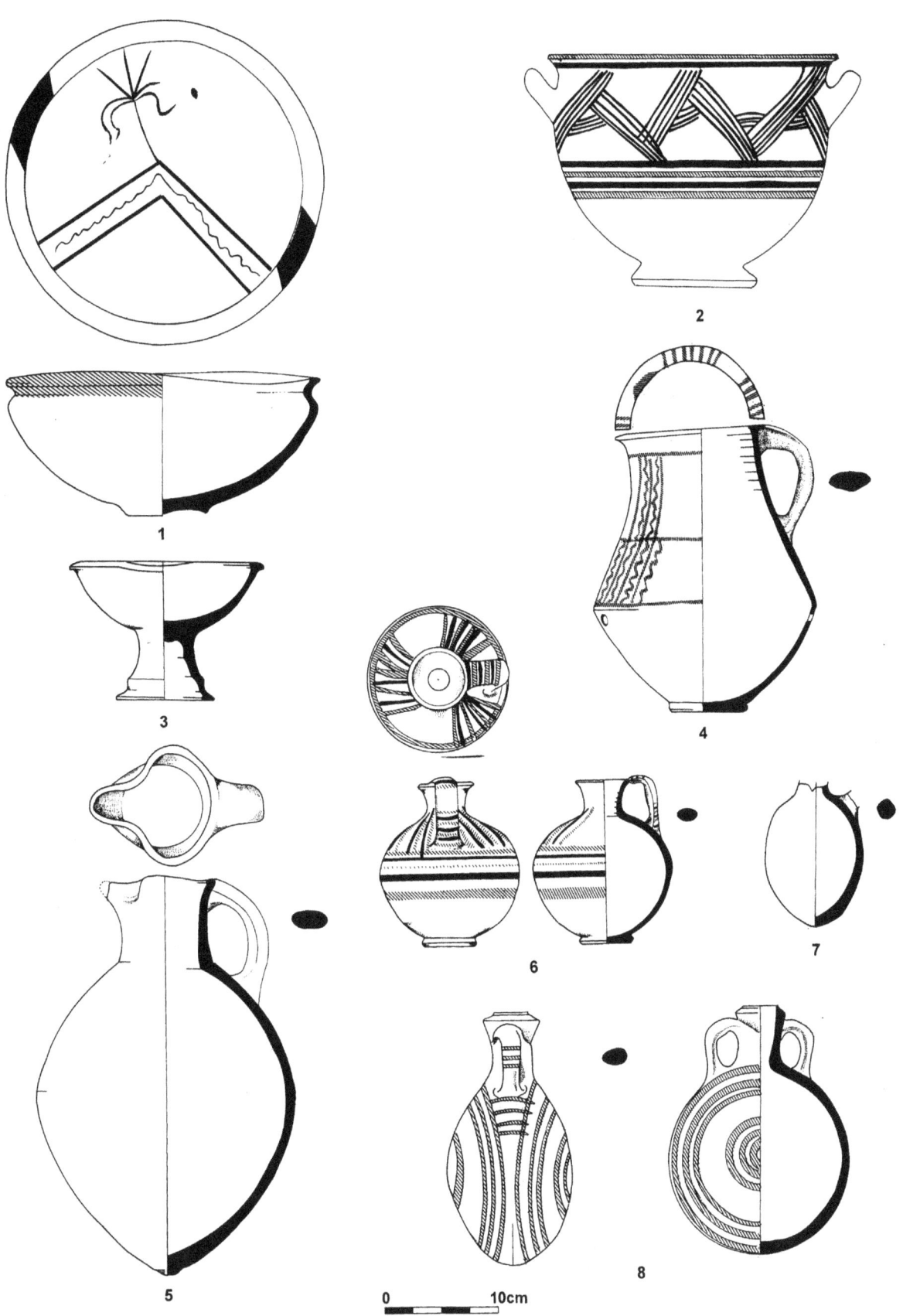

Plate 13 - Line Drawings of the Imported Vessels, Imitations of Imported Vessels, and Other Objects Attributed to Tomb I

No.	CRN	Vessel	Plate
1.	147	Mycenaean piriform jar	8:1
2.	149	Mycenaean piriform jar	8:2
3.	150	Mycenaean flask	8:3
4.	176	Cypriot White Shaved juglet	8:6
5.	129	Cypriot White Shaved juglet (?)	10:129
6.	159	Cypriot Base Ring jug	10:159
7.	157	Cypriot Base Ring jug	8:8
8.	167	Imitation Base Ring jug	9:1
9.	160	Imitation Base Ring jug	9:11
10.	152	Stone "bilbil"	11:1
11.	121	Stone jug	11:3
12.	120	Stone "tazze"	11:2

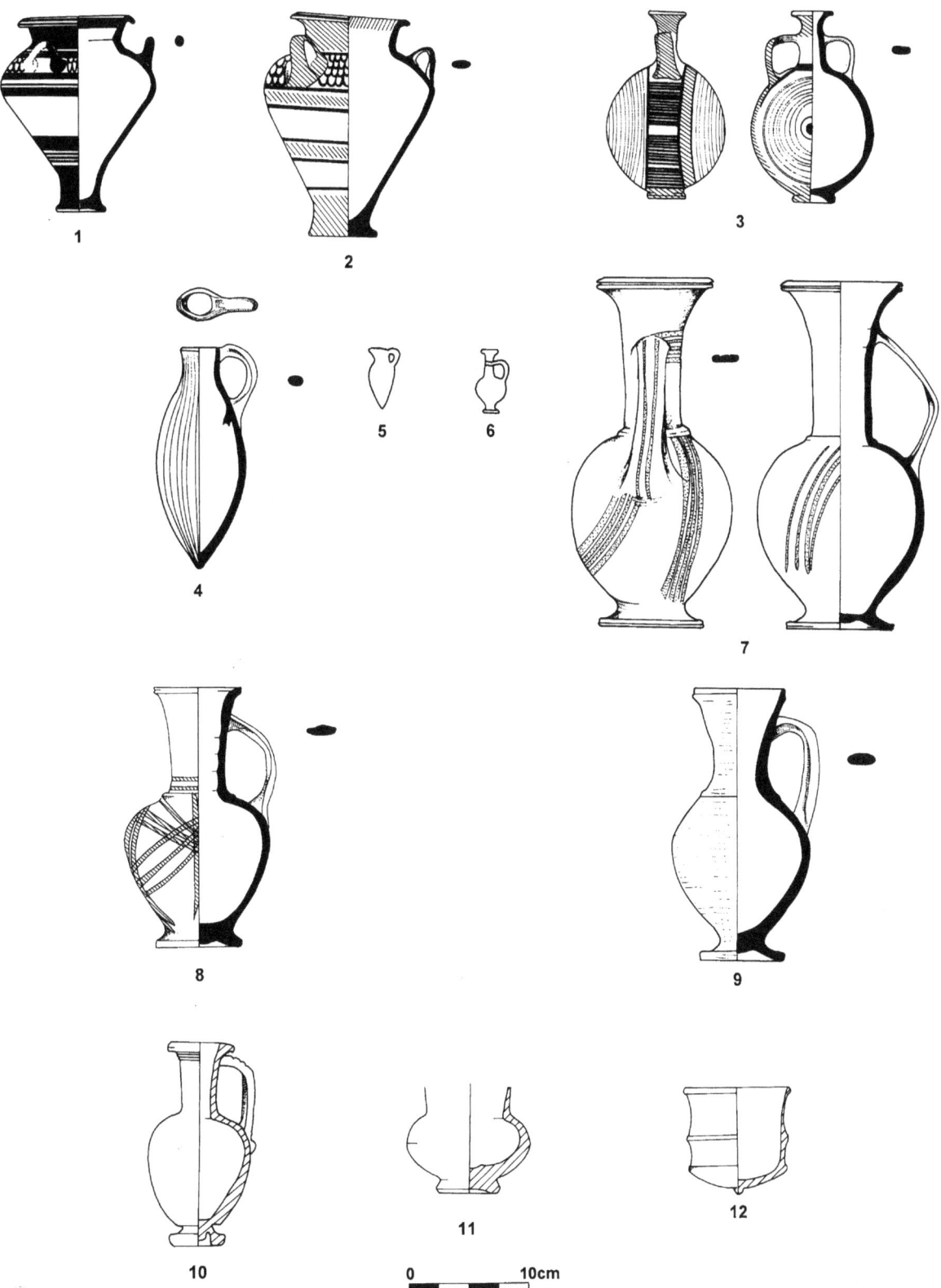

Plate 13

Plate 14

1) Group Photograph of Objects Known to Have Originated from Tomb I
2) Line Drawing and Photograph of the Egyptian Late Bronze Age Glass Vessel (HU 214)

Plate 14

1

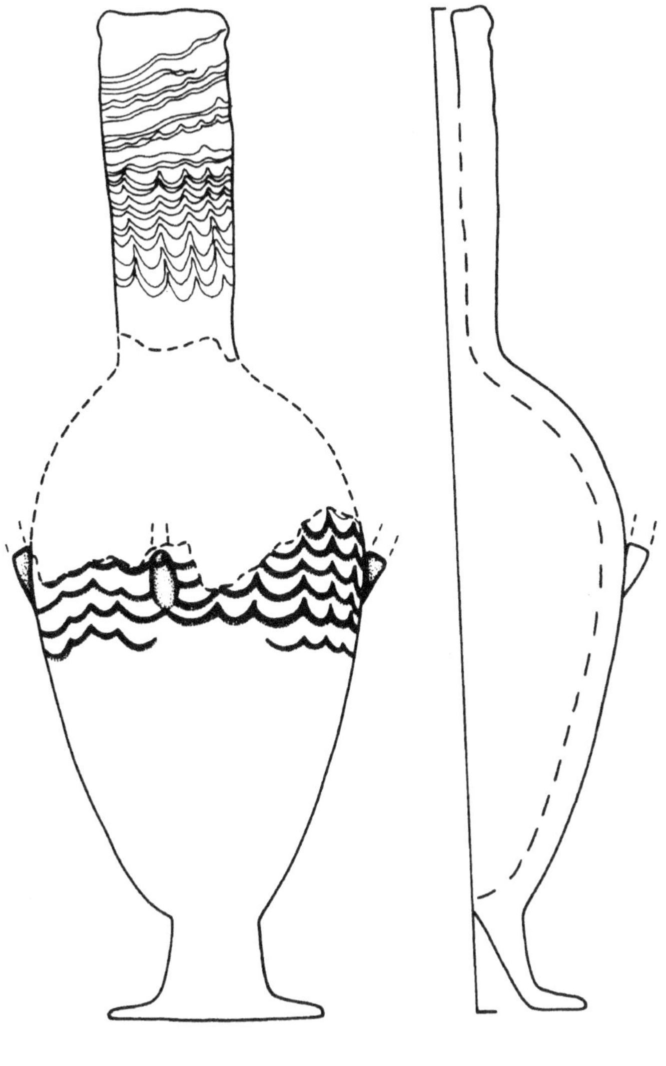

2

3

Plate 15 - Line Drawings and Photographs of the Glyptic Finds

No.	CRN	Comments
1.	111	Scarab
2.	112	Scarab

Plate 15

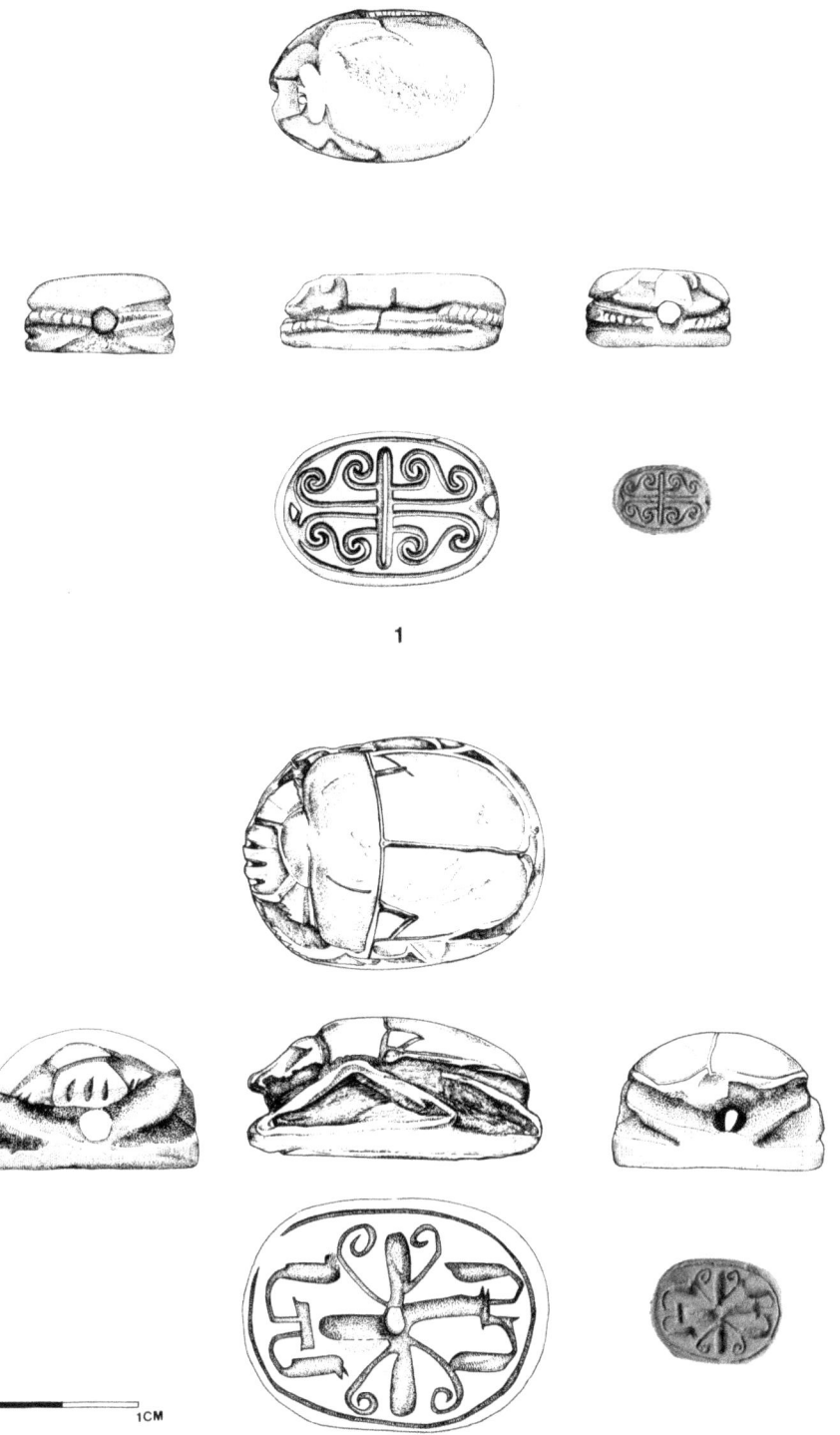

1

2

Plate 16 - Line Drawings and Photographs of the Glyptic Finds

No.	CRN	Comments
1.	113	Scarab
2.	115	Stamp Seal

Plate 16

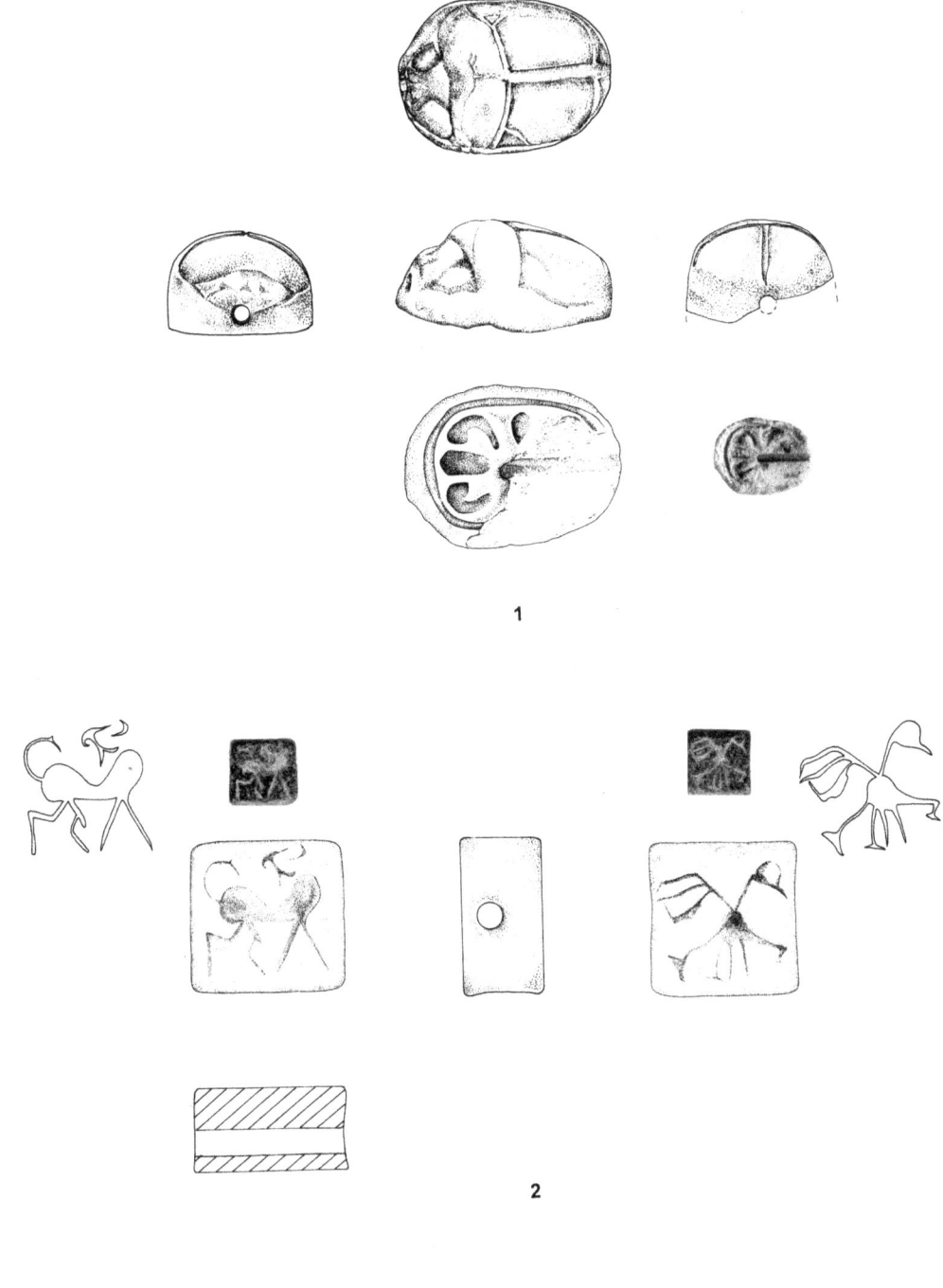

Plate 17 – Photographs of Selected Bowls from Plate 1 (HU Collection)

No.	CRN	Comments
1.	68	= Pl. 1:2
2.	135	= Pl. 1:6
3.	132	= Pl. 1:8
4.	202	= Pl. 1:12
5.	207	= Pl. 1:15
6.	209	= Pl. 1:17
7.	72	= Pl. 1:19
8.	57	= Pl. 1:21
9.	70	= Pl. 1:22
10.	210	= Pl. 1:23

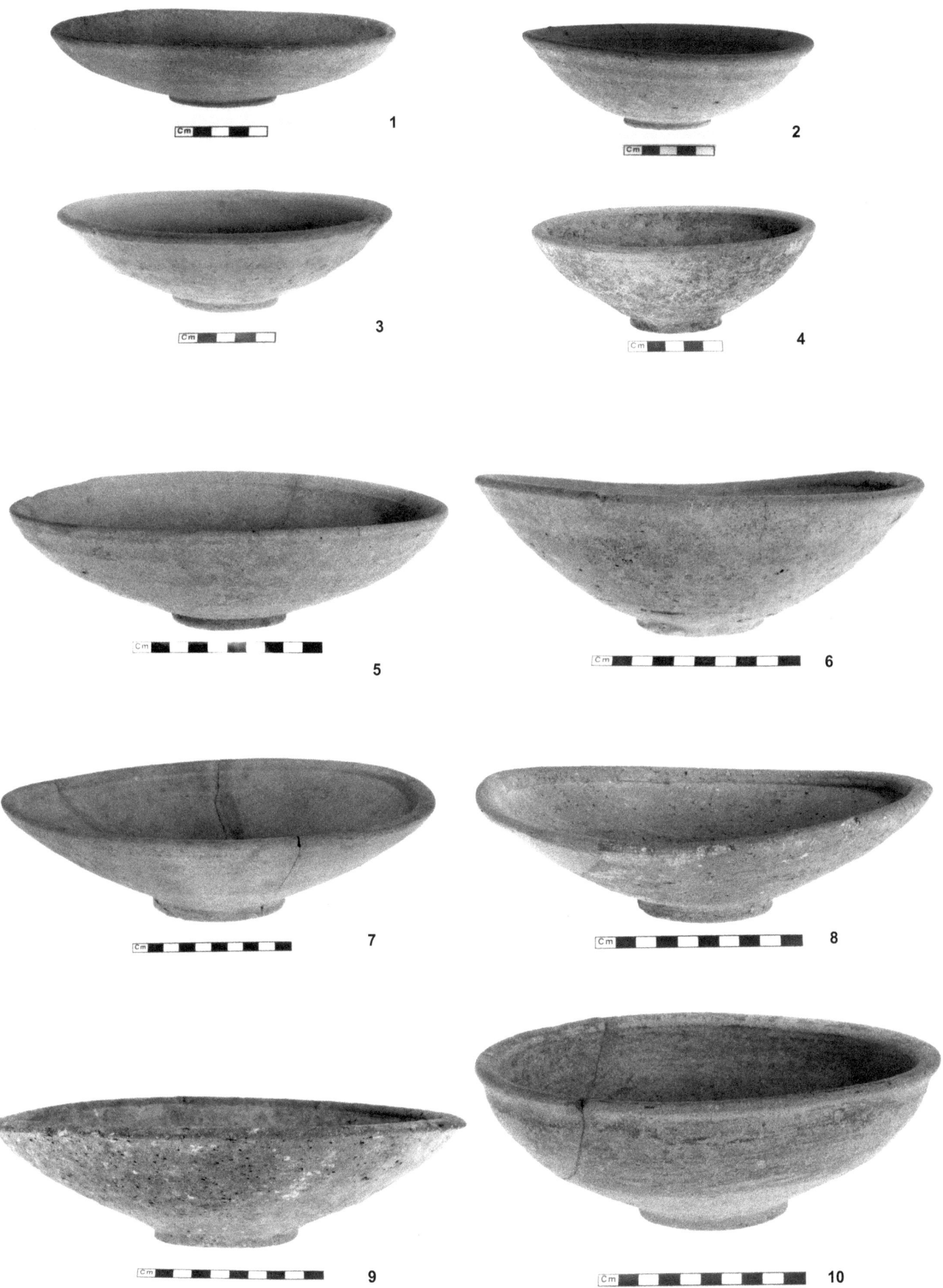

Plate 17

Plate 18 – Photographs of Selected Bowls from Plate 2 (HU Collection)

No.	CRN	Comments
1.	76	= Pl. 2:3
2.	83	= Pl. 2:4
3.	126	= Pl. 2:6
4.	185	= Pl. 2:10
5.	109	= Pl. 2:11 (side view)
6.	109	= Pl. 2:11 (upper view)

Plate 18

Plate 19 – Photographs of Selected Bowls, Chalices and a Krater from Plate 3 (HU Collection)

No.	CRN	Comments
1.	85	= Pl. 3:1
2.	92	= Pl. 3:3
3.	56	= Pl. 3:4
4.	102	= Pl. 3:6
5.	101	= Pl. 3:7
6.	105	= Pl. 3:8
7.	93	= Pl. 3:9
8.	172	= Pl. 3:10
9.	128	= Pl. 3:11
10.	119	= Pl. 3:12

Plate 19

Plate 20 – Photographs of Selected Lamps, Flasks and a Pyxis from Plates 4 and 7 (HU Collection)

No.	CRN	Comments
1.	94	= Pl. 4:1
2.	190	= Pl. 4:2
3.	198	= Pl. 4:9
4.	118	= Pl. 4:13
5.	178	= Pl. 7:1
6.	116	= Pl. 7:2
7.	122	= Pl. 7:3
8.	173	= Pl. 7:4

Plate 20

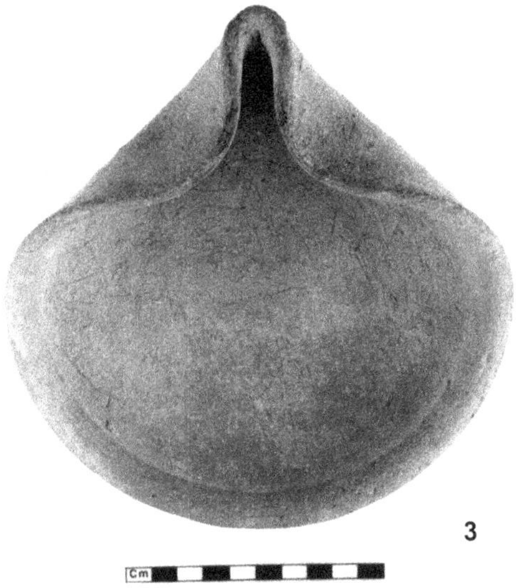

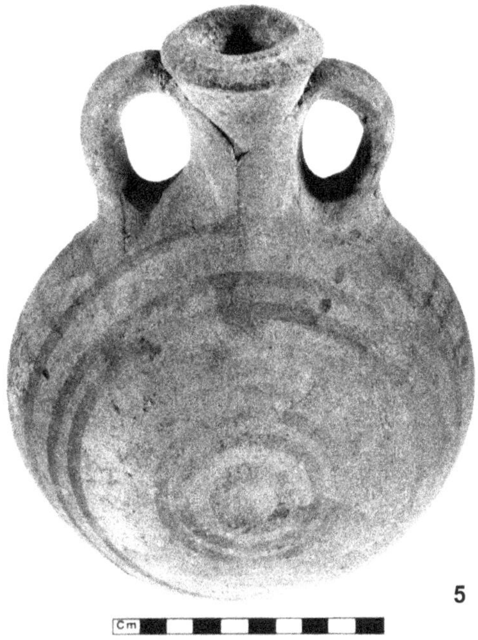

Plate 21 – Photographs of Selected Jugs from Plate 5 (HU Collection)

No.	CRN	Comments
1.	28	= Pl. 5:1
2.	55	= Pl. 5:2
3.	65	= Pl. 5:5
4.	182	= Pl. 5:6
5.	183	= Pl. 5:8
6.	216	= Pl. 5:9
7.	177	= Pl. 5:10
8.	188	= Pl. 5:11
9.	215	= Pl. 5:12

Plate 21

Plate 22 – Photographs of Selected Juglets from Plate 6 (HU Collection)

No.	CRN	Comments
1.	59	= Pl. 6:1
2.	67	= Pl. 6:2
3.	75	= Pl. 6:3
4.	66	= Pl. 6:4
5.	89	= Pl. 6:7
6.	171	= Pl. 6:8
7.	91	= Pl. 6:10
8.	63	= Pl. 6:11
9.	62	= Pl. 6:13
10.	61	= Pl. 6:14
11.	60	= Pl. 6:15
12.	80	= Pl. 6:16
13.	180	= Pl. 6:17

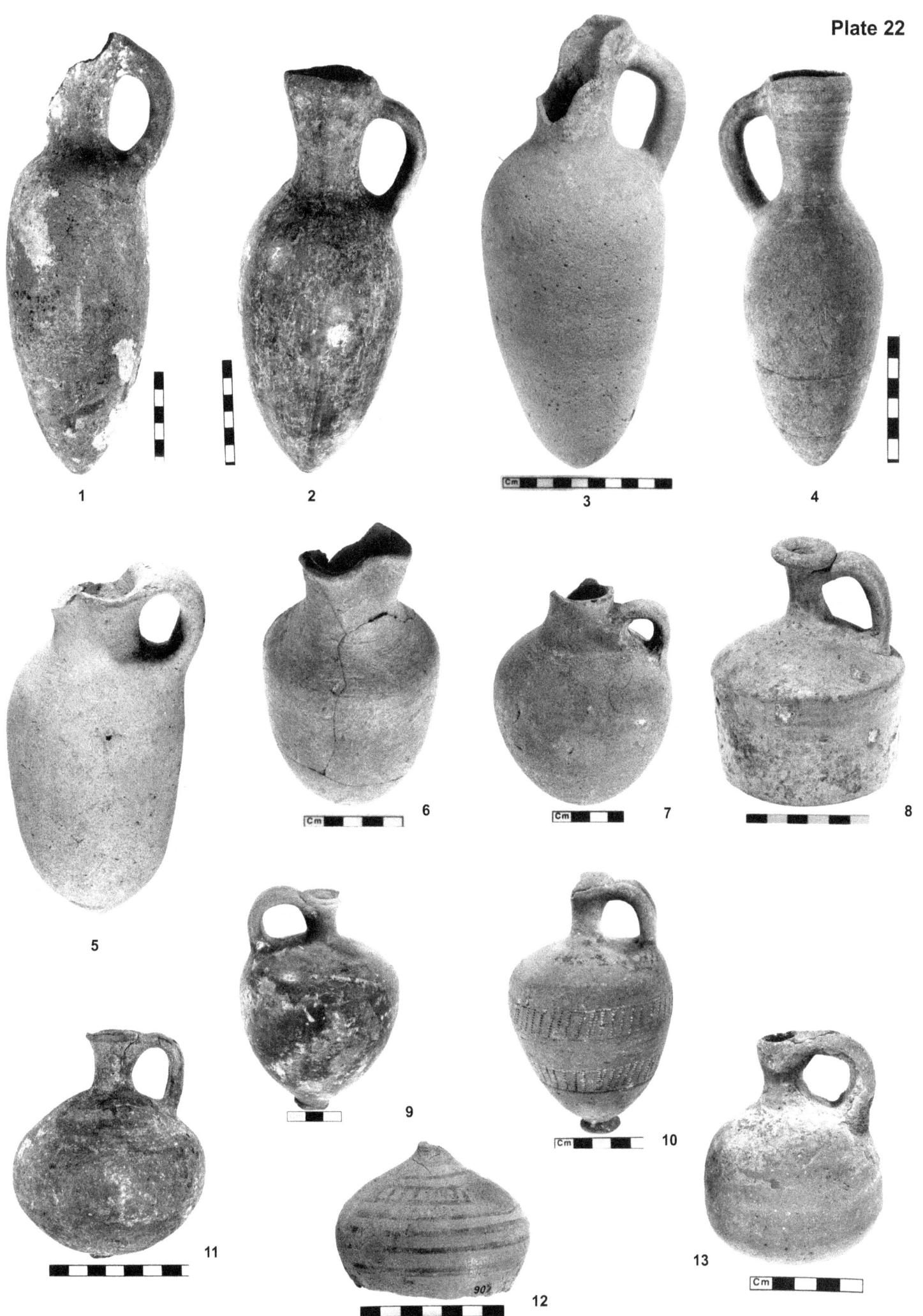

Plate 22

Plate 23 – Photographs of Selected Imported Wares from Plate 8 (HU Collection)

No.	CRN	Comments
1.	147, 150, 149	= Pl. 8:1, 8:3, 8:2 (from left to right)
2.	175	= Pl. 8:5
3.	156	= Pl. 8:6
4.	161	= Pl. 8:7
5.	157	= Pl. 8:8
6.	164	= Pl. 8:9
7.	155	= Pl. 8:10
8.	158	= Pl. 8:12
9.	162	= Pl. 8:13
10.	163	= Pl. 8:15

Plate 23

Plate 24 – Photographs of Selected Imitation Base Ring Vessels from Plate 9 (HU Collection)

No.	CRN	Comments
1.	167	= Pl. 9:1
2.	169	= Pl. 9:2
3.	123	= Pl. 9:3
4.	168	= Pl. 9:5
5.	170	= Pl. 9:6
6.	166	= Pl. 9:9
7.	160	= Pl. 9:10

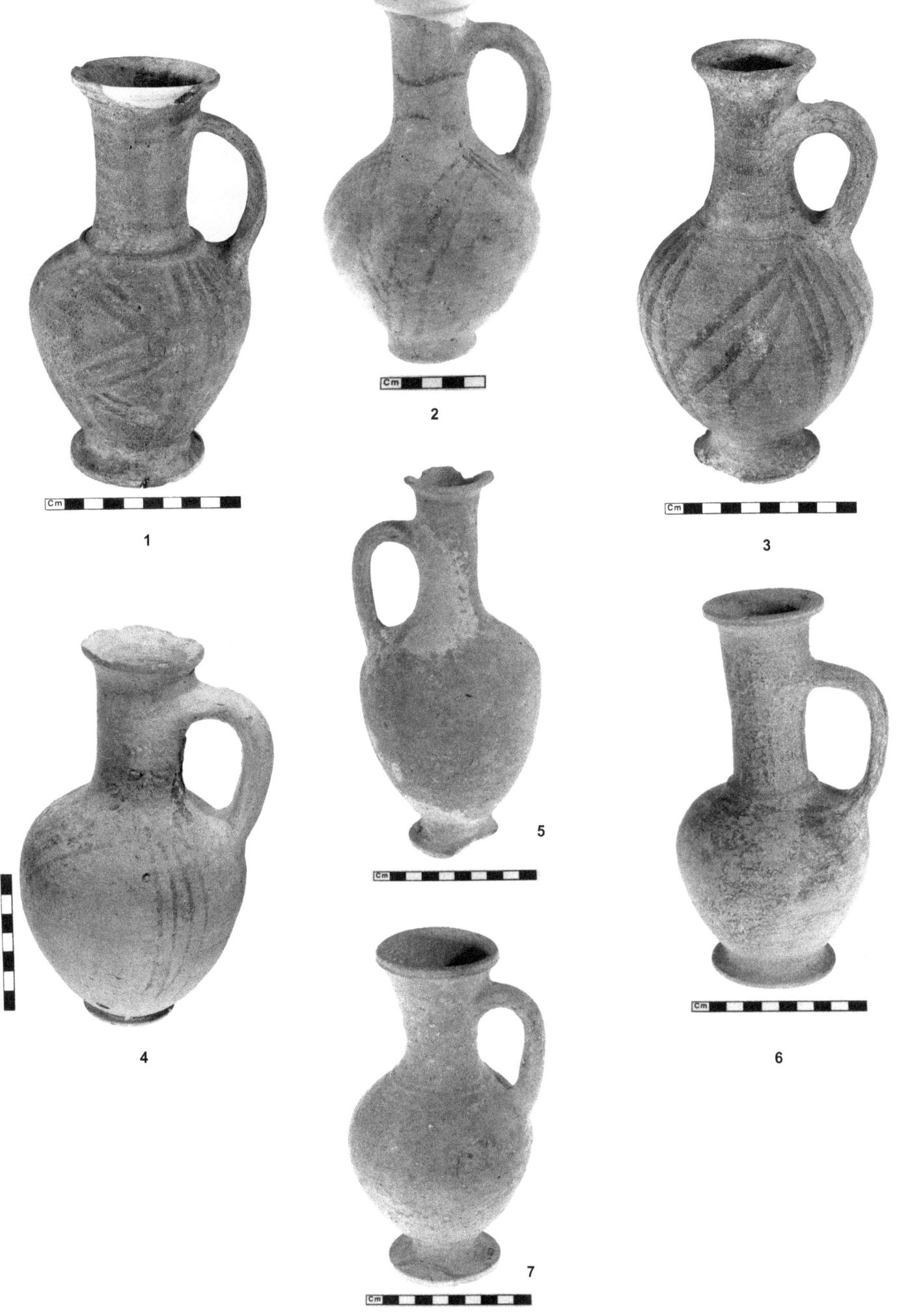

Plate 24

Plate 25 – Photographs of Selected Vessels (SG Collection)

No.	Reg. #	Comments
1.	77.211B	See page 10, note 2
2.	77.211C	See page 13
3.	77.211F1	See page 16
4.	77.211F2	See page 16
5.	72.356b	See page 17
6.	77.211E1	See page 22
7.	77.211I1	See page 24
8.	77.211I2	See page 25
9.	77.211E4	See page 23
10.	77.211E3	See page 23, note 12

Plate 25

Plate 26 – Photographs of Selected Vessels (SG Collection)

No.	Reg. #	Comments
1.	77.211H4	See page 21
2.	77.211G1	See page 21
3.	77.211G2	See page 21
4.	77.211G3	See page 21
5.	77.211G4	See pages 21-22
6.	72.356f	See page 27
7.	77.211H2	See page 30
8.	77.211H3	See page 30

Plate 26

77211 H4
1

77211G2
3

77211G4
5

77211H2
7

77211G1
2

77211G3
4

72356 f
6

77211H3
8

Plate 27 – Photographs of Selected Vessels (AO Collection)

No.	Reg. #	Comments
1.	AO 7001	See page 25
2.	AO 7000	See page 25
3.	AO 7003	See page 25
4.	AO 7003b	See page 25
5.	AO 7002	See page 23
6.	AO 6995	See page 30
7.	AO 6996	See page 30
8.	AO 6997	See page 30
9.	AO 6998	See page 30

Plate 27

Plate 28 – Photographs of Selected Non-Ceramic Objects from Plate 11 (HU Collection)

No.	CRN	Comments
1.	152	= Pl. 11:1
2.	120	= Pl. 11:2
3.	121	= Pl. 11:3
4.	564	= Pl. 11:4
5.	69 (?)	= Pl. 11:5
6.	565	= Pl. 11:6
7.	153	= Pl. 11:7
8.	396	= Pl. 11:8
9.	1647, 1648, 1648/1, 1648/2	= Pl. 11:9-12
10.	1649	= Pl. 11:13
11.	107	= Pl. 11:15

Plate 28

Plate 29 – Digital Radiographic Images of Selected Vessels

No.	Reg. #	See Illustration Plate #	Comments
1.	HU 136	Pl. 1:1	"Surview"
2.	HU 136	Pl. 1:1	Axial Scan of Vessel
3.	HU 136	Pl. 1:1	Transverse Scan of Vessel Body Above Base
4.	HU 136	Pl. 1:1	Transverse Scan of Vessel Base
5.	HU 85	Pl. 3:1	Surview
6.	HU 85	Pl. 3:1	Longitudinal Scan of Vessel
7.	HU 85	Pl. 3:1	Axial Scan of Vessel. Note Vessel-Wall Thickness Above Base (1mm)

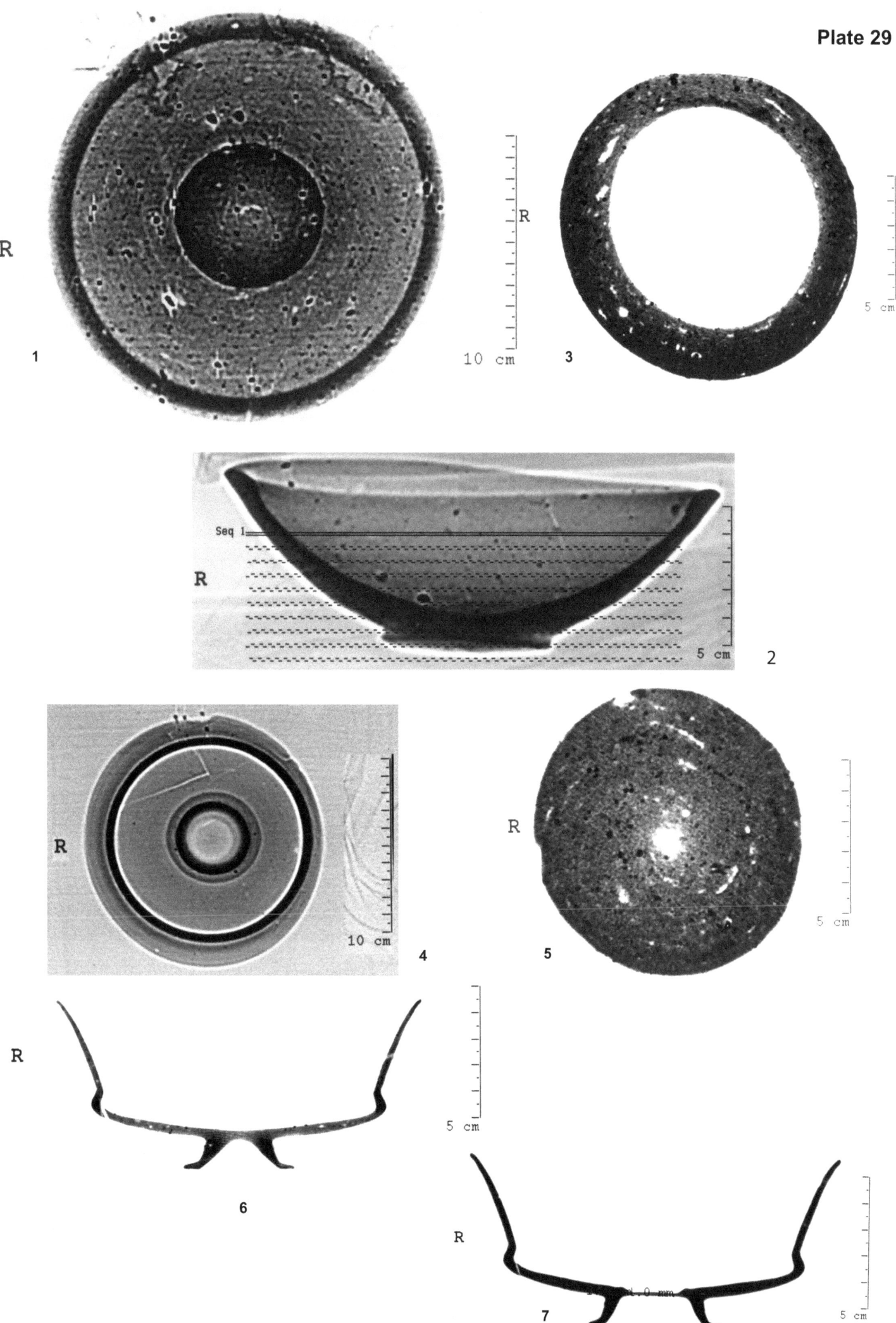

Plate 29

Plate 30 – Digital Radiographic Images of Selected Vessels

No.	Reg. #	See Illustration Plate #	Comments
1.	V1715	Pl. 7:5	Transverse Scan of Vessel at Mid-Height
2.	V1715	Pl. 7:5	Axial Scan of Vessel
3.	HU 149	Pl. 8:2	Axial Scan of Vessel
4.	HU 136	Pl. 8:2	Portion of Transverse Scan of Vessel at Level of Handles. Note Air Void.
5.	V1713	Pl. 8:16	Transverse Scan of Vessel Above Base
6.	V1713	Pl. 8:16	Longitundal Scan of Vessel. Note "Inserted" Handle.
7.	V1713	Pl. 8:16	Transverse Scan of Vessel. Note Air Voids Around "Inserted" Handle.

Plate 30

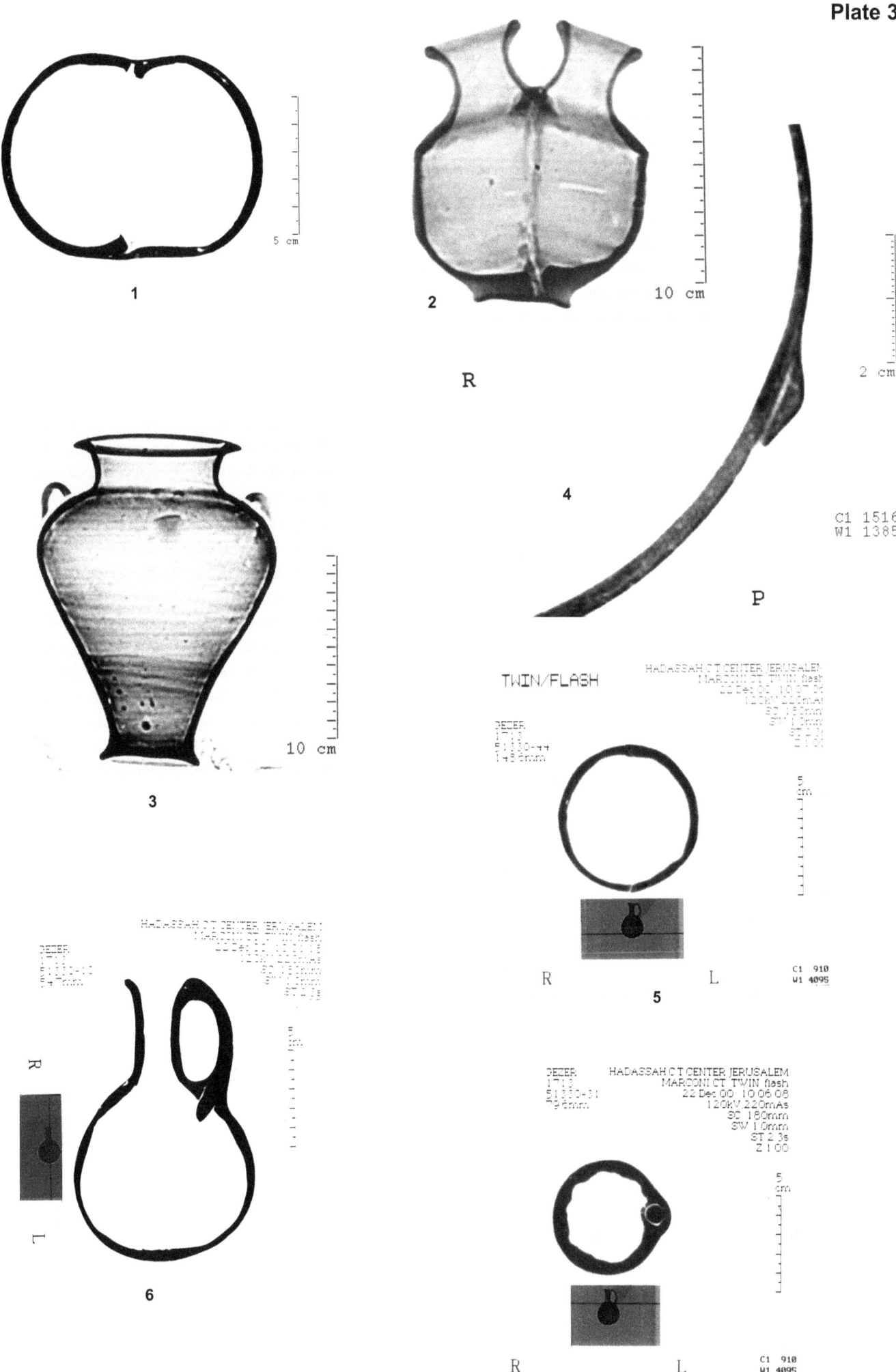

www.ingramcontent.com/pod-product-compliance
Lightning Source LLC
Chambersburg PA
CBHW041703290426
44108CB00027B/2843